W9-CKR-916

Also by Amanda Petrusich

It Still Moves: Lost Songs, Lost Highways,
and the Search for the Next American Music

Nick Drake's Pink Moon (33⅓ Series)

DO NOT SELL AT ANY PRICE

The Wild, Obsessive Hunt for

the World's Rarest 78 rpm Records

———— // ————

AMANDA PETRUSICH

SCRIBNER

New York   London   Toronto   Sydney   New Delhi

SCRIBNER

A Division of Simon & Schuster, Inc.
1230 Avenue of the Americas
New York, NY 10020

First Scribner hardcover edition July 2014

SCRIBNER and design are registered trademarks of The Gale Group, Inc.,
used under license by Simon & Schuster, Inc., the publisher of this work.

For information about special discounts for bulk purchases,
please contact Simon & Schuster Special Sales at 1-866-506-1949
or business@simonandschuster.com.

The Simon & Schuster Speakers Bureau can bring authors to your live event.
For more information or to book an event, contact the Simon & Schuster
Speakers Bureau at 1-866-248-3049 or visit our website at www.simonspeakers.com.

Interior design by Kyle Kabel
Jacket design by Jason Heuer
Jacket art: Record player © La puma/Shutterstock,
ornaments © bomg/Shutterstock, © Clipart deSIGN/Shutterstock

Manufactured in the United States of America

1   3   5   7   9   10   8   6   4   2

Library of Congress Control Number: 2013045926

ISBN 978-1-4516-6705-9
ISBN 978-1-4516-6707-3 (ebook)

Some sections of this book originally appeared in the *Oxford American* and *Loops*.

For my parents, John and Linda Petrusich

"Listening to music, I always have exactly the same feeling: something's missing. Never will I learn the cause of this gentle sadness, never will I wish to investigate it. I've no desire to know what it is. I've no desire to know everything."

—Robert Walser (translated by Susan Bernofsky),
Masquerade and Other Stories

Contents

DO NOT SELL
AT ANY PRICE

An Air of Impoverishment and Depleted Humanity

○

Music Criticism, the Culture of 78 rpm Record Collecting,
Jean Baudrillard, Mouth Breathing, the Lure of Objects

○

I was a pretty good kid with rebellious aspirations. I spent most of my adolescence listening to punk-rock bands on my plastic Sports Walkman and, like many young music fans, I self-identified via my record collection (for me, a sticker-coated trunk packed with cassettes). Because I came of age during the pinnacle of grunge, I further expressed that identity via Doc Martens, Manic Panic, and flannel shirts I pilfered from my father's closet. As I grew older, my communion with music became more complex and less visceral, but it was still my primary method of self-expression: I was what I heard, always, and I eventually parlayed those delusions into something resembling a career as a music critic.

The crowning perk of professional music criticism—the only perk, maybe; it's not a particularly glamorous gig—is that your mailbox is routinely crammed with dozens of padded envelopes containing CD copies of upcoming releases, shipped en masse by labels, publicists, or the artists themselves. That tottering stack of plastic can feel as much like an albatross as it does an opportunity, and practically speaking, the volume of material (at its height, I'd say I was unwrapping between sixty and seventy new CDs each week) is a curious thing to manage. I have to goad a pal into collecting my mail every time I go out of town—even just for a few nights, lest a mound of manila alert the entire neighborhood to my absence—and since my apartment can't possibly accommodate all the CDs that come through, I'm routinely developing new ways of disposing of albums that I don't like or can't write about or never found the time to hear. Getting free records used to at least feel like something of a coup. These days, music fans with no critical aspirations can instantly—and freely—experience the same kind of oversaturation. If you have a computer and a modicum of Web-browsing savvy, it's not difficult to acquire leaked versions of new records months or weeks before their street dates. An unreleased song or album can be detected, acquired, and judged in the time it takes to prepare and eat a grilled cheese sandwich.

Obviously, free promotional material is an absurd thing for anyone to grumble about, but at some point, the process did begin to skew my perception of what music looked like and how it should be valued. It's reductive to suggest that the availability of free or nearly free music—and the concurrent switch, for most of the population, from music as object to music as code—has inexorably altered our relationship with sound, and I don't actually believe that the emotional circuitry that allows us to love and require a bit of music is dependent on what it feels like in our hands. But I do think that the ways in which we attain art at least partially dictate the ways in which we ultimately allow ourselves to own it.

For me, the modern marketing cycle and the endless gifts of the Web had begun to feel toxic, and not necessarily because I was nostalgic for CDs, then the primary musical medium sold in my lifetime, or because I thought the music industry was a beacon of efficiency before. It was because, for the first time in my entire life, I didn't care about any of it.

By all accounts, the first decade of the twenty-first century was a disconcerting time to be a music fan. By 2005, the ritual of consumption had been almost entirely annihilated: acquiring and listening to music was, suddenly, a solitary exercise that involved untangling lots of little white cords. Like many people, I missed browsing record stores, buying albums based exclusively on cover art, hobnobbing with bespectacled clerks in Joy Division T-shirts. I could still do those things, but suddenly it felt like a pose: Here I am! Buying records!

Moreover, I missed pining for things. I missed the ecstasy of acquisition. (In 1993, it took me seven weeks to sniff out a copy of Dinosaur Jr.'s *Where You Been*, and I spent the next seven memorizing every last crooked riff.) I missed making literal investments in music, of funneling all the time and cash and heart I could manage into the chase. I had free CDs and illegally attained MP3s and lawfully purchased LPs, but unless I was being paid to professionally render my opinion, I listened to everything for three or seven or nine minutes and moved on. I was overwhelmed and underinvested. Some days, music itself seemed like a nasty postmodern experiment in which public discussion eclipsed everything else, and art was measured only by the amount of chatter it incited. Writing and publishing felt futile, like tossing a meticulously prepared pork chop to a bulldog, then watching him devour it, throw it up, and start eating something else.

It was around then—the fall of 2007, the apex of my disillusionment—that I met John Heneghan. I was researching a story about the commercial resurgence of vinyl records for *Spin*, and I'd been pestering Mike Lupica, then a DJ and the director of the WFMU Record Fair, for the names of a few prominent collectors who might be willing to speak—forcefully, and on the record—about the relative lowliness of digital music. I was looking for a violent retaliation. Lupica slipped me Heneghan's phone number with a caveat: "These 78 guys are on another *level*."

While vinyl has enjoyed a welcome and precipitous renaissance in the last decade, 78 rpm records—the thick, ten-inch, two-song shellac discs developed around the turn of the twentieth century, and the earliest iteration of a record as we think of it today—are still considered odd and archaic. Because there is so little popular interest in the format, even hunting down a turntable capable of playing one is a challenge. The grooves in a 78 can be two to five times wider than those in a modern LP, so a different kind of stylus is required in addition to a motor that spins at 78 revolutions per minute, rather than the standard 33⅓ or 45 rpm. Even the most ardent vinyl fans are likely to push a stack of 78s aside rather than obtain all the equipment necessary to get one to play. It's not a medium that invites dabbling.

I already knew that 78 fanatics were part of an intense, competitive, and insular subculture with its own rules and economics—an oddball fraternity of men (and they are almost always men) obsessed with an outmoded technology and the aural rewards it could offer them. Because 78s are remarkably fragile and were sometimes produced in very limited quantities, they're a finite resource, and the amount of time and effort required to find the coveted ones is astonishing. The maniacal pursuit of rare shellac seemed like an epic treasure hunt, a quest story—an elaborate, multipronged search for a prize that may or may not even exist.

I also understood that collecting anything was nerdy in a way that would never be fashionable. If cool has a single isolatable signifier, it's the appearance of indifference. To seriously collect 78s, you have to give all that up: you have to admit that you *want*. Accordingly, 78 collectors, like the men who work at comic book stores, are something of a pop-cultural trope. There is a stereotype in place, and it is unflattering: picture, as we do, a middle-aged, balding, socially awkward, slightly plump or disconcertingly skinny basement-dwelling dude who breathes through his mouth and wears stained shorts. Obviously, this is not always true, or even predominantly true. Most collectors have challenging full-time jobs, sustained romantic partners, pleasant social lives, and functional wardrobes. Provided you ask the right questions and don't try to touch anything, they can be charming, funny, and even sweet (at worst they're nostalgic, a sentiment that in recent years has practically birthed its own zeitgeist). Still, the proliferation of reality shows like *Hoarders*—and even the amiable *American Pickers*, where a team of antiques buyers crawls through basements and barns overloaded with stuff—hasn't helped to brighten the collector's reputation. In our era of too-much-ness, minimalism is seen as something of an attribute.

Ironically, I would learn, most 78 collectors *are* minimalists. They're far more persnickety about what records they allow into their homes and onto their shelves than I've ever been. For example, I was willing to accept a copy of *Cat Scratch Fever* into my LP collection because I knew I would enjoy placing it in sensitive places around the apartment—the shower, the medicine cabinet—and waiting for unsuspecting visitors to be startled anew by Ted Nugent's giant, terrifying face. My terrible late-career Waylon Jennings LPs and three identical copies of Pavement's *Crooked Rain, Crooked Rain* don't bother me, even though they occupy valuable space. I'll probably continue cramming records onto my shelves until the whole setup collapses.

Approach a 78 collector, though, with some mundane or particularly commonplace 78—"Yes! We Have No Bananas," say—and request to store it amid his collection, and he will glower at you as if you have announced you intend to slowly disfigure his face with a fork. Just as we sweat over the minutiae of our Facebook profiles and the contents of our closets, collectors customize an identity via the serialization of objects. "It is invariably oneself that one collects," the French sociologist and philosopher Jean Baudrillard points out in his 1968 essay "The System of Collecting." For Baudrillard, the collection, with all its attendant pieces, is a complex, multifaceted statement of self, and the worth of each component is determined by how it interacts with and complements its neighbors. If a specific part of the collection is absent, then a part of the collector is also missing. Who wouldn't hunt down a lost feature as though their life depended on it?

Baudrillard also posits that collectors devote energy to their collections rather than to other human beings (it's easier, cleaner, and requires less negotiation), which inadvertently figures collecting as an inherently selfish and self-obsessed pursuit. "The object thus emerges as the ideal mirror: for the images it reflects succeed one another while never contradicting one another . . . this is why one invests in objects all that one finds impossible to invest in human relationships," he writes. (He later goes so far as to compare the collection itself to "a harem" and the collector to "the sultan of a secret seraglio.") Ultimately, Baudrillard finds collecting both pathological and dangerous. He ends his essay with a chilling little barb: "He who does collect can never entirely shake off an air of impoverishment and depleted humanity."

Baudrillard was right, at least, about how particular and protective 78 collectors can be. They recognize their trade as tremendously fragile. Only a select few are capable of understanding and appraising the contents or condition of a given 78, and that exclusivity both insulates their economy and allows it to survive. Value being a relative function, it's vital that the demand remains low, because the supply is inherently nonrenewable. There is even a vague fear that rare-record collecting could one day become analogous to fine-art collecting—the obligation of wealthy aristocrats whose consumption of art is more a statement of status than a function of love or even understanding. Collectors find that possibility legitimately horrifying, although it's also extremely unlikely it could ever be realized, primarily because there aren't enough records left, and the collectors who have them will probably never sell. For now, though, public ambivalence is both a source of nagging rage for collectors—*Why doesn't anyone else care?*—and the financial linchpin of their entire trade. It is also something they take pride in, insomuch as it feeds their self-identification as outsiders and underdogs.

Accordingly, information-gathering questions that might seem relatively innocuous—if a bit meddlesome—to a layman (Where'd you get that record? How much did it cost? How much is it worth? How'd you hear about it?) can be deeply offensive to a 78 collector. At first, my conversational interest in the minutiae of collecting was reportorial, almost businesslike: I wanted collectors to reveal their desires and methodologies so I could dissect their work and devise grand statements about our cultural moment. In response, collectors sneered, chortled, or told me to fuck off. They were frequently unwilling to share what records they were looking for, what records they'd recently found, what the rarest record in their collection was (on occasion, they'd pull out a bullshit record and try to sell me on its magnitude), where they looked for records, who had which records, how many copies there were of a given record, or how much they'd be willing to pay for it. They already thought too many people were interested in 78s. Consequently, interviewing a 78 fanatic could sometimes feel a little like boxing: bob, weave, duck. Wait till you wear 'em down, wait for one good shot.

What I'd hoped for, at least at first, was to tell the story of a strange, misunderstood community: why the work collectors did mattered so much, what was at stake, how it got done. After a while, though, they were right to evade me. Eventually, I started to want what they wanted.

Like anyone who's ever spent a bright Sunday morning trawling through a crate of old records in someone's driveway (carefully pulling a vinyl disc from its crinkled sleeve, inhaling the damp-dog mustiness of a mottled cardboard cover, squinting for scratches), I understood the rapture of discovery. I wasn't immune to the lure of objects. As a kid, I'd lined up paperback installments of *The Baby-Sitters Club* in numerical order and hovered for hours, gazing at the spines, running my little fingertips along their titles, mesmerized by all that order. My collections made me feel safe and focused; they lent my life purpose and form. They still do: my apartment is loaded with useless sundries, with tottering stacks of books and records, a shelf of globes, a mason jar crammed full of antique wedding-cake toppers (grooms only). On a good day, even writing can feel like a form of collecting—of gathering words, images, and ideas and arranging them in an order that feels right.

// One //

That's Mine Now, I Got That Before You Could Get It

○

John Heneghan, "Devil Got My Woman," Dreams,
Analog Playback, "Davey Crockett," Do Not Sell at Any Price

○

The living room of John Heneghan's East Village apartment is crammed with dusty American artifacts: antique wooden furniture, kitschy paperback novels, a *Beverly Hills, 90210* pencil case with matching ruler and eraser. All available surfaces are littered with collectibles; all accessible closets are bursting with vintage clothes, discerningly acquired by Heneghan's striking live-in girlfriend, Eden Brower. I sat on his couch with my hands folded in my lap and sucked in the smell: old. Two skittish housecats, both rescues, nipped in and out of cardboard boxes, eyes wary and wide.

Alongside the far wall, sixteen squat wooden cubes—each filled with about a hundred 78 rpm records, most recorded before 1935— loomed, parsed into genres like Hillbilly, Blues, Hawaiian, and Comedy and organized alphabetically by artist. Each section was blocked out with a neatly labeled cardboard divider. Individual 78s were housed in unmarked brown paper sleeves. It was an impeccable display. I asked

Heneghan if he ever sat in his living room and gazed at his record collection, mesmerized by each flawless row. "All the time," he answered.

Every last person alive right now came of age in the era of recorded sound, which makes it extraordinarily difficult for any of us to properly conceive of a time in which music was not a thing we could hear whenever we felt like it. The 78 rpm record was introduced in the 1890s, about ten years after Thomas Edison developed his phonograph machine and revolutionized the ways human beings thought about sound. Initially, Edison's phonograph played cylinders—little tubes, smaller than a can of soup, that were crafted from metal (later wax, and then hard shellac), stored in cardboard canisters, and coated with a strip of tin foil. Sound transcriptions were pressed into the foil with a cutting stylus, and the phonograph translated the textures back into sound. After a dozen or so plays at 160 revolutions per minute, the cylinders wore down and became unlistenable.

In 1887, the German-born inventor Emile Berliner patented the gramophone, which worked similarly to Edison's phonograph but played flat, grooved discs instead of stumpy cylinders. Berliner's disc records—which were five to seven inches across, made of various materials (often rubber), and whirled, on hand-cranked players, at around seventy to seventy-eight revolutions per minute—were easier to produce and store than cylinders, and Edison's tubes were nearly obsolete by 1929. Around the same time, the production of disc records became somewhat standardized, although there were still hundreds of rogue labels recording and manufacturing dozens of different kinds of records. Most were ten inches wide (which yielded about three minutes of sound per side) and crafted from a precarious jumble of shellac, a cotton compound, powdered slate, and wax lubricant. 78s would remain in relatively wide use until the 1960s, when they would be gradually replaced by seven-inch, two-song 45s and twelve-inch, long-playing 33⅓ records—themselves ousted by cassettes, to be eventually supplanted by compact discs, which have now been succeeded almost entirely by digital audio files.

The first day we met, John Heneghan was careful to establish a disconnect between 78 collectors and the folks who stockpile LPs or 45s—for Heneghan, the distinction is acute, comparable to collecting pebbles versus collecting diamonds. But his own collection began with an LP—a reissue of a Charley Patton record, which he acquired when he was sixteen years old. Heneghan can still describe, in remarkable detail, the subsequent epiphany: picking up the record, feeling its heft in his hands, squinting at the photograph on the cover, flipping it over to read the date printed on the back, placing it on his turntable and releasing the needle into the groove, feeling transported, feeling changed.

"I'm not even sure that I liked it at first," he admitted. "I liked the idea of it. It was really hard to listen to. But I was a guitar player—I had played the guitar since I was a kid—and I thought, 'What is this? What is he doing?' It was only a matter of time before I started seeking out the original records, the 78s. I resisted it for a long time because I knew it would be nearly impossible, and I knew it would be a financial burden beyond what any rational mind would consider a wise decision."

The price of a 78 ranges from a few cents to a fair amount of cents—in some cases, up to $40,000—depending on the cachet of the artist, the condition of the record, the rarity of the pressing, and the fervency of a collector's desire. Because 78s are objectively worthless and because collectors are so particular about what they want, a record's archival value often trumps its monetary value. But that archival value can still be astonishing. Because they weren't produced in huge quantities (although a CD or MP3 player is a fairly common accessory in most American homes now, gramophones were hardly standard in the early 1920s) and because for so long, so few people were interested in salvaging them, a good portion of the world's remaining 78s—and it's impossible to say how many are even left—were also singular representations. Often, no metal masters of these recording sessions survived, meaning that if the records themselves were to break, or be crammed into a flood-prone basement, or tossed into a Dumpster, then that particular song is gone, forever.

Most of Heneghan's collecting peers, including the famed illustrator Robert Crumb, are the types who went door-to-door in the 1960s, asking people if they had records in their attics and snatching up 78s for a quarter apiece. When I asked Heneghan where he scored the bulk of his collection, he looked at me as if I'd commanded him to disrobe. "You don't expect me to answer that question, do you? I'm not sure I should answer *any* of these questions," he guffawed, his voice incredulous. "Do you realize how limited . . . These aren't LPs! All it takes is a dozen more people interested and . . ." He trailed off again. "It amazes me. It's American musical history and it's forgotten about, and there are only a handful of people out there preserving it."

Heneghan wasn't being particularly hyperbolic. He and his pals are often uncovering and heralding artists who were previously unknown, and who would have remained that way had a collector not bothered to listen and share his finds. "The amazing thing about 78s is that so much of the music is one hundred percent undiscovered," he said. "There are still so many records out there that are so rare there are only one or two copies, or no copies—you've never heard it. I'm still often discovering things. You find some weird band name, you don't know what it is, and you take a chance on it, put it on, and it's some incredible masterpiece."

John Heneghan was glib and, at times, aggressively self-deprecating about his fanaticism, but his collection was, independent of its personal worth, an extraordinary cultural document. Collectors of 78s, maybe more than any other curators of music or music memorabilia, are doing essential preservationist work, chasing after tiny bits of art that would otherwise be lost. Even though their pursuits are inherently selfish, fueled by the same untempered obsession that drives all collectors, without Heneghan and his peers a good slice of musical history would be absent from the contemporary canon. And while academics, anthropologists, archivists, and reissue labels all assume roles in the preservation and diffusion of early songbooks, the bulk of the material being released or reissued is still being sourced from the original

78s—which are found, almost exclusively, in the cramped basements and bedrooms of 78 collectors.

Still, the historical heft of his effort didn't mean Heneghan was free from the neuroses that characterize so many collectors: his collection was historically significant, but it was also deeply personal, even pathological. Collectors, like everyone, get seduced by the chase.

"I have a recurring dream about finding Skip James's 'Devil Got My Woman,'" Heneghan said, leaning in, his voice low and solemn. "It's so vivid, so clear—the first time it happened I woke up in the middle of the night certain that I had the record. I was like, *This is amazing.* So I got up to check, and it wasn't there, and I was like, *Fuck.* So then I have the dream again, and it's so vivid the second time, and I think maybe the part about *not* having it was the dream. So I get up to check. Then I have the dream the third time, and the fourth time . . ." He shook his head, leaned back in his chair, and scratched a craggy blond goatee. Heneghan is a formidable physical presence, and his narrow, slate-gray eyes betrayed an intolerance for certain strains of bullshit; he was exceedingly pleasant but uninterested in pleasantries, and it occurred to me that I wouldn't ever want to be standing between him and a copy of "Devil Got My Woman."

"On a good day, you look at yourself like, I'm preserving American history: I'm an archaeologist. But the bottom line is that there's seriously something wrong," he continued, adjusting the black bowler hat he frequently sports. "The first time I bought a record, I remember thinking, I have to see if this band has any other records. And then when I got the other records, I thought, I need to figure out which one came first so I can put them in order. I remember going to friends' houses and they just had their records anywhere, and it was like, 'How can you *do* that? They have to be in order!' I just spent so much time thinking about the perfect way to put everything in order."

Heneghan finally asked me what I'd like to listen to, and we huddled around his turntable, taking turns pulling 78s from his shelves. My hands shook. Unlike vinyl records, which are forgivingly pliable,

78s are thick, brittle, and heavy. Drop one on the wrong surface at the wrong angle, and it'll shatter like a dinner plate.

The bulk of Heneghan's collection consists of early blues and hillbilly records, and they range in quality and tone. Up until about 1925, recordings were made acoustically, meaning the musicians would have to bellow and pluck directly into the phonograph's diaphragm cone, where the resulting sound vibrations would nudge the cutting stylus and create a transcription, which could then be played back. There were considerable drawbacks to the technology: drums and bass were rarely recorded because the depth of their vibrations would knock the cutting stylus from its intended groove, and things like cellos, violins, and even the human voice didn't always resonate enough to be properly rendered. By 1927, engineers had figured out how to use a carbon microphone—another Edison gadget, from 1877—which could then be amplified with vacuum tubes and used to power an electromagnetic recording head, meaning a far wider range of frequencies could be picked up and reproduced, yielding a richer, more authentic sound. Still, if you are not prone to romance and nostalgia, the process can seem silly in the face of today's error-free digital recording, where analog sound is converted into clean streams of binary code. To a modern sound technician, things like styluses and diaphragm cones are about as clunky and outmoded as the iron lung.

But for traditional record collectors—ones who, like Heneghan, came of age in the late 1970s—the upsides of digital recording are largely irrelevant. Although he owns an iPod (he bought it for Eden, who said she rarely used it) and a few shelves of CDs (mostly from the reissue label Yazoo Records, which was founded in the late 1960s and is now run, in part, by his friend and fellow collector Richard Nevins, who works exclusively from original 78s), he was not particularly interested in consuming digitally produced music. I could see how Heneghan might find MP3s a bit unsettling (those intangible streams of zeros and ones are about as far from cumbersome shellac discs as possible), but even the CD, the MP3's doofy, moonfaced older brother, was inherently unappealing to him. "If I find a great record, and a friend of mine says, 'How about I keep that record and just make you a CD of it?' it's like, 'Are you *insane?*' " he snorted.

Heneghan pulled Mississippi John Hurt's "Big Leg Blues," the Cannon Jug Stompers' "Walk Right In," and a 1920s test pressing of Frankie Franko and His Louisianans' "Somebody Stole My Gal" from his shelves. He laid the John Hurt record on his turntable, flipped a switch on a receiver, and dropped the stylus. The room filled with crackle. I held my breath.

The thing is, I wasn't exactly an analog rookie, even then. I owned plenty of LPs, and while my initial interest in vinyl was driven by mathematics (I could pay twenty-five cents for a *Led Zeppelin III* LP at my local Salvation Army, or slap down fourteen dollars for a plastic CD version at the record store), I secretly appreciated all the tender platitudes—Warmth! Texture! Authenticity!—spewed about analog sound. But because the bulk of my collection was lazily sourced from junk shops (I can still identify a three-LP set of Handel's *Messiah*—that brown-and-yellow thrift-store staple—from approximately forty-five feet away), I was never captivated by rare records in particular. My expertise regarding coveted vinyl consisted mostly of ribbing my pal Clarke for his pristine copy of *The Anal Staircase*, a three-song, twelve-inch EP released by the British industrial band Coil in 1986 and worth around eighty dollars to the right customer. (There's a photograph of a human anus on the cover.)

So while I possessed a working understanding of what 78s were and when they were produced, I had never purchased or played a single one. Still, I loved scrappy, prewar country blues in the same way I loved punk rock—something about the tenuousness of the entire enterprise, the threat of spontaneous dissolution, the immediacy—and had always been more than content to listen to it via digital reissue. Prior to this moment, it had never occurred to me that I was doing anything wrong. That I might be chasing an approximation.

Right now, there are 78 collectors working to gather and preserve all forms of prewar music—jazz, opera, classical, gospel, country, dance, pop—but there's something particularly seductive about the way blues music played on an acoustic guitar between 1925 and 1939—the so-called country blues—sounds on shellac. While playing the country blues can require a staggering amount of technical prowess (no other genre, except maybe rap, is as routinely underestimated), the most important component of any country blues song is still the performer's articulation of blues "feeling," that amorphous, intangible, gut-borne thing that animates all music and gives it life.

The necessity of emotion obviously isn't unique to the country blues, but because most prewar blues songs were assembled rather than composed (performers were often working with the same old folk songs as bases, tinkering with and rewriting verses to suit their needs), and because many performances were barely captured, let alone manipulated, it's often the only difference between a middling blues side and a transcendent one. Critics and scholars can pontificate at length about the technical dexterity of a country blues performer like Robert Johnson— the way his long fingers curled around the fret board, what his left foot was doing—but blues feeling is a lot trickier to dissect, in part because it runs counter to the very notion of analysis. It becomes the singular challenge of blues critics (of all critics, really) to articulate some sense of that bewildering force. It becomes the obligation of the fan to hear it.

That afternoon, sitting upright on Heneghan's couch, I was playing it real cool. But by fifty seconds into "Big Leg Blues"—right around the time John Hurt coos, "I asked you, baby, to come and hold my head" in his soft, honeyed voice—I felt like every single one of my internal organs had liquefied and was bubbling up into my esophagus. Even now, I'm not sure there's a way to accurately recount the experience without sounding dumb and hammy. I wanted to curl up inside that record; I wanted to inhabit it. Then I wanted it to inhabit me: I wanted to crack it into bits and use them as bones. I wanted it to keep playing forever, from somewhere deep inside my skull. This is how it often begins for collectors: with a feeling that music is suddenly opening up to you. That you're getting closer to it—to blues feeling—than you've ever gotten before.

The aesthetic superiority of analog playback has been so thoroughly and aggressively trumpeted that it feels almost silly to talk about it now, but if you're accustomed to low-quality MP3s, and if you primarily route them through your computer's speakers or cheap headphones, listening to a vinyl record on a proper stereo is still something of a revelation. It's luxurious rather than serviceable—like delicately consuming a fancy French chocolate when you've only ever gnawed on Hershey bars in the parking lot of a Piggly Wiggly.

Prewar 78s, though, are not particularly easy to relish, or at least not at first. Depending on the quality of the recording and the condition of the disc, there's often a high and persistent background hiss. The melody might be fully obscured by a staticky sizzle that feels otherworldly and distant, like the song had been buried in the backyard and was now being broadcast from beneath six solid feet of dirt.

I'd heard "Big Leg Blues" before; in 1990, Yazoo Records had released a CD of the thirteen tracks Hurt recorded for the Okeh Electric Records Company in 1928, and I'd picked up a used copy at a local record store a few years earlier. Not only was I familiar with the song, I'd experienced an expert digital rendering of an actual 78. My reaction to hearing the 78 itself played four feet in front of me felt wild and disproportionate even as it was happening. I like to think that I was reacting to the song, and that the record was just a conduit, a vehicle of presentation. But I suspect I was also seduced by the ritual—by the sense of being made privy to something exclusive, something rare.

The record ended. Clutching my notebook to my chest, I tried to think of a professional-sounding thing to say. "Wow!" I yelled. Heneghan looked at me. I stared at my list of handwritten questions for a beat or two too long before finally asking him if he thought that, given technological advancements in the way music is disseminated and stored, record collecting was a dying art.

"I think it's funny that you even call it an art," he answered. "I think it's more of a disease. There has to be something really wrong with you to want to possess these objects in the first place. You have to have them, and it's never enough, and you get that strange, tingly feeling when you get one. Anyone who collects anything is obsessive-compulsive and neurotic. The need to put things in order, to file by number, to alphabetize and label, to be constantly reassessing how you've ordered things—that's neurotic behavior. I've always thought I was really crazy, that there was something really wrong with me. Especially when I started collecting 78s, because I didn't know anyone else who collected them, and I felt really isolated and weird," he continued. "But then when I met guys like Crumb and Nevins, everyone was like, 'Yeah, we're all crazy.' I've never met [another 78 collector] who wasn't like, 'This is sick, we're all sick,'" he said. "When I finally gave in and started buying 78s, it was a conscious decision to embrace my sickness and do what I always wanted to do. It's probably like when someone dabbles in drugs their whole life and finally decides to shoot heroin. There has to be something in your mind that says, 'I give up.'

"If I really wanted a big house in the suburbs, I wouldn't be able to buy records as often, if ever," he conceded. "But the thing is, I don't really want a house in the suburbs. I'm happy, which is a little bit of a problem."

●

Heneghan and I kept in touch, and a few months later he invited me to a 78 listening party in his living room. On a gleaming afternoon in early May, I plodded down Second Avenue toward Heneghan's apartment, toting a warm six-pack of Brooklyn Lager.

I was the first to arrive. As Heneghan handed me back a beer, he pointed out a new acquisition: a small, weathered banjo, signed in fading pencil by the 1920s folksinger Chubby Parker. The banjo was hung above Heneghan's computer, alongside a framed headshot of Parker. A tiny silver star, inlaid deep in the instrument's head, shined. It reminded me of a Christmas tree.

Heneghan explained that he had recently scored an extremely rare 78 of Parker's "Davey Crockett" on eBay. Parker was one of the first performers to be featured regularly on Chicago's *National Barn Dance*, itself a precursor to *The Grand Ole Opry*, but his legacy was middling at best, and he is mostly known, when he is known at all, for chirping goofy folk songs like "Nickety Nackety Now Now Now." As was often the case, Heneghan was the only serious bidder. "When I first saw it on eBay, I had a weird panicky feeling," he said. "This was it, this was the day I'd been waiting for. But you just don't know. All it takes is one other person. I have my archenemies on eBay—I don't know who they are, but their monikers haunt me. When I saw 'Davey Crockett,' I didn't sleep that well for a week. I knew this was it—I was never gonna see it again. All my crazy friends saw it and knew that I wanted to get it and valiantly stayed away, and then they congratulated me when I got it." He smiled.

Until Heneghan manages to locate a copy of Skip James's "Devil Got My Woman"—his Holy Grail—he placates himself with smaller victories like "Davey Crockett." That may be all he ever gets. There are only three or four known copies of "Devil Got My Woman" remaining, two of which are so damaged as to be inconsequential. The song was recorded in February 1931 in Grafton, Wisconsin, for a small record label called Paramount Records. James created eighteen sides (or nine double-sided 78s) in Wisconsin that winter, but they were commercial nonstarters, and soon after, he quit playing blues music and became a choir director in his father's church. James wouldn't record again until the 1960s, when he was "rediscovered" in a county hospital in Tunica, Mississippi, by an enterprising trio of blues enthusiasts who persuaded him to come out of retirement. ("Well, that might be a good idea. Might be. But right now Skip is awful tired," he was quoted as saying.) In 1964, a sixty-two-year-old James appeared at the Newport Folk Festival, and he continued to perform sporadically until his death in 1969. Because his records weren't especially popular or very widely sold, few copies were made, and now, more than eighty years later, collectors have a slim-to-improbable shot at finding one in playable condition.

Still, "Devil Got My Woman" exists in infinite quantities in a re-mastered digital format and can be purchased instantly on iTunes for ninety-nine cents, thanks to the collector Richard Nevins, who possesses an original copy. As Nevins explained to me in an e-mail, almost any time anyone listens to "Devil Got My Woman," regardless of the individual source, chances are good that the recording they're hearing originated from his personal 78: " 'Devil Got My Woman' was first reissued on LP in the 60s, and, like for almost all old 78s of backcountry music, no masters have survived," he wrote. "I'd say that all reissues of this came from my copy, which is close to new and which previously belonged to [late Yazoo founder] Nick Perls. Many of the European labels that reissued this just dubbed it off the Yazoo release [1994's *The Complete Early Recordings of Skip James*]."

"Devil Got My Woman" is meandering and almost structureless, composed of little more than a three-bar vocal phrase and variations on two guitar chords, which are embellished and augmented by vocal and instrumental flourishes. That's the technical description. I can't really explain the rest. His falsetto careens, soaring and plummeting as if it were powered by some unseen, disreputable force. "Aw, nothin' but the devil changed my baby's mind," James whimpers over a bit of nefarious-sounding guitar. My favorite part of the 2001 film *Ghost World*—directed and adapted by the 78 devotee Terry Zwigoff—is when Enid, a recent high school graduate played by Thora Birch, asks Seymour, a 78 collector played by Steve Buscemi, if he has any more records like "Devil Got My Woman," and Seymour looks back at her, duly appalled: "There are no other records like that!" he yelps. When Bob Dylan featured the track on his *Theme Time Radio Hour*, he introduced it by declaring, "Skip had a style that was celestially divine, sounded like it was coming from beyond the rail, magic in the grooves . . . rare and unusual, mysterious and vague, you won't believe it when you hear." "Devil Got My Woman" is so strange, so volatile and wraithlike, I can understand why James's biographer Stephen Calt called the song "one of the most extraordinary feats of vocalizing found in blues song." I can see why Heneghan has been consumed by it.

While we waited for the rest of his guests to arrive, Heneghan and I dipped crackers in the small tub of hummus he'd set out on his coffee table. I admired his walls, which were covered with framed pieces of sheet music, hung just inches apart to ensure maximum capacity. Heneghan was self-effacing about his collecting habit; he recognized the practice as maniacal and his interests as outmoded. Still, he fancied himself an amateur historian of sorts—which was not entirely unreasonable—and was also convinced that, on some level, having interesting stuff around made him a more interesting person. Ironically, it was a very twenty-first-century approach to identity: broadcasting in lieu of communicating.

"When people come to my apartment, some walk in and get really silent, and I can tell they think it's creepy," he said. "And I think, Okay, your house is like the Ikea catalog, and so my stuff seems really strange. But I'm a little uncomfortable when I go to someone's house and it looks like the Ikea catalog. This is the most thought you could put into the stuff you want to be around?" he asked, his voice rising. "Give me that, give me A, B, C, and D, because they're on the same page? To me, that's why George Bush was president. That's why everyone eats at McDonald's."

Even though he rarely framed it as such, collecting had clearly become, for Heneghan, a functional way of rebelling against mainstream culture. Like getting a tattoo or jamming a titanium post through your septum, packing your apartment with old records and sheet music was a semipublic way of establishing a countercultural identity, of rejecting a society that felt homogenized and unforgiving. Heneghan frequently spoke of collecting as a form of submission, as a way of giving in to basic urges and desires that other people stifled, and when he did, it wasn't without a certain amount of pride.

Heneghan earned his cash as a freelance video technician, setting up cameras for television shows and concerts; when pressed, he gently grumbled about the artless nature of the gig. He was particularly disgusted by the extent to which backing tracks were employed by pop stars paid mounds of cash to sing their songs live. He considered the entire enterprise an epic charade: "It sounds like the album because you're listening to the album," he'd spit. When he wasn't working, Heneghan was performing with Eden; together they comprised John and Eden's East River String Band, a beguiling old-time outfit featuring John on guitar and Eden on ukulele and vocals. When they played, they sported period-appropriate garb and strummed antique instruments. (Heneghan collected old guitars, too.) Each time I saw them perform—at bars and small clubs downtown or in Brooklyn, mostly—they enthralled the room with their charmingly antiquated odd-couple rapport. That afternoon, Heneghan told me he'd been endeavoring to get their newest self-released album, *Some Cold Rainy Day*, issued on 180-gram vinyl with a gatefold cover, a cardboard sleeve that opens like a book. He ran into a snag when the kid who answered the phone at the pressing plant didn't understand what "gatefold" meant. "I finally had to ask, How old are you? I told him to find the oldest person who worked there and to ask them."

We ate some green grapes. A few minutes later, Heneghan buzzed in Sherwin Dunner, a jazz and blues collector who worked with Richard Nevins at Yazoo. He sat in a chair. "I notice that your Starkist lamp has a different shade than mine," he said, surveying a Starkist tuna–brand promotional lamp perched on Heneghan's bookshelf. He and Heneghan had identical carrying cases for their 78s, each marked with a little plaque that read MUSIC APPRECIATION RECORDS. Dunner set his box of records on the floor. The handle had been reinforced with duct tape. He had been amassing 78s for years, and, like Heneghan, understood collecting as a way of insulating oneself from a culture that was not always especially welcoming. "It's the way you cope with feeling like an outsider, feeling alienated from pop or mainstream culture, which has gotten more and more controlled and oppressive and dehumanized. So you create your own world, using whatever you think has meaning or aesthetic value. It's a world that can save you from the modern world," Dunner told me later.

Both Dunner and Heneghan were fervent, focused music fans with comprehensive knowledge of the various subgenres of early American music, and, accordingly, their collections were more functional than decorative. These records were not squirreled away in Plexiglas cases or sitting silent in locked boxes. They were handled with care, but they were *handled*—frequently and with enthusiasm, spun for friends and in private. Consequently, Heneghan had little interest in 78s that were so severely worn they no longer played properly. Both men also expressed deep vitriol for anyone who didn't share a similar keenness for the music, like some of the more investment-minded 78 collectors who procured records because of their potential for financial appreciation. For Heneghan and Dunner, such fetishistic thinking failed to acknowledge the wealth inherent in the songs themselves.

"That's a level of collecting that I despise," Heneghan said. "The guys who just buy [a record] because it's worth something and they're speculating that it's going to be worth more. But with something like 78s, there's so few of them available in the first place, and if [Sherwin] gets a good record, I may be envious or whatever, but I don't feel like, Oh, that's so horrible. There are other people who get a record and it's like, Well, that'll just sit on a shelf. No one's enjoying it, it's out of circulation, no one can hear it. With some of these records, there are so few copies [remaining] that really, *no one can hear it*," Heneghan seethed. "There's just something really despicable about that mentality. Those people tend to be the most, you know, 'That's mine now, I got that before you could get it.' "

Heneghan, accordingly, is generous with his records. He is periodically approached about loaning songs to documentary films—he had just given Cleoma Breaux and Joseph Falcon's "Fe Fe Ponchaux," a Cajun song from 1929 of which he has one of the better known copies, to the BBC—and routinely posts requested tracks on his Facebook or

MySpace page. If you manage to land an invitation to his home, he will play you anything you want to hear.

Three more guests arrived and settled into chairs. Dunner and Heneghan realized they owned two different 78s festooned with identical stickers foreswearing future commerce. In careful, handwritten block letters, someone had printed DO NOT SELL AT ANY PRICE and affixed it to each record's label. Considering that both 78s were purchased (in separate transactions) with the stipulation already in place, only two scenarios made sense: the author had changed his mind, or—the more likely option—he was long gone, and his estate hadn't been terribly concerned with his posthumous wishes for his precious discs.

I was subsumed by a strange gratitude, just then, for that faceless person and his little white stickers, for his vehemence, for his commitment to music as a thing to work for and revere and treasure and save, till death do you part. And even then, a desperate posthumous incantation, a plea: DO NOT SELL AT ANY PRICE. It felt poetic. It felt certain.

In some ways, the parameters of the collector's search—looking for one specific, tangible thing—made for an infinitely easier passage, a more satisfying arc, than blindly stumbling through life, trying to figure out what else would make you happy. These guys *knew* what would make them happy. Whether that happiness actually manifested itself at the end of the quest didn't necessarily matter—I believed in all those old, insipid chestnuts about the journey trumping the destination, about the process being more important than the product.

I realized then it was about the knowing, and the wanting.

at a house party. I paused at the door. An older woman was seated at a folding table near the entrance, eating baked beans directly from a tin can. She asked me for my name and I gave it to her, spelling it out carefully even though I hadn't preregistered for anything. She told me there was a ten-dollar entry fee. I dug some bills out of my skirt pocket. While I counted them out, she cheerfully admonished me for my late arrival: "You missed the gala," she clucked. "They had a lot of fun last night."

Record fairs—including this one, which is small but still relatively esteemed among collectors—are not particularly monumental occasions within the 78 community. All the major sales and trades are conducted privately, beyond the callous glare of fluorescent lights. But a record fair is also not a terrible place for a newcomer to seed a collection. Vendors, knowing their audience, have usually brought out their best, most coveted merchandise. Gone are the faded *Best of Bread* LPs; present, suddenly, are the psych rarities, the aberrant soul 45s, the 78s. After meeting with Heneghan, I was curious about the acquisition of rare records, where they came from, how they moved. I wandered from table to table, eavesdropping on conversations. The spirit was genial, but I felt unmoored, unsure of what to do with my hands and convinced everyone was giving me side eye. There was only one other woman on the floor.

Collectors shopping for records spend a lot of time assessing the condition of potential purchases, and at any moment I could see one or three or five of them holding a platter toward the light, carefully tilting it back and forth, like a mischievous fourth grader incinerating a line of ants. Collectors and vendors assign letter grades to records using a schematic known as the VJM Record Grading System, so named because it was refined by an editor of *Vintage Jazz Mart* (the world's oldest ongoing jazz and blues magazine) in the early 1950s. It is readily available on VJM's website and hasn't changed in half a century. For 78s, the scale technically ranges from N (for new or unplayed, an improbable grade for a 78) to P (for unplayable), although most collectors are only interested in records that fall between V ("moderate, even wear throughout, but still very playable; surface noise and scratches audible but not intrusive") and E ("still very shiny, near new looking, with no visible signs of wear, but a few inaudible scuffs and scratches"). Some collectors will determine a grade just by eyeballing the surface, but a 78 should be played before a decree is announced; because the composition of the shellac varied so wildly between labels, some records look significantly better (or worse) than they sound.

I stopped at a table of 78s and picked up a record featuring the tamburitza, a stringed, mandolin-like instrument that my father, the son of Croatian immigrants, has kept hung near his bed for as long as I can remember. The dealer standing behind it was in his early sixties, with curly, dark gray hair and a paper name tag stuck to his T-shirt: Elliot Jackson. He had come to the Hilton from New Hope, Pennsylvania, and to America from England before that. Jackson had gotten into 78s as a teenager. Blues records, mostly. "I remember buying some records at auction from the States, and unless I'm completely mistaken, I believe the person selling them was John Fahey—*that* John Fahey," he said.

Born in Washington, DC, in 1939 and raised in Takoma Park, Maryland, John Fahey is frequently invoked by 78 collectors as a kind of rogue idol. In pictures of him from his young adulthood, he has a confrontational slant to his face, blue eyes so sharp it almost smarts to look at them. He would later become feted for his instrumental acoustic guitar figures—rich, distantly tortured compositions that were idolized by rock musicians with avant-garde leanings, like Sonic Youth and the producer Jim O'Rourke, who heard something ghostly and eternal in them. There is a sense, in his work, of deep heartache and vexation. ("Fahey and myself are playing frustrated little symphonies on guitar," his friend and colleague Robbie Basho once said.)

Before he was a guitarist with a name worth dropping downtown, Fahey was a 78 rpm record collector; the two practices were acutely intertwined. He started canvasing for 78s under the tutelage of the musicologist and collector Dick Spottswood, scouring the South first for country and bluegrass records, then for primitive country blues 78s by the likes of Skip James and Charley Patton. In 1964, Fahey was part of the team (along with Henry Vestine of Canned Heat and Bill Barth of the Insect Trust) that found James convalescing in a Mississippi hospital. James and Fahey did not become fast friends. ("I didn't like him, and he didn't like me," Fahey later told the writer Eddie Dean, and confirmed his virulence in his part-autobiographical, part-fictionalized book *How Bluegrass Music Destroyed My Life*, in which he calls James an "obnoxious, bitter, hateful old creep.")

Fahey eventually wrote a master's thesis on Patton (*A Textual and Musicological Analysis of the Repertoire of Charley Patton*) for UCLA's folklore program. He already had a sense of the ways in which white blues fans were unduly aroused by the supreme otherness of black, prewar blues musicians. Years earlier, in 1959, he'd thought up a performance moniker for himself: Blind Joe Death. It was a vicious send-up. He would totter onstage wearing dark sunglasses, someone helping him to his chair by the elbow. Blind Joe Death, it was written, played a guitar made from a baby's coffin.

By the end of his life, Fahey was spherical and angry, living in a welfare motel near Portland, Oregon. In 1994, when the writer Byron Coley visited Fahey to profile him for *Spin*, he was discovered "vast, white and shirtless across a queen-sized bed," listening to a record of General Douglas MacArthur's farewell speech with all the lights in his room flipped off. Coley believed Fahey's situation—his obscurity—said "as much about the paucity of the public's imagination as it does about any of his personal failings." Fahey died in February 2001 at age sixty-one, from complications following a sextuple coronary bypass.

Jackson and I started talking about the sorts of people who frequent record fairs in suburban hotel conference rooms. "There are loads of weird people who are doing this. The majority are fairly strange," Jackson said. There was warmth in his voice. "I occasionally have people around to the house to buy stuff. My wife will say, 'I don't ever remember anyone coming around who's an ordinary person and can have a normal conversation,'" he said. "You have to be a little strange to be obsessed by something."

I bought the tamburitza record from Jackson and spent another hour milling around, until the existential stress of spending a bright summer morning inside a New Jersey Hilton started to trouble my stomach and I retreated to the elevator. I carted my 78 home and spent some time staring at it. I admired the way it looked on my shelf. I played it relentlessly. I thought, a lot, about getting another one.

A few days later, I received an e-mail from Art Zimmerman, the owner of a jazz label called Zim Records, who had hosted the bash with Jim Eigo, the founder of a publicity company called Jazz Promo Services. Its tone was unusual in its precision—almost poetic. I would eventually come to recognize this as the collectors' voice, an exacting, thorough, and thoughtful mode, unconcerned, perhaps, with elegance, but always useful, and sometimes even kind:

"This message is intended for those who attended the Jazz Record Collectors' Bash this past weekend. Many of you who did not attend are receiving this message simply because it is less labor intensive to send this to the entire Bash customer list than to filter the contact information for only the attendees. Several items (summarily described below) were left in the vendor room at the Bash. If any belong to you, please contact me by return email or by phone. 1. A volume of one of the Rust discographies with much wear to the binding. 2. Sunglasses 3. A small quantity of 78s purchased from Lloyd Rauch, mainly popular vocal items, but possibly including a disc by Pasquale Amato."

The sunglasses might have been mine.

Three

This Is One of the Things
I Would Say Is Inexplicable

●

Christopher King, Geeshie Wiley, Blind Uncle Gaspard, Matchsticks,
Facebook, the Hillsville VFW Flea Market and Gun Show, Death

●

I first met the collector Christopher King on the same afternoon Hurricane Irene came whipping through central Virginia. I spent most of the drive to his home dodging cracked branches and other tree-borne detritus, eventually parking my rental car in a giant puddle and booking it to his doorstep. King, then forty-one, had short dark hair that he combed back and to the side, and a pale, round face that suggested a certain kind of old-fashioned innocence, although in actuality he was sharp and acerbic, quick with an eye roll and unlikely to let anyone get away with saying anything stupid. He had a tattoo of Betty Boop on his right bicep, which he acquired while working as a janitor, in an everlasting bid at solidarity with his colleagues. He smoked stubby cigarettes he rolled himself from a baggie of tobacco he kept in his front pants pocket. King was precise but open-minded, which was good, because he would eventually end up spending a terrifying amount of time walking me through the nuances of various recorded phenomena. I was grateful for that. If I wanted to learn about records—where they were, how they got there, why it mattered—I knew I would need a tolerant sensei, a patient guide.

King worked as a production coordinator at Rebel Records, a bluegrass label, and County Records, an old-time label, both based in Charlottesville; he was also the owner of Long Gone Sound Productions, a sound-engineering and historical music production company. On his office desk, alongside a supplementary-seeming desktop computer—in my memory it was an archaic, Commodore 64–looking behemoth, although in actuality it was likely a contemporary PC—sat a green Remington typewriter. His eyeglasses were of another era. He didn't own a mobile phone, and referred to mine as a "smart-thing." His house in rural Faber, which he shares with his wife, Charmagne, his daughter, Riley, and a bug-eyed Boston terrier named Betty, was outfitted with an assortment of carefully vetted antiques and oddities. Like many collectors, King had insulated himself from the facets of modernity he found most distasteful. At one point he asked me if Lady Gaga was, indeed, "a lady." He was not being coy or funny.

King was flummoxed by my interest in collecting, which he insisted was a mundane if not static hobby, and he answered my questions with barely contained bemusement. What he *was* compelled by was listening, and the myriad ways people required and employed sound: "The question that never gets answered, or maybe that doesn't even get asked, is what is it about being human that makes us desire this thing that is so ephemeral?"

Music, he pointed out, was a universally recognized salve, and it was worth considering the mechanics of *that* exchange, because understanding it was the only way anyone could ever begin to explain why he collected 78s. "There's some sound or some group of sounds or some line of sounds that evokes something cathartic. I think every single human being has that, from one end of the spectrum to the other," he said.

Accordingly, King insisted he wasn't collecting records so much as performances. He liked the things, but he needed the songs, the cathar-sis—the records were a vehicle. I would eventually hear a version of this speech get recited by dozens of different collectors, and it usually felt like bullshit, but I believed King when he insisted that listening to a 78 (rather than an LP or a digital reissue) proffered him a more thorough and transformative experience. He didn't try to define it any further. "It's a fidelity thing and it's also an aura, an intangible. I'm one of those people who don't think there's much that is inexplicable, but this is one of the things that I would say is inexplicable," he said.

King was born and raised in Bath County, Virginia, and he's never lived outside the state, save a brief, errant stint in Steubenville, Ohio, during which he completed three days of a PhD program in philos-ophy at Franciscan University. He'd previously studied philosophy and religion as an undergraduate at Radford University and learned the practice of collecting from his dad, Les King, a local teacher and musician who steadily accrued upright music boxes, antique books, Victrolas, 16-millimeter films, records, and other curiosities. His father, who passed away in the winter of 2001, remained a consider-able presence in his life, and King mentioned him frequently, with a mix of devastation and approbation.

As a kid, King was often toted along to yard sales and flea markets, but his own collecting began when he serendipitously encountered a stack of 78s in an abandoned shack on his grandparents' land. It's a good story, cinematic: "My grandmother had died, so my grandfather wanted me to come there and help clean out the sharecropper's shed. I remember opening the door to this tar-paper shack, and there was a dilapidated Victrola in the room. I knew what a 78 was and I knew how to play them, but I had never had a profound attraction to them. Maybe what Dad was playing didn't tug at the strings in the right way. So I opened the lid and I'm going through records and there's Blind Willie Johnson, 'God Don't Never Change.' Then there's Washing-ton Phillips's 'Denomination Blues.' Then there's 'Aimer et Perdre' by Joe and Cleoma Falcon, a Cajun lost-love song. Dad helped me wash them. I was in eighth grade and became obsessed with going in people's basements and looking under their porches. I can't tell you the stacks of 78s people would put under their porches back then."

King started out looking for hillbilly records, which bled into blues, which splintered into a profound affinity for the raw and rural sounding. "If there's any one continuous thread through everything that I have, it's deeply, deeply rural and backwoodsy. It's almost like it turns its back to the city. There's something about that," he admitted. King was also preternaturally drawn to narratives of longing and discontent, to performances that sounded unhinged and uncontrollable. It was a preference, unfortunately, that I recognized in myself—a base, possibly shameful desire to hear someone so overcome by emotion that they could no longer maintain any guise of dignity or restraint. I suppose the idea was that it made us feel less alone, hearing someone else unravel. Or maybe it was a yardstick by which we could measure our relative damage. Or maybe it just sounded good and liberating—a kind of proxy wilding. King was listening for it, constantly.

He was also a guy who thought frequently about dying (he worked, briefly, as an undertaker) and was prone to saying things like "I prepare for death every day. I'm obsessed with it." It made sense that King, a collector, would be fixated on the passage of time, and his preoccupation with his legacy—as a curator, a producer, a father—fueled much of his work. "Look at all the blatantly transient things that, ultimately, are never going to last, like Facebook postings," he complained to me one day on the telephone. "I'm definitely obsessed with the notion that it could end just like that. What's going to be left behind?"

In actuality, the question of what will endure has never been more complicated to answer. Although King would have scoffed at the notion, it's possible to argue that our digital legacies (all those dopey Facebook posts) will ultimately prove infinitely more enduring than our material legacies. They are, after all, replicated and indissoluble—such is the way of the Web. These days, there are even services to help with the posthumous management of a digital legacy; now, when people draft wills and name executors, they can also make arrangements with companies like Legacy Locker, "a safe, secure repository for your vital digital property that lets you grant access to online assets for friends and loved ones in the event of loss, death, or disability." It's hard not to assume that this is how future generations will engage with and be edified by the past—that this is the way they'll come to understand how humans used to live.

But I knew what King meant about endurance, about capturing something true. Maybe what he was actually looking for on all those records—what I was actually looking for—were songs that somehow captured the tenuousness of even being alive in the first place. Songs that recognized, either explicitly or implicitly, the threat of swift and complete termination that all living creatures are forced to contend with. And it's not just that our existence is friable. Our happiness is, too. Anything can fall apart.

King had been involved, in one way or another, in many of my favorite reissue collections, but the one that seemed closest to his heart (and that best encapsulates his particular worldview) is *Aimer et Perdre: To Love & to Lose, Songs, 1917–1934*, which was released in 2012 on the Tompkins Square label. King produced and remastered and fussed it into being; all the 78s were sourced from his private collection, and his introductory essay is an earnest paean to what he refers to as "our inexplicable mulishness in seeking out relationships that we know will ultimately both enrich us and devastate us, more often at the same time." I think King found solace in the idea that bad love was an ancient human pastime, and that our desperate search for (and epic bungling of) intimate relationships was somehow hardwired into our DNA— that heartache was a kind of biological inevitability. In any case, he had assembled a record collection that seemed to very clearly say as much. Or, as he wrote in the same notes: "Many of the songs in this collection convey the deep despair of abandonment and loss as if the only precondition of *our being* is our ability to suffer, to hold multitudes of contradictions such as regretting having done and not done the same thing at different times and under different conditions." It was dark, but it was true: we suffer, therefore we sing.

King's records are neatly contained on squat, custom-built shelves lining the north wall of his music room, itself a dark and mystical spot—a small, cooled space packed with vintage audio equipment, instruments, artwork, and books. (If you are prone to romanticizing such things, a gasp upon entry is inevitable.) King controlled one of the best assortments of prewar Cajun 78s (his friend, the collector Ron Brown, had the other), and his stock of Albanian folk records, a newer preoccupation, was inimitable. Now that most of the coveted prewar blues records had been discovered or at least named, many collectors had moved on to more "exotic" fare, although the musical through line running through all of it remained clear: these were outlier records, frenzied and raw.

More important—to me, at least—was that King is also the keeper of one of three known copies of Geeshie Wiley's "Last Kind Words Blues" and one of three known copies of Blind Uncle Gaspard's "Sur le Borde de l'Eau," arguably two of the saddest, strangest songs ever recorded, a fact he summarized thusly: "So, I have two of the world's most rare and most depressing 78s ever . . . if I were to be swallowed up, would all the sadness disappear with me?"

King was joking, and I had not yet sunk so far as to believe that the whole well of human despair—that eternally flush reservoir—was somehow being sustained or directed by two old records, but they did feel imbued with a certain otherworldly import. I first heard "Last Kind Words Blues" on a 2005 Revenant Records compilation called *American Primitive, Vol. II: Pre-War Revenants (1897–1939)* (King, incidentally, had remastered that collection). By then, collectors and researchers had figured out the song was recorded in Paramount Records' Grafton studio in March 1930, but nobody knew how its creator, Geeshie Wiley, had gotten to Wisconsin, or where she came from (she might have spent time in Natchez, Mississippi, or at a medicine show farther north in Jackson, or—as King suggested after noting the particular way she pronounced "depot"—been born and reared somewhere along the Texas-Louisiana border), or even what her real name was ("Geeshie" was likely a nickname, indicating she had Gullah roots, or was a descendant of West African slaves brought to South Carolina and Georgia via Charleston and Savannah). Wiley played with a guitarist named Elvie Thomas, and they recorded six sides for Paramount between 1930 and 1931. Beyond that, there wasn't even significant conjecture about her life—who she loved, what she looked like, how she died. Wiley was a specter, fiercely incorporeal, a spirit suggested if not contained by shellac. King thought that was part of her appeal—that we could project whatever we needed onto her—but "Last Kind Words Blues" is also so odd and chilling an accomplishment that it effectively transcends its own mythology. Or at least renders it mostly subordinate.

Wiley's lyrics and phrasing aren't idiosyncratic, exactly, but they're rhythmically baffling in a way that makes her performance feel singular if not entirely unreproducible—to the extent that it almost makes sense that the record itself is so rare. In his essay "Unknown Bards," John Jeremiah Sullivan called the song "an essential work of American art, sans qualifiers, a blues that isn't a blues, that is something other, but is at the same time a perfect blues, a pinnacle," and the confusion Sullivan references—the psychic disorientation stirred up by Wiley's performance—is maybe the only quantifiable thing about it. King chided me about my inability to articulate precisely what it was about "Last Kind Words Blues" that I found so undeniable—why it worked on me; why, by the time she arrived at the "What you do to me, baby / It never gets out of me" bit, I was half-breathing and glassy-eyed—but that mystery was a fundamental part of its allure. In "O Black and Unknown Bards," the James Weldon Johnson poem that gave Sullivan's piece its title, Johnson wrote of his own bewilderment regarding the composition of certain spirituals, presenting the only useful question one can really ask of Wiley: "How came your lips to touch the sacred fire?"

"Last Kind Words Blues" was the first record I ever asked King to play for me, and I suspect it's the one most people request if they ever make it past his front door and get a chance to start demanding things. There's even an online video—shot by the 78 Project, a pair of Brooklyn-based filmmakers who traveled around recording new artists to blank lacquer discs on a 1930s Presto Direct-to-Disc recorder—titled "Christopher King Plays Geeshie Wiley," which is, incredibly, just that: three and a half minutes of King spinning "Last Kind Words Blues" on a turntable and looking uncomfortable. At one point he scratches his nose.

If Wiley is an enigma, Blind Uncle Gaspard is a wisp. The guitarist and curator Nathan Salsburg sent me an MP3 of "Sur le Borde de l'Eau" one October, after I told him I'd never heard it; to his credit, he included fair warning ("The end of [the] side sounds completely like he's choking up and can't go on and thank God the record's over. He's probably just got a frog in his throat . . . But it sure as shit doesn't sound like it, reaching through the years and kicking you in the face."). Gaspard was born in 1880 in Avoyelles Parish in Dupont, Louisiana, recorded a handful of Cajun ballads and string-band songs for Vocalion Records in two sessions in the winter of 1929 (one in Chicago, one in New Orleans), and died in 1937. I'd heard "La Danseuse," the Gaspard and Delma Lachney track the collector and producer Harry Smith included on *The Anthology of American Folk Music*, and I thought it was a very sweet guitar and fiddle tune, but "Sur le Borde de l'Eau" is something else entirely. I don't know what Gaspard is going on about (I don't speak enough French), but I'm certain the payoff isn't narrative. His voice is so saturated with longing that it seems to hover midair, a helium balloon that's lost too much gas. It is tenuous and malfunctioning and then it disintegrates entirely, like the best/worst relationship you've ever had, like a ghost disappearing into the mist.

King acquired a copy in a trade with a collector he will still identify only as "Paul" ("It sounds more *Mr. Arkadin*-esque that way . . . Jeez, I don't want to give up all my secrets!") in late 2012. When I visited him in November of that year, a few days before Thanksgiving, he didn't make me wait very long to hear it. We decamped to his music room with tall glasses of Turkish iced tea and he let me have the good chair, the one behind his desk, the one that faced the speakers. I made him play it for me again several hours later, right before I left, and I sat and stared at the turntable, watching the record spin, feeling flabbergasted anew that anything so alive-sounding could be carved into a slab of shellac. I had sipped some stronger drinks by then, but still: the entire experience was so disorienting that I lurched off into the icy Virginia night without my coat and scarf.

King is well regarded as an engineer—he'd been nominated for six Grammys and won one in 2002, which he now stores in a cardboard box labeled ACCOLADES—and his ability to wrangle usable sound from gouged and battered records was astonishing. It was so astonishing, in fact, that I periodically questioned both its origins and its manifestations. What did King hear when he listened to his records? What did I hear? Those discrepancies, when and if they existed, were they physical or metaphysical? Had I just blithely annihilated my eardrums via a catastrophic combination of punk-rock records and shitty headphones, an end-of-day blaring ritual that had eased me through several years of life and work in New York City? Or was it more complicated—was it a function of need? Did King hear more because he needed more?

"I can hear stuff that's on a different frequency than a lot of other people," King said. "It's also really irritating. I can be in the living room reading with fans going and Betty could be in the library lying on the floor, but I can hear her heart beating. She's a small dog. I have an intense, acute sense of hearing. It's selective; I can turn it off when people are talking. Is it a form of autism? I don't know."

What was certain was that his work required a great deal of ingenuity. The turntable in his music room was littered with oddly sized bits—matchsticks, tongue depressors, little plastic ice-cream spoons—that he used to weigh down the tone arm based on assumptions he'd made or things he'd learned regarding certain studios or recording sessions. He accommodated for factors like ambient humidity, or a tilt in the floorboards, or a distraction on the part of the original engineer, who may have been daydreaming or hungry or new at the studio. When he was working on remastering records for Revenant Records' *Screamin' and Hollerin' the Blues: The Worlds of Charley Patton*, an epic, seven-CD compendium of Patton's work, he managed to suss out a second voice on Patton's "I'm Goin' Home"—a whole other person, singing along from a different room. "It's definitely there," he shrugged. "No one knows who the hell it is."

What King did, in these instances, was something akin to translation, and it was useful, generous work. Sonically speaking, 78s can be intimidating—the music they contain is often ancient sounding, so obscured by years and circumstance that it becomes too distant, too historic, to be properly felt. Shrouded by mythology and crackle, it's easy to forget that Charley Patton sang about fucking and heartbreak and shit that pissed him off—all the same stuff people sing about now. King humanized and demystified the performance by isolating a breath, a foot stomp. Some goon waiting outside.

Sometimes King's mission had to do with how a record was played and the shape it was in when he got it. Was the Victrola crooked, were people dancing so vigorously that the needle kept jumping, was the record stored in a damp basement or a drafty attic? Mostly, though, he was compensating for the shortcomings of a then-nascent technology (most records weren't recorded precisely at 78 rpm, and some weren't recorded anywhere near that speed). The same night King played me his Gaspard we also listened to Robert Johnson's "Hell Hound on My Trail," a song I'd heard hundreds of times before, only it sounded different, clearer, more vigorous. I asked King about it. He smirked. When I looked at his turntable, I saw it was spinning at 79.4 rpm and that he had placed a Popsicle stick on top of the stylus. It felt like a magic trick. A conjuring.

○

I've since consumed several of the most gluttonous meals of my adult life with King, a dubious gastronomical streak that began in the front seat of King's Volkswagen, then parked outside Dudes Drive-In in Christiansburg, Virginia. The aftermath was bleak, spiritually speaking.

"I feel like I just ate a small child," King announced. The remnants of a hamburger steak sandwich quivered in his lap. I squirted more ketchup packets onto a cardboard boat of tater tots, which I'd strategically positioned on the dashboard for continued ease of access. A typewritten track listing for *Mama, I'll Be Long Gone*, a collection of songs recorded by the prewar accordionist Amédé Ardoin and recently reissued by King, was Scotch-taped to the glove box. I was careful not to smear it. "I'm gross," I mumbled to no one in particular. I took a long pull of Coke. My mouth was still crammed with cheeseburger. King had warned me about the culinary limitations of our destination—the way he put it was, "If you flew over at night, the area would be illuminated with the lights of a thousand deep fryers"—but we didn't try especially hard to circumvent that proclamation. Cursory consideration was paid to the barbecue restaurant next door, but their evening's scheduled entertainment (a pair of longhairs strumming the Statler Brothers' "Flowers on the Wall") had functioned as an instant appetite suppressant for King. I could see that much on his face.

A few weeks earlier, I had convinced King to let me tag along on a junking mission—the procurement of records from people who don't know or care to know their worth, financial or otherwise—to the Hillsville VFW Flea Market and Gun Show in Hillsville, Virginia, a sleepy little town in the eastern foothills of the Blue Ridge Mountains, about twenty miles from the North Carolina border. King had been lucky there before, although he also warned me that it might be a tremendous bust: "I've gone almost every year for fourteen years," he wrote in an e-mail. "Some years I've done quite well . . . Scored a [Charley] Patton once, several Henry Thomas records another, a Reeves White County Ramblers another, a large stack of Polish string bands another. Last year I came back with nothing . . . It's just like that. But it is a stinky, dusty, terribly early trek (you have to hit it, and hit it hard, early on Friday just as the sun comes up)." This, I knew, was how good records got found—not by belatedly stopping by the Jazz Record Collectors' Bash in suburban New Jersey. And while I wanted to watch King work, I also wanted to see what sorts of things I could find for myself.

On the Thursday before the market opened, I met King in his office at County Records. Getting to Hillsville on time required driving the two and a half hours from Charlottesville to Christiansburg, spending the night, and waking up before six to finish the trip. King was a good traveling companion, not above friendly ribbing (he immediately gave me shit about the size of my duffel bag—which I still contend was reasonable—as he hoisted it into his trunk), amenable to frequent stops (in part so he could smoke), and prepared to discuss, at length, all the grand failings of humankind, both as they related to our individual lives and to the whole of the species. ("It seems like I only enter into an abysmal depression every year and a half or so, and it's usually because of having to go to Whole Foods.")

We also talked about records. King had developed a marked disdain for collectors who issued compilations of their finds but failed to procure the necessary support documents—the ones who didn't provide meaningful context for the music they were promoting. As far as King was concerned, collectors should embrace research, and the ones who refused to were dilettantes. "They don't feel like they need to fill in any information, and so it creates this imaginary, artificial mythology," he said. "It's a pretense that covers up a banality that they don't want to reveal to others. 'We just like this—we don't want to tell you about it.' The people who impress me are the people who become so obsessed with the music that they do everything in their power to get the best-condition copies of the discs, and then find out everything they possibly can about some really obscure, arcane musician or type of music. Then they provide it. They don't withhold it."

I still hadn't quite worked out how I felt about most 78 collectors' obsessive desire to contextualize—in the worst instances, to synthesize spotty research into quasi-academic narratives—and I still wanted to believe that these records were significant on their own merits, independently of any applied historical heft. It was music, after all. Why distance ourselves from it? Modern listeners, I insisted, didn't have many chances to experience art in a vacuum, devoid of cultural currency and freed from the constraints of time and place. Wasn't it an opportunity? A thing to treasure?

He didn't say as much, but I'm fairly certain King thought I was being naïve, if not willfully oblivious. There were some eye rolls. I brought up Wiley. Didn't he believe "Last Kind Words Blues" was good enough to devastate a roomful of, say, rural Swedes who didn't know anything about the country blues or Mississippi or rare 78s? Who hadn't yet engaged in a spirited debate about whether she says "bolted meal" or "boutonniere" or "broken will" at the end of that early verse? He made a face at me. "There's just too much richness to be derived from the context of the original recording," he said. "Reckon it makes me a pessimist or killjoy, even though I'm a true believer in the redemptive power of Geeshie."

Ultimately, King and I would end up spending more time bickering about this than anything else—I had taken to arguing that Wiley could destroy anyone, anywhere, regardless of what he or she knew or didn't know—and a few months after I got back from Virginia, when I started up about it again, he sent me the following e-mail:

"Here's a thought-experiment. Rather than the 78 being presented to a bunch of rural Swedes, Albanians, or Greeks, why don't you have the actual Geeshie Wiley show up in Albania and [the Albanian clarinetist, violinist, and singer] Riza Bilbyl show up in Jackson, Mississippi? Do you think that the reaction of a bunch of rural Albanians to Wiley's music or a bunch of sharecroppers in Mississippi to Riza Bilbyl in the 1930s would differ from their reaction right now? If so, why? Now, remove Geeshie and Riza and replace them with a battered, only-known copy of their respective 78 but retain the two different date spreads . . . would the reaction to their greatness be diminished or intensified by the introduction of this base artifact rather than the real thing?"

I mean, he was right: time and circumstance shape our understanding of art in substantial ways. But what I still couldn't unpack—probably because I often caught myself conflating the two—was whether my subjective context (the fact of me, where I live now and when I was born, my understanding of heartache and what I ate for lunch) can or should be trumped or augmented by a more objective context (the fact of the song, of how and where and why it was made). I remain a staunch believer in the subjective experience, but I am skeptical, sometimes, of objective significance. As an engineer, King was tasked with balancing all contexts: what he wanted to hear, what he was supposed to hear, what was actually audible. John Muir's famed assertions of interconnectedness—"When we try to pick out anything by itself we find that it is bound fast by a thousand invisible cords that cannot be broken, to everything in the universe," he wrote in his journal in 1869—felt applicable.

That Thursday night, after we'd arrived in Christiansburg and scrounged supper at Dudes, King and I commandeered a pair of beige-colored, $49-a-night beds at an Econo Lodge near the highway. The hotel was set up like an old motor inn, with two levels of rooms emptying onto concrete balconies. A fleet of cable repairmen were tailgating in the parking lot, slapping wads of hamburger meat onto hibachi grills and emptying endless cans of Pabst Blue Ribbon beer. I entertained a handful of cheery solicitations while wandering around with a plastic bucket, hoping to ice the bourbon I'd brought from Charlottesville. When the timbre shifted from jovial to menacing, I darted back to my room, piled all the unbolted furniture in front of the door, unwrapped a plastic cup, poured myself a drink (neat), and fell asleep horizontally with all of my clothes still on.

King and I had agreed to meet up in the lobby at six A.M. sharp. Before I'd left New York for Virginia, I'd asked King if I needed to bring anything in particular with me. He'd sent this advice, which I was tempted to print out and tape to the inside of my closet door, like Joan Didion in "The White Album":

> So, you should pack:
> a) water-bottle
> b) knapsack
> c) comfortable shoes that you can burn afterwards (I've read that ladies in New York do this all the time, so this is more of an afterthought)
> d) handkerchiefs (viewed from the moon, Hillsville at noon would appear to be a dust storm, as if it were over the Sahara)
> e) change of clothes or two (I even offend myself after three or four hours at the market)
> f) a disbelief in what humanity can bear

It seemed comprehensive—and applicable to a variety of reporting scenarios. I dressed in a pair of cutoff Levi's, a white tank top, and my old Converse sneakers. I filled my water bottle from the bathroom tap, secured it in my backpack with my cell phone, notebook, pens, and recorder. I pulled my hair into a knot on top of my head. I rubbed my eyes. I felt like I was preparing myself for battle, or for indoctrination into some brotherhood of shared trauma. I dragged the furniture away from the door, strapped on my backpack, and walked outside and toward the lobby.

The moon—a blue moon, incidentally, which felt portentous even from the Econo Lodge parking lot, typically a romance-obliterating sort of place—was still sunken and teeming in the sky. Despite the lack of sun it was already hot, or maybe just moist; every time I inhaled, I felt bloated, sticky from the inside out. While I waited for King to appear, I poured myself a cup of tepid coffee from the lobby pot and watched the local news on TV. A skinny teenager named Levi Moneyhunt was being interviewed regarding his participation in something called the Catawba Farm Fest, which seemed to involve him playing "old-time music" on a yellow Flying V electric guitar. I was underlining the words "Levi Moneyhunt" in my notebook when King arrived. He was dressed in jeans and a tucked-in brown T-shirt. His leather-and-canvas rucksack contained an antique record-carrying case, complete with cardboard separators, where he could stow and protect his purchases.

Following a brief consultation, we decided to take breakfast at the Waffle House on the other side of the parking lot. I ordered a plate of fried eggs and smothered hash browns. The toast—wheat, a concession that now strikes me as absurd—was so thoroughly saturated with butter that it could no longer ably support itself. I gobbed a tiny tub of grape jelly on top of it and shoved it into my mouth anyway. It seemed smart to renew our resources, bank some energy. While we forked our eggs, King outlined his plan for the day. We'd head directly to a record dealer he'd had luck with before—a guy named Rodger Hicks who trekked to Hillsville every year from Forest Hill, West Virginia, a couple hours north. King knew where his table was typically located, and he knew we needed to get there early. After that, we'd walk around for as long as we could stand it, looking for records concealed amid other relics. I asked King what I should expect, broadly speaking. "You'll want to take a picture," he said. "You'll be stunned. By how many people, how thick the people are, how thick the tents are, how big the whole thing is, and I guess by how disgusting it is." I told him I'd seen some pretty grody displays in Brooklyn, like this one time a guy in track pants vacated his bowels on the sidewalk outside my apartment. I received an eye roll. We tossed down some cash for our meal, climbed back into the Volkswagen, and sped off.

King and I approached Hillsville from the north, rolling through miles of bucolic countryside, up and down, smoothly, like a surfer straddling his board at sunrise. There is a moment in late August, in the South, where the landscape gets nearly obscene—overfed and cognizant of what comes next—and unleashes a final, boasting parade of virility. Abundance was in the air. Just a few miles outside of town the yard sales started, driveways and porches crammed with junk. Out-oftowners were coming, with cash, in pursuit of they-ain't-sayin'-what, and anyone lucky enough to own property along the primary artery to the market was taking full advantage of the sudden influx, luring shoppers off-course with renegade wares. Entire houses appeared to have been turned inside out. Traffic slowed. There was some aggressive browsing. People were caffeinated. King, for his part, was stoic, unswayed by the siren call of unregulated product, and by 8:40 A.M. we had parked at a lot in town (five dollars to the man in the overalls) and were marching, briskly, toward Rodger Hicks's tent, past the vendors with fanny packs of small bills, past the women tearing open packages of gas station donuts and unleashing tiny puffs of powdered sugar. The air was airless—heavy and close, like a wet sheet.

Tramping through a flea market with Chris King is oddly thrilling, like getting tied to the back of a heat-seeking missile, or being RoboCop. As we moved steadily toward our target, King scanned various tables and booths, pointing out any vendor with a gramophone—to King, the most obvious signifier of a potential shellac windfall. I can't overstate how good he is at this; he can turn a corner and point out a Victrola in about 1.5 seconds. I, meanwhile, was distracted by nearly everything ("Oh, I had this exact Alf doll when I was a kid!"), and for each whiskey decanter shaped like the Great Chicago Fire that I paused to admire, King discovered another sagging box of old media tucked inside a teak midcentury buffet. At this point, he was only making mental notes of spots to revisit. We needed to get to Hicks by nine A.M., when the flea market officially opened and vendors could begin selling their goods.

By the time we found Hicks's booth, there were already a few shoppers milling about, including a collector King recognized—a soft-spoken older gentleman with a mustache and a buttoned-up shirt named Gene Anderson. After I introduced myself, Anderson let me flip through his want lists, which he'd slipped into clear plastic pages and assembled in a binder—based on the contents, he had what appeared to be a solid collection of prewar country and blues records on his shelves already. King, meanwhile, nodded hello to Hicks—a middle-aged man with thin brown hair pulled into a ponytail and a pair of tiny, oval-shaped sunglasses—leaned over a box of 78s, and began thumbing away. On a piece of cardboard, someone had written GOOD 78S BE CAREFUL, but rivulets of dew had already dripped through the tarp Hicks had strung up, saturating the sign. King snorted and pushed it aside.

Most of the tent was filled with used rock LPs, 45s, and CDs. Rodger Hicks seemed to have some passing sense that certain old 78s were worth something, although he also hadn't really bothered to follow that thread to any logical pricing conclusions. The bulk of his 78s were marked at just a couple bucks, although a few in especially good condition were randomly priced at $100 to $300. Some negotiation was expected. Almost immediately, King nudged me and handed over a Paramount pressing of Blind Lemon Jefferson's "That Black Snake Moan," which he already owned and wasn't interested in—it was marked $250, which was probably about $100 more than most collectors would pay. It's a powerful, groaning song—the black snake, in this case, being both exactly what it sounds like and a useful metaphor for Jefferson's fear of everything he couldn't see—but was also popular, meaning an awful lot of copies were pressed. I was tickled by the idea of having it in my clutches, but I wasn't particularly seduced by the song or its price. I set it down.

King chatted amicably with Anderson and kept on pulling out records. I stood a few feet away, jotting impressions of the crowd in my notebook ("A woman in a visor holding an LP and yelling, 'Jim, look, Steve Miller!'") and occasionally peeking over King's shoulder. I felt acutely aware of wanting to stay out of his way, lest I complicate a delicate acquisition process. At some point, King faux-casually asked Anderson what he'd picked up so far, then appeared relieved when Anderson showed him his selections. (Watching two collectors interrogate each other about recent—or, in this case, ongoing—purchases is a little like watching two high-achieving middle school students warily prod each other about a grade: "What'd you get?" "What? What'd you get?" "What?")

Finally Anderson paid for his records and ambled off, and King showed me the 78s he'd pulled, which included two notable rarities: Eddie Head and His Family's "Down on Me" / "Lord I'm the True Vine" (one of two, maybe three known copies; it was priced at two dollars) and Sylvester Weaver's "Guitar Blues" / "Guitar Rag" (less rare, but in notable condition—an E copy, which would replace King's E-minus copy). After a bit of gentle bargaining, King paid Hicks $100 cash for a total of nine 78s. He knelt down in the grass and gently tucked the records into his case. He was pleased. I picked up a few of King's cast-offs, including 78s from Stick McGhee, Washboard Sam, and Blind Boy Fuller, and a stack of Victor pressings of early Carter Family tunes. I paid around forty dollars for all of it. I was beaming. King was proud.

Before we walked away, King stopped to ask Hicks what else he'd sold that morning. Although vendors weren't technically supposed to open for business before nine A.M. on Friday (those hours would change to seven A.M. the following year), many had been camped out in Hillsville for a couple days already. With the profit margins on hocking old shit hovering somewhere between slight and undetectable, you couldn't really blame a guy for entertaining early offers. While readjusting his shorts, Hicks, already gloriously sweaty, unpinned a grenade: he'd sold $1,600 worth of "blues records" to "someone from Raleigh" earlier in the week—probably Wednesday. He'd been in the field since Sunday. He didn't recall the specific titles. King, I could tell, was ruffled. Not miffed, exactly, but disturbed. Hours later, when we stopped for a late lunch and several gallons of sweet tea at the Blue Ridge Restaurant in Floyd, Virginia—King ordered "country ham" and I ordered "city ham" and we both got the brown beans and fried squash—he brought it up again. "I won't sleep for several weeks," he sighed. I couldn't tell if he was being serious. For now, though, the information was filed away. We trudged off, once more unto the breach.

In retrospect, it occurs to me that if one was interested in compiling the world's most comprehensive collection of sweat-soaked T-shirts, the Hillsville VFW Flea Market and Gun Show would be an unqualified

Mecca. Here, the gradual darkening of preshrunk cotton mirrors a darkening of the soul. It is unconscionably hot and crowded, and attendees are forced to contend with several miles of gently used detritus, all the bits and bobs—a thousand riffs on colored plastic—humans have designed to ease our long, slow crawl toward death. Surrender is required, or else you will crumple under the weight. When a portly man sporting strained cargo shorts and an orange GUNS SAVE LIVES sticker unleashed an epic, undulating belch a couple inches from my face—we were both digging, somewhat frantically, through a mound of state-shaped refrigerator magnets—I found myself not only not repulsed, but almost wanting to shake his hand.

Hillsville allows for (and perhaps even encourages) sudden reinvention, and you could probably outfit an entire one-bedroom apartment here for $500, particularly if you subscribe to the "odd old stuff" aesthetic (which seized Brooklyn, at least, several years ago, and to which I continue to shamefully adhere). But even if you don't, there is copious bounty to be ravaged: hand-carved Victorian bed frames and kitschy Atomic Age knickknacks and gold-and-ivory pocketknives are plentiful, but so are dented Ikea nightstands and used Cabbage Patch dolls and Duracell batteries of unknown origin. It is a feast of accumulation, presented without judgment or categorization. I was instantly reminded of Donovan Hohn's "A Romance of Rust: Nostalgia, Progress, and the Meaning of Tools," a 2005 *Harper's* essay in which the author visits the barn of an antique tool collector and is struck by how zoological his collection appears. "Divorced from usefulness and subjected to morphological classification, they looked like the fossils of Cenozoic mollusks or the wristbones of tyrannosaurs," Hohn wrote of his subject's prizes.

There is no sense of genus or species at Hillsville—everything is everything—but product, detached from both its intended use and the codified retail experience, becomes ungrounded, ill defined, and increasingly absurd: all parts and no corresponding whole. After less than an hour of browsing, the merchandise at Hillsville resembled a word I'd said too much—as if I'd accidentally subtracted all meaning via blind repetition, as if it had never had any meaning at all. Particularly upsetting were objects of recent vintage: piles of video games from 2011, hardcover installments of *Harry Potter*, an unopened Cuisinart panini press. Hohn, at an estate auction, remarked how an ink-jet printer, still in its original box, had "already passed into that limbo of worthlessness that exists between novelty and nostalgia," and, looking across the fields, I recognized that vast and endless void—the terrain of the freshly outmoded, of that which is neither useful nor evocative.

Obviously, none of this slowed us down. Existential duress has no place at Hillsville; it is softened or eradicated by the consumption of deep-fried foodstuffs. Available at one tent near the entrance were deep-fried Reese's peanut butter cups, Oreos, Twinkies, Milky Way bars, Snickers bars, Three Musketeers bars, and—for dessert—"frozen cheesecake hand-dipped in chocolate." Near the gun section of the market (an old VFW hall overloaded with every kind of assault weapon imaginable, some in shades of pink for the lady in your life), a scrum of hunters in tank tops were selling taxidermy and assorted sundries (dustpans, bathroom scales, plastic nativity figures) from the back of a pickup truck. I paused to admire a white-tailed deer head mounted on a slab of oak, a steal at twenty dollars, and scratched it behind its ears until King gave me a look that said, "Don't do that." Later, he did nod approvingly when I purchased an old puzzle, copyrighted in 1981 and called Feelings. It consisted of five wooden cutouts of a young girl in varying throes of emotion—Sad, Afraid, Angry, Happy, and Love—and required users to match her face with a corresponding title. Still, as I was paying, he couldn't resist this: "That would be so much better if it had been made in 1975."

We also looked for 78s—in Victrola cabinets, under piles of John Denver LPs, wrapped in sheets of yellowed newspaper, in the backseats of vendors' cars, shoved under tables, in blue Tupperware bins labeled OLD RECORDS, stacked indiscriminately in the high, bleating sun—but despite several hours of thorough digging, little else of note emerged

Four

A Form of Protection Against the Loss of Self

◦

Pete Whelan, 78 Quarterly, *Florida, Willie Brown, Kid Bailey,*
Scholarship, the Question of Context, How to Master What Masters You

◦

Pete Whelan, one of the earliest collectors of rare blues and jazz 78s, is also the founder and editor in chief of *78 Quarterly*, a magazine created in the late 1960s by and for 78 collectors. In the pre-Internet days especially, *78 Quarterly* was a default bible for the trade, purchasable at small record stores or via mail order. Besides features, it ran want ads, discographies, and irate letters to the editor, and in the renegade spirit of many countercultural periodicals, it never actually appeared quarterly, as promised by its title. There was a twenty-five-year break, for example, between volumes two and three.

Although some of its articles are objectively insane—in volume six, a Paramount Records pressing is described as "Black as a nun when mint (it shines with pale moon lettering), demure as a French whore at a cocktail party wearing a tight maid's uniform"—*78 Quarterly* is a tremendous resource and a surprisingly energizing read. There are in-jokes and self-deprecating asides (in volume three, a cartoon of an evil, vampiric-looking figure has a thought bubble saying, "Big overcoats with wide, large pockets are *in* this year!," while a photo of Fidel Castro has been appended with a "My focus is on Autograph . . ." caption, a reference to the 1920s jazz label), and plenty of service-oriented auction announcements. Most useful, perhaps, are the alphabetical lists of "The Rarest 78s," which, as far as I know, are the only published compendiums of who owns what, and of how many copies of certain records exist. The collector James McKune once called it "an annoying feature about records some of us will never own," while Whelan himself referred to it as "a dredging operation." The lists are somewhat outdated now (the last issue of *78 Quarterly* came out over a decade ago), but not as outdated as you might think: rare 78s don't move from shelf to shelf that quickly.

I got in touch with Whelan by mailing a typed letter to the address printed on the magazine's masthead. He responded promptly with his telephone number, and I called him up a few days later. At eighty-one, Whelan had decided to officially retire *78 Quarterly*, which had become less vital—if no less beloved—in the wake of online forums and e-mail listservs. By the time we spoke, he'd been involved with the 78 community on and off for seventy years, both as a collector and a de facto organizer.

Whelan was born in New York City but grew up in Pennsylvania. "Mainly a place called Plymouth Meeting, Pennsylvania, which is outside of Philadelphia," he explained. "That was in the 1930s, and it was farmland. Later on, of course, it became suburbia. It was starting to turn into a suburb when I was a child, even. Originally that area was composed of old, late-eighteenth-century stone farmhouses and farmland, and occasional woods."

He didn't have a particularly musical family. "Nobody liked blues or jazz," he said. "My mother and stepfather pretended to like classical music. My mother liked opera because of the Italian men." Still, the record-collecting itch hit him quickly, first with jazz records, then with blues: "[The collector] Bernie Klatzko once described rare blues like the sexual surge of a teenager," Whelan said, laughing. "It comes out of nowhere."

Whelan was eleven and living in Asbury Park, New Jersey, when he bought his first 78. "I was trying to find this kind of music that I liked. I didn't know anything about it. So I went into this record store and I tried to describe the music. I said, 'Well, it sounds kind of sweet.' And so he brought out Glenn Miller. And I said, 'No, no, that's not it.' And he kept bringing out different records until finally he said, 'You mean race records. Those are under the counter.' And he reached under the counter and brought out a bunch of blue-label Vocalion records from the late 1930s." And so it began.

In 1970, Whelan decided to sell his collection to finance a move from New York to Key West, and he took a full decade off before starting up again. "I managed to get a lot of those rare ones back," he said, almost wistfully. I asked him if it was hard—selling all his records, then methodically trying to coerce them back onto his shelves, as if they had never left, as if he had never pushed them away. The connotations were, of course, romantic. "It's sort of like a loss," he said, "that you don't want to think about too much."

Whelan had played me a few 78s over the telephone, but even I knew that was a pitiful approximation. A few months later, while I was vacationing with my parents on the Gulf Coast of Florida, I decided to drive across the Everglades and down to the southernmost tip of the continental United States, to where Pete Whelan lived in a shady wooden bungalow on Canfield Lane, surrounded by his records.

○

To get to Key West from Miami, motorists have to take the Seven Mile Bridge—one of the longest bridges in the world—from Knight's Key to Little Duck Key, crossing the Moser Channel, chugging directly into the Gulf of Mexico, speeding farther offshore than might seem advisable. Although it has a reputation for wantonness, I found Key West genteel and jovial, more culturally southern than I'd anticipated. There was endless pie and sweet tea. There was a sharp saltiness to the air.

Pete Whelan had invited me over for lunch, and he answered the door in loose khaki trousers, a long-sleeved yellow shirt, and flip-flops. His gray hair was cropped close. Whelan's home was surrounded by rare palm trees, which he had been collecting since 1975. We walked the perimeter and he pointed out different species while I spastically swatted away clouds of bugs.

"This is the second-largest palm in the world," he said, gesturing toward a massive, rough-looking trunk. "It's from Vietnam. A palm collector managed to get into Vietnam in the middle of the war. He went thirty miles inland to get this one palm that seeds once and dies after it seeds. It takes three years, and it throws out three tons of seeds in three years, and that's it," he explained. "So he somehow found out about it and went in and got the seeds and sent them around."

We circled back, Whelan still narrating the landscape, which was unlike anything I'd ever seen: lush, impenetrable, untamed. "There are some very exotic-looking palms that don't look like palms that came out of Cuba," he said. "Cuba underwent a severe climate-change dry spell about thirty thousand years ago, and some of the palms there, called Copernicias, became water-catching systems. They look like giant funnels with petticoats. One of them might even be semi-carnivorous because of the arrangement of spines," he said. "You can stick your hand in, but you can't pull it out."

Eventually, we took refuge in his record room, a cool, dimly lit space with books and papers and records piled atop every surface. An old-fashioned-looking fan sat in a corner, permanently at rest; a sea-foam-green antique safe was pressed against one wall, tall enough that I could have stood inside it if I'd hunched a little. Whelan said he'd acquired it to protect his record collection against hurricanes, but it was empty right now ("Thank goodness!"). On an adjacent wall, near a pair of glass doors, were cubes and cubes of 78s, all tucked inside unmarked paper sleeves.

We chatted about collecting for a few minutes. Almost immediately, Whelan stood up and started taking records down to spin; he was more eager to listen than to talk. He played a few jazz pieces, and then, at my request, pulled Skip James's "Drunken Spree"—which, according to 78 *Quarterly* volume six, is the only known copy in the world. Before I'd left for Florida, Chris King had told me to make sure to ask Whelan to play it for me, and to lodge a gentle plea on his behalf: "Please say hello to Pete for me and remind him that my life is relatively incomplete and fraught with emptiness without a Skip James guitar 78," he'd written. "Really it is, no shit. I have a nice copy of each of the Delta (and Hill Country) greats except for James. Pete has a beautiful copy of 'I'm So Glad' / 'Special Rider Blues' but, jeez, I'd love to have his 'Drunken Spree.' Do me a favor, pal, and remind him of my desperation."

"Drunken Spree," like "Devil Got My Woman," was deserving of covetousness: James would eventually rerecord the song in the 1960s, recasting it as a sweet, almost flirtatious ballad, but the 1931 version is an unimpeachable encapsulation of the regret that occasionally accompanies the robust consumption of alcohol. You can practically hear the dehydration in James's vocals—the humiliation.

I was still agitated from "Drunken Spree" when Whelan played me his favorite country blues record, a song called "Mississippi Bottom Blues" by a particularly obscure performer named Kid Bailey. It was recorded at the Peabody Hotel in Memphis in 1929, in a session for Brunswick Records, a Dubuque, Iowa (and later Chicago)–based label founded in 1916. So far, only one Kid Bailey 78 had been resurrected: "Mississippi Bottom Blues" / "Rowdy Blues" (Brunswick 7114). For years, there were rumors—hissed between collectors—that Bailey may have been a playing partner of Charley Patton's or, more intriguingly, that "Kid Bailey" was actually a pseudonym for Willie Brown, another blues singer who had confounded and titillated collectors for decades.

According to the company's surviving ledgers, a guitarist named Willie Brown recorded six songs for Paramount Records in 1930—"Grandma Blues" / "Sorry Blues" (Paramount 13001), "Window

Blues" / "Kicking in My Sleep Blues" (Paramount 13099), and "M&O Blues" / "Future Blues" (Paramount 13090), the latter being the only one of Brown's records presently extant, the others having somehow evaded rediscovery entirely. "Future Blues," at least, is a masterpiece: "Can't tell my future, and I can't tell my past," Brown growls over a quick, spindly guitar bit. "Lord, it seems like every minute, sure gonna be my last," he declares, striking the bass string so hard it bounces back off the fret board. It's that syncopated bass line—smacked into being—that makes "Future Blues" unshakable. Those descending notes somehow convey (precisely, efficiently) the rather unpleasant feeling of being unstuck in time.

Brown's other records have remained mythical objects, fretted over, imagined. Someone (I suspect John Heneghan) even constructed a Facebook profile in their honor. The page features a rigged-up photo of one of the still-unseen sides, with the words "Kicking in My Sleep Blues" and "Willie Brown" transposed, via Photoshop, onto a black-and-gold Paramount label. When I tried to befriend it—"Friend request sent to The Missing Willie Brown"—my invitation languished unanswered for weeks until, one night, it was mysteriously received.

Besides his partnership with Patton, Brown may or may not have also played second guitar for Robert Johnson—"You can run, you can run, tell my friend Willie Brown," Johnson keens in "Cross Road Blues"—and Son House. Collectors disagree about exactly what's going on with the Kid Bailey record: if Bailey was Brown, if there was a second guitar, if the second guitar was Patton, if the second guitar was Brown. "There's a second guitar in there, I think—maybe Willie Brown, who was kind of a midget. Patton was sort of a short man, too. They were known as the two midgets, and they would play at different barrel-houses," Whelan said, adjusting his turntable. "And Kid Bailey figures in there somewhere, but nobody seems to be able to find out the real information." It's worth noting that Bailey's "Rowdy Blues" is a very close analog of Brown's "M&O Blues," itself a reworking of Patton's "Pony Blues"—although, of course, the blues just moved like that.

Later, when I was back in New York, I e-mailed around for more details. I knew that there were gaps in our knowledge of early blues history (written accounts of most commercial recording sessions either weren't kept or didn't survive), but I hadn't realized how contentious certain narratives were and the extent to which those mysteries were solved—or at least puzzled over—by collectors. "Well, in MY opinion, it is indeed Willie Brown. Just listen to it and compare the vocals—just about identical to me," the collector John Tefteller responded. He was an admirer: "The Kid Bailey Brunswick is one of my TOP TEN all time favorite pre-war blues records and I own a mint copy! Now, bear in mind, there is NO proof whatsoever that Kid Bailey and Willie Brown are one and the same. I base my opinion on just listening and comparing voices and playing styles. Others have come to the same conclusion, but we probably will never know for sure, as there is no Brunswick file card for that session and no one alive who was there," he continued. "Since we only have the one [Willie Brown] Paramount to compare to, I think that when the other two finally surface (and I firmly believe that they will), we can compare those songs to Bailey and again, I bet it's him."

King was far less sure; I could practically hear his snort through the computer screen. "Everything that is 'known' about Bailey and partner is either based on aural speculation or interviews with [the blues guitarists] Robert Wilkins and Furry Lewis, both of whom were recorded on the same day at the Peabody Hotel in Memphis," King wrote. "They described Bailey and partner as short, very black men and did not know them," he continued. "The rumor that was started is that the style of [playing a guitar] 'up the staff' in D and the revamping of [Patton's] 'Pony Blues' in C were solely the domain of Patton and Brown, and so therefore these mysterious dudes must be Patton and Brown. I wholeheartedly disagree.

"First, Brown, but especially Patton, were outrageously uninhibited in both their playing and their singing, full of dynamics, bass-string slapping, hollering and bending of the treble strings. These two sides by Kid Bailey and Unknown are exactly not that . . . they are quite subdued and very subtle in the interplay of the guitars," he continued. "In fact, 'Mississippi Bottom Blues' has only one contributing factor by the 'seconding' guitar; a sustained, eerie, single note played as a dissonant interval during the first four measures of the I and IV part. If this were Brown and Patton, then it would be them at their most uninspired and timid. Second, plenty of other Jackson and Delta guitarists played 'up the staff' and variations of 'Pony Blues' including Mattie Delaney, Tommy Johnson, and Ishman Bracey. It was probably just two guys that had worked up clean arrangements of these proto-Delta blues pieces and then were swallowed up by the void," he finished.

Perhaps unsurprisingly, few collectors were ambivalent on the matter. Dr. David Evans, the director of the Ethnomusicology/Regional Studies doctoral program at the University of Memphis, agreed with Tefteller's take. Writing in *Blues Revue* in 1993, Evans admitted he'd once been skeptical, or at least dismissive of the notion: "Many researchers, myself included, asked Son House if he had ever heard of Kid Bailey and played the two pieces for him. The name didn't ring a bell with Son, but he insisted without wavering that it was the voice of his good friend and partner Willie Brown. Nobody at the time put too much stock in Son's opinion. The voices sounded different. Brown's was rough, gravelly, and forced; Bailey's was lighter and rather airy, suggesting that the nickname 'Kid' befit him." But years of methodical listening had changed Evans's mind. He now cited a "great number of similarities and musical and lyrical correspondences"—which he outlined in spectacular detail in his essay—as evidence that Brown and Bailey were the same person. He was emphatic.

"One important thing to note is that 'Bailey' is capoed up about three frets on the guitar," he told me in an e-mail. "Assuming he sang the same melodies as he would have sung with the same guitar part un-capoed, his voice would become significantly higher pitched and perhaps lighter in texture (as is actually the case of Bailey compared to what we definitely know of Willie Brown). Presence or absence of alcohol at the recording session could also have been a factor in voice quality. Compare melodies, guitar parts, and vocal rhythmic phrasing, then imagine Willie Brown singing toward the top of his range maybe on a day when he wasn't so stirred up by alcohol and rowdy buddies in the studio," he suggested.

My instinct, for what it's worth, was to agree with King. The two voices sounded similar, but all blues of a certain era hews to idiom, and there was a wildness missing from Bailey's performance—attributable, perhaps, to the performer's relative sobriety, or to the particular tuning of his guitar. But I liked to think that the ferociousness that animated Brown's recordings couldn't be so easily distilled. That it didn't leave him, not in the sobering light of the Peabody, not on his mother's porch.

But listening to the record in Whelan's music room in Key West, its windows shaded by strange and colossal palms, I wasn't thinking about Brown, or any mysteries not directly contained in Bailey's delivery— more staid than Brown's, perhaps, but no less brutal. His voice was clear and resolute, with a tiny quiver that emerged only when he was running low on air. I was already curious about why collectors were so deeply invested in the historical minutiae of certain recordings when the performances themselves were so staggering. It was intriguing to think that Brown and Bailey might be the same guy, but it was also the exact sort of fact I'd mull for a moment or two—because who was Willie Brown, anyway?—and then promptly forget.

I felt both guilty and foolish about that. As a young critic, I'd had to learn the language of criticism: the genres and microgenres, the makes and models of guitars and vintage organs, the allusions to obscure labels and sold-ten-copies compilations. I'd dutifully memorized facts about amplifier settings and pedals and filters and microphones and producers and years of release, even when it felt depressing and hollow, like I was methodically teaching myself exactly how to miss the point. When I wondered whether I just listened *differently*—whether my experience of music was somehow more emotional, more divorced from its technical circumstances, more about the whole than its pieces—I chastised myself for being arrogant or stupid. (I blanched, in fact, at catching myself using a word as treacly as "emotional.") And yet: I could love a record more than anything in the world and still not make myself recall its serial number.

That chasm—between a studied response and a gut-borne one—seemed even more palpable in the specific context of prewar blues music, where the hunt for (and especially the subsequent analysis of) the records appeared to run directly counter to the lawless spirit of the work. With a few notable exceptions, blues music was rowdy and social, and its creators led brash, lustful lives. They drank and roamed and had reckless sex and occasionally stabbed each other in the throat. There was something incongruous about sitting in a dimly lit room, meticulously wiping dust and mold off a blues 78 and noting the serial number in an antique log book. Why not dance or sob or get wasted and kick something over? Some collectors, I knew, did exactly that, but for others, the experience of a rare blues record involved a kind of isolated studiousness, which of course was fine—there's no wrong way to enjoy music, and I understood that certain contextual or biographical details could help crystallize a bigger, richer picture of a song. But I continued to believe that the pathway that allowed human beings to appreciate and require music probably began in a more instinctual place (the heart, the stomach, the nether regions). Context was important, but it was never as essential—or as compelling—to me as the way my entire central nervous system involuntarily convulsed whenever Skip James opened his mouth.

I was beginning to suspect that the collector's focus on ancient minutiae was a way of mitigating that desire: our relationship with music is intense, but it can be combated, at least in part, by an arsenal of historical truths. In his book *Retromania*, Simon Reynolds suggests that a proclivity for record collecting and its attendant memorization of facts and figures is "perhaps related to the impulse to master what masters you; containing music within a grid map of systematic knowledge is a form of protection against the loss of self that is music's greatest gift." According to Reynolds, because collectors tend to wield such little societal authority, they "*become* authorities through their taste and cultural expertise." This both protects them and makes them powerful. (That same desire—to create authority for oneself—is also at the very heart of music criticism. I may have had to learn that behavior, but I was hardly innocent of it myself.)

It was possible, then, that the collector's concentration on scholarship—on knowing things like whether Kid Bailey and Willie Brown were really one and the same—was actually just a veiled attempt at insulating the entire practice of 78 collecting from unwanted amateurs. Like a wild-eyed grizzly circling her cubs, collectors were protective of their hobby.

What felt incredibly clear to me, though, was how these records worked in their present contexts, what they did for me right now. "Mississippi Bottom Blues" is a sad song about letting people down and then succumbing to their expectations of you—assuming your failures, wearing them like a mask. "I'm going where the water drinks like wine / Where I can be drunk and staggering all the time," Bailey sings. The most remarkable thing about his delivery is that he doesn't sound resigned; he sounds free. There is an inertia to his guitar playing, as if to suggest that certain things can't be stopped or slowed, no matter how hard we try.

/ / Five / /

Suck All the Blossoms and
He Leave You an Empty Square

○

*Edison's Tone Tests, the Wisconsin Chair Company, the Rise and Fall of
Paramount Records, Charley Patton, "High Water Everywhere"*

○

"The Phonograph knows more about us than we know ourselves," Thomas Edison wrote in 1888. "For it retains the memory of many things which we forget, even though we have said them."

Edison had some prescience regarding his invention's importance—"It will teach us to be careful what we say," he warned, "for it imparts to us the gift of listening to ourselves as others might listen to us"—although it's hard to say whether anyone could have predicted the extent to which it would alter our cultural systems. It took decades for folks to catch up with the repercussions. Music was previously a temporary, lived experience—practiced, perhaps, but extemporaneously rendered. Sound was fleeting. Songs and voices were remembered or they were lost.

On September 17, 1915, Edison Records organized an invitation-only concert in Montclair, New Jersey, booking the contralto Christine Miller, the flautist Harold Lyman, and the violinist Arthur Walsh. It was the first of Edison's so-called Tone Tests, in which someone placed an Edison Diamond Disc phonograph in the center of a stage and cued a 78. (That night, it was Miller singing "O Rest in the Lord," an aria from Felix Mendelssohn's *Elijah*.) Then Miller (or whomever) would begin performing along with the recording. Periodically, the singer or player would stop moving his or her mouth, or lower the bow. Audiences gasped when they realized they couldn't tell the difference: a collective breath, snagged. As Greg Milner clarifies in *Perfecting Sound Forever*, the singers and musicians likely fudged it a bit, imitating the recording rather than trusting it would reflect the live performance, but even that shift felt profound. "From now on," Milner wrote, "Recordings would not sound like the world; the world would sound like recordings."

In the 1910s, the Wisconsin Chair Company, a small, Port Washington–based furniture company, began assembling and selling wooden phonograph cabinets under contract from Edison. The production and sale of phonographs was a newly booming industry, and between 1914 and 1916, more than 150 phonograph-related companies formed in the United States, bringing the total up from fourteen to a robust 167 (in 1914 about 540,000 Americans owned a player; by 1919, that number had swelled to over two million). Like many manufacturers of phonograph cabinets, the WCC eventually opted to dip into the still-burgeoning record business, building phonograph machines (under the name Vista) to cram inside its cabinets, then cranking out records to accompany the players.

This wasn't such a wide leap, strategically speaking. In its early years, the phonograph was promoted almost as a piece of decorative furniture, a showy homage to modernity that could also tie a room together. Phonograph records were sold at furniture stores as accessories; the record shop, as we think of it today, hadn't yet been conceived. As Paramount historian Stephen Calt wrote in *78 Quarterly* volume three, "Record executives could not entertain the notion that people bought phonographs in order to play records . . . it was believed that customers bought records for the sake of operating their Victrolas."

In the summer of 1917, the WCC launched a recording company called the New York Recording Laboratories (the "New York" bit was aspirational; the "laboratories" was a pretentious affect borrowed from Edison) and began releasing 78 rpm records. According to *Paramount's Rise and Fall* author Alex van der Tuuk, the NYRL was initially just a way for the company to more effectively push its furniture. Records were an added-value marketing ploy: if you bought a player, the company would toss in five or ten free 78s. Using established studios in New York and Chicago, the Wisconsin-based NYRL released popular cuts by novelty or vaudeville artists like Helen Clark and Arthur Fields and German-language tracks imported from Europe to appease its home state's considerable German-immigrant population. The recordings were released on a handful of imprints with names like Famous, National, Broadway, Blue Bird, Puritan, and Paramount.

Because records were still something of an afterthought, the WCC didn't funnel a significant amount of time or money into their production. Bigger, more dedicated labels like Victor, Columbia, and Brunswick paid higher rates and made better-sounding releases, thus drawing greater talent. For the WCC, a 78 was a little like the free plastic umbrella you get when you sign up for a high-interest credit card: not entirely insignificant, but sort of beside the point. Most early Paramount employees knew next to nothing about records or recording; they were chair salesmen. As Calt wrote, "It was this continued reliance on amateurs, more than its accomplishments in producing black music, that made Paramount a unique company."

Paramount was launched by the NYRL on June 27, 1917 (it bore no relation to the American movie studio, which was founded in 1912), and after four floundering years as a flailing pop enterprise, Paramount executives, led by the sales manager M. A. Supper, decided to cash in on a sudden boom in black vaudeville, jazz, and blues. Paramount, it was decided, would make a fine test dummy for the company's speculative "race records" series, and the project began in 1922 with the release of Paramount 12001—Alberta Hunter's "Daddy Blues" / "Don't Pan Me." The series was a savvy move: besides serving a relatively untapped market, race artists didn't command high prices, meaning Paramount could keep its costs low. Getting Al Jolson behind your microphone might cost $10,000, but a blues singer required a payout of only twenty-five to seventy-five dollars per side, and sometimes as little as six dollars.

Paramount was born from a mercenary impulse: at no point in the company's history were its founders intent on performing any grand cultural service or nobly distributing overlooked music to an underserved community. Like any functional capitalist enterprise, the WCC was only trying to make as much cash as possible. When early record executives thought about music as an edifying force, it was about exposing indigent populations to "sophisticated" white art, and never the other way around. Race records became popular only after African-Americans became record buyers, which happened mostly in the early 1920s, after portable phonographs, a novelty intended for World War I soldiers, suddenly allowed folks who couldn't necessarily afford an ornate Victrola to dip into the home-audio scene.

The notion of black performers recording music for black audiences was still rogue and untested in 1922, although a few enterprising labels had been experimenting with similar projects. A few months earlier, in 1921, the New York City–based Okeh Records had initiated its first race series, with serial numbers starting in the 8000s. A year prior, Okeh (then the General Phonograph Corporation) had taken a chance on a thirty-seven-year-old black singer and actress named Mamie Smith, releasing Smith's "Crazy Blues" / "It's Right Here for You (If You Don't Get It . . . 'Taint No Fault of Mine)," possibly the first recording of a vocal blues by a black artist. It sold a whopping 75,000 copies in its first month of release. By 1923, Columbia had its own race series, and by 1926, the entire industry had caught on.

A year after its launch, a twenty-eight-year-old talent scout and part-time sportswriter named J. Mayo Williams was selected to oversee

Paramount's race series from Chicago. A Brown University graduate and former track and football star, the charismatic Williams was Paramount's only black "executive" (he didn't receive a salary, only royalty payments) and had effectively volunteered himself for the job, traveling to Port Washington and bluffing his way through a meeting ("I just jived my way into the whole situation," he later told Calt). Williams is credited as a composer on many of Paramount's race releases, sometimes under the pseudonym Everett Murphy, and has since become a contentious figure for blues enthusiasts. He purportedly plied rural performers with liquor and often assumed false ownership of their songs, crediting himself as a co-composer (it was, after all, his only way to make cash). Williams's scheming was hardly aberrant—according to van der Tuuk, Williams's secretary, Aletha Dickerson, also snuck her name onto forty-three titles listed for copyright—and besides, most artists readily agreed to a flat recording fee and waived all rights to future royalties. Whether they fully understood the financial repercussions of the contract should they have landed a hit is unclear; in the money-now vs. money-later debate, most chose money now. Interestingly, Calt credits Williams's "aloofness"—he wasn't much for banter, particularly if his conversational partner was uneducated—for his sour reputation among artists of the era.

Still, Williams was something of a gatekeeper for black musicians, who, in the early 1920s, didn't have many options for recording their work. As Sarah Filzen notes in the *Wisconsin Magazine of History*, "Because Williams was one of the very few black music representatives in the recording business, he had the luxury of having many black artists come to him to be 'discovered.'" He frequented local theaters, held auditions, and entertained suggestions from Paramount talent scouts scattered throughout the South. Men like R. T. Ashford, who owned a combination shoe-shine parlor and record shop on Central Avenue in Dallas, often sent local artists north to Chicago to record for Paramount. In 1925, Ashford referred the blues great Blind Lemon Jefferson, whom he purportedly discovered playing on a street corner;

Jefferson eventually became Paramount's most-frequently-recorded race artist, laying down a total of ninety-two sides in a period of three and a half years.

A good chunk of Paramount's race releases were captured by a producer named Orlando Marsh, who worked out of a studio on the sixth floor of the Lyon and Healy building in downtown Chicago. According to *The Country Blues* author Samuel Charters, Marsh was "a conscientious, imaginative recording engineer, but everything about the Paramount business operation was cheap, and the quality of the recordings was very poor." Marsh's original studio was close to the city's elevated train tracks, and recording had to stop every time a train rattled by. Even after the business moved to a building farther down the block, Marsh could be a sloppy manager (supposedly he once left a box of wax masters in a hot room filled with mice—they scrambled through and scratched the inscriptions, leaving the masters unusable). Recording sessions usually lasted three to four hours and yielded three or four songs. Artists, who were cued to start and stop by a series of lights, often under- or overshot, ignoring the warning to wrap up altogether or abruptly cutting themselves off midverse. The technology was still new, and it could be confounding. If artists couldn't get it done in fewer than four takes, they were usually dismissed.

When Marsh was finished, the wax masters were shipped to a pressing plant in Grafton, Wisconsin, a small, predominantly white town on the Milwaukee River, about a hundred miles north of Chicago and just south of the Wisconsin Chair Company's corporate hub in Port Washington. The Grafton plant had previously cranked out chairs, but in 1917 it was remodeled for the manufacture of 78 rpm records. The wax masters of Paramount's recording sessions were sent to intermediaries on the East Coast (first a company in Bridgeport, Connecticut, and later one in New York), where they were converted into metal stampers that could be used to mass-produce 78s. When the Grafton plant finally became capable of making its own stampers, the wax masters were packed in dry ice and delivered there by train.

Employees in the plating department used a camel's hair brush to carefully apply graphite to the grooved surface of the wax; it was then hung in a tank of copper sulfate, where the graphite attracted iron oxide, resulting in copper plating. This so-called negative master was then stripped from the wax, which was discarded, and used to make a positive master. Known as a "mother" or "matrix," the positive master had ridges instead of grooves and was coated with nickel or silver. Eventually, a negative stamper was made from the mother master and fitted to a press, where it could be used to fashion brand-new 78s. As Filzen wrote, a fresh record would then pop off the press like "a very thin, delicate waffle."

Workers sanded and cleaned the new records, then slid them into brown paper sleeves. Old stampers and masters were often melted down and reused for the creation of new records. The whole process took about four days. Test pressings of each record were dispersed to the company executives, who decided—based on, one assumes, a somewhat arbitrary set of rules—whether or not a given record was suitable for release.

Early on Paramount had about ten presses, but by the mid-1920s—the company's commercial peak—there were fifty-two presses squishing wads of shellac, ground stone, and local clay into flat, grooved 78s. Each press could theoretically produce around seven hundred records per day, but because Paramount's pressing plant was run with a rope drive from a water wheel in the river rather than an electric motor, it only operated at partial power. Most things about the Grafton plant were slipshod or half-cooked, and while it was functional, it was hardly producing lauded product. Even Paramount's earliest customers griped about the quality of the pressings, which seemed to contain an odd and aggravating amount of surface noise. Most historians chalk it up to the plant's cheap shellac mixture, which was heavy on filler—Wisconsin stone is good for lots of things, but not for being ground up and crushed into blues records.

An initial pressing typically demanded a run of 1,200 78s, which were packed into wooden crates (twenty-five per box) and priced at seventy-five cents apiece. Paramount releases were often reissued by the company's subsidiaries, so a recording made in Chicago for Paramount might also appear, later, on a WCC-owned sublabel like Puritan, Famous, or Broadway. These were made of an even crappier shellac compound and typically went for fifty cents each, or sometimes three for a dollar.

Once they were pressed, packed, and stacked, Paramount's race records sold mostly via mail order (for a while, Broadway pressings were even on offer in the Montgomery Ward catalog). In 1999, Dorothy Larson Bostwick told Alex van der Tuuk that she remembered processing orders for Paramount as a high school student: "We assembled several pieces of printed advertising, which were mailed to customers or prospective customers in the Southern states. In order to secure the records, the customer would be required to pay in advance, with a post office money order," she said. Potential buyers filled out a short form with their name and address, checked off the records they were interested in, and handed it all to their mailman, along with payment. Paramount covered the shipping on orders of two or more records. If you ordered only one, you were expected to pay "a small COD fee" when the record was delivered.

Aside from its direct-marketing campaigns, Paramount placed advertisements in the *Chicago Defender*, an African-American-run newspaper founded in 1905, with a considerable black readership and an impressive masthead (both Langston Hughes and Gwendolyn Brooks wrote for the *Defender* in the early 1920s). In addition, stock was sent out with traveling salesmen who plonked down $4.50 for the honor of peddling Paramount 78s (that bought you ten records, which you could then pitch to buyers for seventy-five cents each, clearing three dollars' profit), and, on occasion, with Chicago-based Pullman porters, who tended to sleeper-car passengers and sold records to buyers living along the railroad routes.

Paramount also shipped its wares directly to a handful of record distributors, but most traditional music stores were uninterested in the label's marginal-seeming goods. As such, Paramount got crafty with its promotions. In 1924, the label pressed a slow, moody blues record by the popular Georgia-born blues singer Ma Rainey and dubbed it "Ma Rainey's Mystery Record." The company claimed it was so spectacular that no one could conceive of a title, then launched a contest to find one (a woman named Ella McGill, from Jefferson, Indiana, won with "Lawd I'm Down Wid De Blues"—although what McGill heard as "down" in Rainey's lyrics, I've always heard as the comparably grim "dyin'"). According to Filzen, a dealer named Harry Charles once conjured a scheme that involved "hiring a group of African-Americans to follow him into a record store and having them show great enthusiasm for the records he was trying to promote."

In the 1920s, race records typically sold around five thousand copies each; a hit record would move twenty thousand to fifty thousand units. For singers to earn a follow-up session with Paramount, they would have to sell ten thousand copies, proving their financial worth to a company that didn't much believe in artistic worth as an end in itself.

Paramount didn't exclusively release blues music—in 1924, it started issuing country and old-time songs by artists like Earl Johnson, the Dixie String Band, and the Kentucky Thorobreds, and it had been releasing dance, jazz, and jazz-influenced records since its inception. But by the end of the 1920s, no Paramount releases were selling very well. As musicologist Dick Spottswood explains in the notes for *Screamin' and Hollerin' the Blues*, rival firms were scouring the South and producing better, locally made versions of the blues records Paramount had built its tenuous reputation on, and profit losses had led to decreasing promotional and distribution budgets. "By 1930–31, Paramount records were either selling by word of mouth or not at all," he wrote. When Charley Patton arrived in Grafton in 1929, Paramount was nearly lifeless.

Patton, who died in 1934 on the Heathman-Dedham plantation in Mississippi, has long been considered an originator of the Delta blues (or at least its finest practitioner), and he's as elusive a figure as he is esteemed. In his book *Deep Blues*, the scholar Robert Palmer claimed Patton "personally inspired just about every Delta bluesman of consequence . . . he is among the most important musicians 20th century America has produced. Yet we know very little about his formative years, and practically nothing about how he learned his art."

We know this much: in the summer of 1929, Patton—who was itinerant in the manner of all classic blues singers—was living in Jackson, Mississippi. He was an acquaintance of Henry C. Speir, a white music store owner who, like R. T. Ashford, acted as a makeshift talent scout for a few record companies. Speir arranged for Patton to travel to Richmond, Indiana, to record in a studio owned by Gennett Records, for sessions underwritten by Paramount. Palmer described the space as a "barnlike frame building just a few feet from a railroad track," and noted that it also housed a pressing plant, meaning "the freshly pressed records could be conveniently dispatched by rail, but recording had to stop whenever a train approached."

On Friday, June 14, Patton, then thirty-eight years old, recorded fourteen tracks at Gennett studios. There's a decent chance Patton was drunk—"most companies gave 'race' and 'hillbilly' artists liquor to loosen them up," Palmer wrote—but Patton's performance is still riveting. In July 1929, the label issued Patton's first release, "Pony Blues" / "Banty Rooster Blues," and the record sold well enough that the label devised an elaborate promotional plan for Patton's next record, "Mississippi Boweavil Blues," an old folk ballad about a little black beetle that bores into cotton buds and prevents them from blossoming. ("Suck all the blossoms and he leave you an empty square, Lordy," Patton sang in his heavy, garbled voice.) The record, Paramount 12805, was credited only to the "Paramount Masked Marvel," and handbills featuring a caricature of a figure that looked sort of like Patton—or a superhero version of him, wearing an extra-large suit and a black wraparound eye mask—were shipped to Paramount dealers. Customers were asked to discern his identity, and anyone who guessed correctly received a free record of their choosing. (Patton being something of a singular singer, the answer would have been blindingly obvious to anyone who had heard ten or more seconds of "Pony Blues.")

The contest was advertised in the *Chicago Defender* on September 7 and 14, and ended on October 15. Ten thousand contest entry forms were printed, and researchers guess that around the same number of records were pressed. Copies have since shown up featuring Patton's proper name on the label rather than the Masked Marvel, meaning Paramount likely re-pressed the song after the original run sold out. Spottswood points out that Patton was "Paramount's most prolific recording artist for 1929, an indication of the confidence that the company had in his sales potential."

Soon after, Patton was invited to record at Paramount's brand-new studio in Grafton. Built in 1928 or early 1929—mostly as a way to save cash, allowing the company to circumvent studio fees—it was located on the second floor of a building directly across the street from the pressing plant, at Twelfth Street and Falls Road. No photographs of the interior have surfaced, but it reportedly housed a piano, a guitar, a few wooden chairs, and a wall of rudimentary recording equipment, some of which may have been handmade. The space is often described with limp euphemisms like "rustic." There were two rooms—a control room and a studio room, where the performers worked—and the walls of each were lined with stretches of burlap, towels, and blankets to reduce echo. As the dance-band leader Sig Heller, who recorded in Grafton in 1931, told van der Tuuk, "Even the door was padded. There was no big room resonance, echo, or acoustics. It was rather difficult to play when a note was gone as soon as [it was] played." The studio was hot and clammy or damp and cold, depending on the season. It was not a luxurious place.

In October 1929, Patton recorded "High Water Everywhere Part 1" and its sequel, "High Water Everywhere Part 2"—a harrowing account of the 1927 Mississippi River flood—in Grafton, along with twenty-four other songs. "High Water Everywhere" was released in April 1930. Three years earlier, in April 1927, the Mississippi River had busted through a levee in Mound Landing, Mississippi, about twenty miles north of Patton's hometown of Greenville. That same spring, the Delta had been pummeled by a series of spectacular weather events (tornadoes, earthquakes, merciless rains) and the levees were taxed, trembling under the weight of a thrusting, overfed river. When they finally acquiesced, a massive wall of muddy water—some reports claim it was well over twenty feet tall—ate up much of northwest Mississippi, blanketing 27,000 square miles of land. According to *Rising Tide* author John M. Barry, the now-unleashed river carried in excess of three million cubic feet of water each second. Even attempting to harness a river as brawny and robust as the Mississippi demanded a certain amount of hubris; in this case, it backfired. The flooding didn't let up until August. By then, at least 250 people were dead, maybe more.

"The whole round country, Lord, river has overflowed," Patton moans in "Part 1," his voice loose and rich over a three-note, open-G guitar melody. There's a vague bit of percussion—Patton smacking his guitar or thwapping his foot on the ground—in the background; his delivery is knotty and almost unintelligible. Patton may have been recording in the world's shittiest studio, seven hundred miles from his hot Delta home, but the performance is tough, aggressive, certain. "The whole round country, man, is overflowed," he snarls. Patton sounds angry and indignant, the way we sing when we are singing about things that are out of our control, things that feel too large and too devastating to also be true.

In a print advertisement for the record, Paramount's copywriter boldly extolled its virtues: "Everyone who has heard this record says that 'HIGH WATER EVERYWHERE' is Charley Patton's best and you know that means it has to be mighty good because he has made some knockouts. You're in for a real treat when you hear this record at your dealer or send us the coupon."

Even though he was a commercially viable blues artist, a physical record of Patton's work has not endured, or at least not in its purest form (the same goes for nearly all of Paramount's blues artists). As Edward Komara wrote in the notes to the Revenant set, "Listening to Patton's records today is challenging, given the battered state of many of the surviving discs, the provincial nature of Mississippi before World War II, and the changes in music since his 1934 death." Consequently, exactly how many copies of "High Water Everywhere" were pressed, how many were sold, and how many remain is tough to definitively ascertain. Richard Nevins guesses there are about fifteen copies still in existence. All anyone knows for sure is that if you find one, you'd best hold it close to your chest.

Between 1929 and 1932, a slew of scout-recruited blues singers, including blues giants like Son House and Skip James, trekked to the Grafton studio from small towns in the South. The company was fading, but Paramount's final three years were arguably the most fruitful, creatively speaking, of any American record company in history. Paramount's discography from this period—from Wiley's "Last Kind Words Blues" through James's "Devil Got My Woman" and Patton's "Moon Going Down"—is astonishing.

Still, Paramount remained notorious for its poor sound fidelity and shoddy pressings, and it wasn't terribly surprising when the company issued its final recordings, the Mississippi Sheiks' "She's Crazy 'Bout Her Lovin'" / "Tell Her to Do Right," in 1932. By then, J. Mayo Williams had left Paramount for Brunswick Records and been replaced by the white, Port Washington–based executive Arthur Laibly, who didn't know much about blues music or its audience. As Filzen notes, "the firm was becoming a dumping ground for mediocre or unknown artists." By the following year, the label had been swallowed up whole by the Great Depression, remaining dormant until it was purchased and briefly revived by the collector John Steiner in the late 1940s. When the Grafton plant closed, some of its remaining dead stock was sold off in wholesale lots and some was offered to retailers at a deep discount, although exactly what happened to the bulk of the company's records—and their metal masters—is unclear. Rumors abound: some folks claim that the factory burned 78s for fuel or used them to patch holes in the walls, but the reigning theory is that disgruntled Paramount employees, upon hearing of their termination, furiously hurled stacks of records into the Milwaukee River.

When I called up Alex van der Tuuk and asked him what he thought might have happened to Paramount's metal masters, he was ready for my question. "In 1944, when the company closed, all the metal masters had either been sold or scrapped to a local junk dealer in Milwaukee," he said. "They did that because there was a lot of corrosion on the metal masters, and the building where the metal masters had been stored didn't have any insulation. Pigeons came into that building and you can imagine what a bird does on a metal master."

The ones that weren't corroded or caked with guano were eventually hauled to a storage facility in Port Washington. They sat there until 1942, when the War Productions Board launched a massive scrap-metal drive with the goal of gathering seventeen million tons of metal for Allied use in World War II. Most of Paramount's masters were subsequently melted down, but a batch of about a hundred were leased to the Chicago-based producer Jack Kapp, who would eventually helm an American subsidiary of the British label Decca. After he purchased Paramount, John Steiner contacted Decca to reclaim the remaining masters. "He called up Decca," van der Tuuk explained, "and he said, 'You have metal masters that belong to me. Ship them back.' And much to his own surprise, they did, and he kept them in his house up until his death in 2000."

Those masters—the only ones left—are supposedly archived with the rest of Steiner's papers in the Regenstein Library at the University of Chicago, although when I wrote to Julie Gardner, head of reader services at the Special Collections Research Center, she sent me the following reply: "While we have lists of various Paramount metal masters, I have not been able to locate the physical masters themselves. For instance, Box 33, folder 12 of the John Steiner Papers has a folder with a list of metal mothers for Paramount masters, 1931–32, but not the actual masters. Similarly, Box 46, folder 1 has photocopies of index cards listing the masters, but again, not the physical pieces. I am sorry we could not be of greater assistance to you."

I felt a little twinge. Of exasperation, maybe, but also of narrative possibility. What did it mean?

Paramount ephemera is hard sought, and in 2006, the PBS television series *History Detectives*, following a tip from a local historian and blues fan named Angela Mack, decided to direct a professional scuba-diving team to the bottom of the Milwaukee to scour the silt for precious Paramount remnants. They dug for a while (and somewhat indiscriminately) but came up empty.

Paramount's blues 78s—particularly records by country blues singers like Patton, James, and Son House—are now extraordinarily rare, trading among collectors for preposterous, life-changing sums of money. In late 2013, the collector John Tefteller paid $37,100 for a copy of Tommy Johnson's "Alcohol and Jake Blues" / "Riding Horse" (Paramount 12950) after an anonymous seller who may or may not have known its potential worth posted it on eBay. It was one of two known copies; the other, which Tefteller had also previously purchased, was found in what he described as "hammered condition." This one, though, he called beautiful.

●

Although I understand that Paramount 78s are prized because they're nearly impossible to find (and, in fact, some have yet to be found at all), I also believe that whatever mysterious, inexplicable thing happened in that Grafton studio has something to do with their particular pull. Were these performances inadvertently fueled by the discomfort of displacement—having been recorded, as they were, by rural southern singers in an unfamiliar northern city? Could those performers have felt the incertitude of recording for a company so clearly on the brink of dissolution, and then responded to it with incredible fearlessness?

I also couldn't help but think about the records possibly deteriorating at the bottom of the Milwaukee, providing shelter for crawfish alongside crushed Schlitz cans and rusted car parts. It seemed eerie and surreal—a cold, watery death for the hottest music on earth. Nearly everyone who had worked in the pressing plant in the late twenties and early thirties was gone, and while a handful of researchers—Calt and van der Tuuk in particular—had worked tirelessly to gather first-person accounts through the 1990s, few revealing stories had emerged. According to John Tefteller, the game of Frisbeeing records into the river wasn't even unique to the day the factory closed. "When they had excess plates or excess recordings that were going to be thrown away, what they would do is take them out and sail them into the Milwaukee River," he told me. "It was the employees having fun on their lunch hour. They didn't do it against the wishes of their bosses or anything like that. It was just excess material they didn't need."

Well, I thought. That's pretty interesting.

Six

We Are Not Drowning

●

Scuba Diving, Claustrophobia, Money,
Goonies, *the Milwaukee River*

●

I had a sense, by now, that if you were around in the first part of the twenty-first century and wanted to assemble a 78 rpm record collection of moderate consequence, you needed to start praying for a windfall. The records would not emerge organically. Things were spoken for. All the obvious routes had been exhausted. All the less obvious routes had also been exhausted.

Only preposterous routes remained.

If you've never cold-called a scuba shop in Wisconsin with the intention of convincing the gracious Midwestern stranger who answers the telephone to personally accompany you while you scour river silt for a pile of old, brittle records that may have been hurled into the Milwaukee River eighty years ago, and that, yes, you do want to dig around for them in shallow water while wearing a rented wet suit and rig, but no, you don't know where, exactly, they were thrown from, and no, you've never been scuba diving before because you live in New York City, and actually, you're really not all that athletically inclined, and also, this one time you were medically treated for debilitating claustrophobia?—honestly, I wouldn't recommend it.

I assembled a list of every scuba shop in the greater Milwaukee area, prepped a rousing speech that omitted certain damning details, and started dialing. After a few humiliating misfires ("You're looking for what? Records of what?"), I was eventually given the phone number of a sea captain I'll call Lenny—an old salt, to borrow a bit of sailing parlance—who led diving tours of shipwrecks in nearby Lake Michigan. He politely tolerated my long-winded introduction. As I continued talking, I was mortified to hear my voice growing progressively higher. I was basically squeaking; it's possible he believed he was speaking to a small child. "Diving in the river is not something people do," he finally said. "But."

I wouldn't necessarily categorize what followed as a unilaterally positive response, but it wasn't a definitive denial, either. He told me to call him again a few weeks before my trip and said good-bye before I could make any more high-pitched demands. The click of the receiver felt like a mercy bullet. I sighed.

●

I had a tenuous lead, but I needed training. I figured scuba instruction would take an afternoon or two. I'd been to tropical resorts, I reminded myself. Tourists in silly shorts sign up for a ten-minute lesson on the beach and then plunge nose-first into the reef! Thousands of people do it every day! It could not be that grand of an investment.

This was the first in a long string of idiotic assumptions about scuba diving. Learning how to dive is not particularly easy, nor is it cheap. (I was later reminded of John Heneghan's fears about his own descent into collecting: "I knew it would be a financial burden beyond what any rational mind would consider a wise decision.") Scuba certification is a grand, multifaceted endeavor requiring many hours of classroom instruction, a few full days of confined water training (usually in a swimming pool), and four open water dives (those can be completed over a period of one to two years). I was spooked by the commitment, but I convinced myself to carry on. I wanted records.

Scuba diving is not a pastime typically associated with New York City, but this being a place that readily fulfills misguided fantasies, a cursory Google search revealed a handful of Manhattan-based dive shops that also offered lessons. I picked Pan Aqua, on Forty-Third Street and Tenth Avenue, and signed myself up for a three-night intensive class. The course would cost $295, I was told, and I would also be required to purchase a $65 textbook, a $38 DVD (the most expensive story ever committed to film), and around $225 worth of scuba equipment. Those prices did not include the open water dives (they run around $160 per day, plus gear rentals), which would also require traveling to a place—any place—more amenable to underwater exploration and spending at least two full days propelling myself down and back up.

Prior to this particular moment, I'm not sure it's even possible to overstate how uninterested I was in scuba diving. I panic in confined spaces. I find the texture of sand unpleasant. And while I pride myself on not being an especially hysterical person, if a fish swims within twelve inches of my exposed skin, I've been known to stage the kind of epic meltdown typically reserved for two-year-olds on airplanes. Although I can appreciate the athletic prowess involved, I'm so aggressively dispassionate about "extreme" sports that I shudder when confronted with an open bottle of energy drink. I am not a thrill seeker. I realized quickly that I couldn't do this alone.

I presented my case to my husband, Bret; it ended with my favorite argument-winning bon mot ("In conclusion, I will probably die"). He gave a spirited retort—pointing out that I was becoming worryingly delusional, consumed by nonsense, et cetera—but ultimately conceded to join me, in part because I think he half believed the part about me dying. I now had a reluctant partner.

The afternoon I went to pick up the training materials and equipment at Pan Aqua, New York was in the midst of a weeklong springtime downpour—an ominous sign, but I persevered in earnest. Squishing back to the Times Square subway station in the warm, whipping rain, trying my best to balance an inverted umbrella, a bag of textbooks, and two three-foot-long mesh sacks (each stuffed with a mask, scuba booties, a snorkel, and fins) while also mentally calculating how many peanut butter sandwiches I would be required to consume as meals in order to justify the amount of money I had just spent, I felt the quick creep of doubt. And as I stumbled into a wall of wet tourists huddling near the subway stairs, bags slipping off my shoulder, bangs plastered to my forehead via a toxic paste of sweat and rain, I panicked fully. What the fuck was I doing?

Here's what I knew: the chance of actually finding any playable Paramount 78s or metal recording masters at the bottom of the Milwaukee River was essentially zero. Had I fully explained my plan to any close friends, I suspect every last one of them would have told me there wasn't enough potential for success to justify the emotional, physical, and financial expenditures. But collecting isn't a rational man's game, and I had immersed myself in a community of single-minded men who'd dedicated their entire lives to improbable ventures, channeling vast amounts of time and cash and brainpower into their respective quests. At this particular moment, the only thing I had going for me was a willingness to do idiotic stuff. And, I hoped, a body still pliable enough to tolerate it.

I practiced meditation techniques the entire way back to Brooklyn. I practiced the same meditation techniques while watching the endless instructional DVD, which I paused every few minutes so I could compose myself. (Apparently, even a video of someone breathing sixty feet underwater is enough to spur an anxiety attack in more delicate viewers.) I practiced additional meditation techniques the night before our first class, after I reminded Bret that he would have to meet me at a swimming pool after work, wiggle into a borrowed wet suit, perform inhuman acts until 11:30 P.M., get back on the subway, journey the forty-five minutes home, eat a slice of cold pizza, sleep, and do it all again the next day (twice more, actually).

The morning of our first class, I received the following e-mail from my mother: "How's the scuba diving?????? Are you ready? Good luck with it. Maybe someone will throw records in the pool." I was a kid in a dunce cap, hunched in the corner, being laughed at by her own mother.

The training itself—we spent the first half of each night in an empty day-care classroom and the second half in a health-club lap pool adjacent to the shop—was led by an uncannily serene man named Tom who handled my periodic breakdowns with seasoned aplomb. The first time I assembled and strapped on all my gear—a seven-millimeter wet suit, scuba booties, fins, a life vest–like buoyancy control device known as a BC, a forty-pound air cylinder, a mask, a regulator hose, a twelve-pound weight belt, and a snorkel—and stood, trembling, at the edge of the pool, I felt like Houdini, shackled in handcuffs and chains and preparing to leap off the Weighlock Bridge. Wet suits squeeze and compress your chest and limbs in ways I previously thought physically impossible; scuba masks completely seal off the top half of your face, including your nostrils. With a breathing regulator blocking my mouth, I was so claustrophobic I could barely stand to keep any of it in place ("Amanda, put your mask back on!" became a refrain familiar to my classmates). My fingers were numb. My throat was arid, scratchy. My panic response—talking as much as possible to anyone within earshot—kicked in. I needed a magical intervention. I turned to Bret, but he was sporting a similar look of distress, which only made me feel guilty on top of terrified. How had I gotten us here, swaddled in neoprene, cowering beside a swimming pool in midtown Manhattan at eleven on a Tuesday night?

I took a clumsy breath of canned air, pressed my mask to my face, extended a lone fin, and stepped in. Fifteen seconds later, I climbed back out. Intellectually, I understood how a regulator works—it converts pressurized air into breathable air via a mechanical system of one-way valves—but inhaling underwater for the first time is a deeply disconcerting experience, like sticking your bare hand into an open flame and holding it there. I gave myself a stern pep talk invoking gods and expletives, tumbled back into the water, and gripped the side of the pool. I closed my eyes. I bit my regulator. I went down, and I forced myself to stay underwater.

After a series of half-tentative, half-frantic breaths, I was able to temporarily retrain my body—*WE ARE NOT DROWNING*—and almost immediately, diving became significantly easier (although still not fun). All I could think about was getting air. In and out: a muffled sucking sound, a stream of bubbles. *We are not drowning.* I took a tentative tour of the pool, distracting myself from the facts of my situation by counting the lost hair ties congregating by a drain. Finally, Tom signaled for us to gather around him, and we began moving through the exercises outlined in our textbooks. Soon I was doing absurd things like removing my regulator from my mouth while sitting cross-legged in the deep end (a scene rendered more preposterous by the health-club patrons swimming after-work laps twelve feet above me). Eventually, I even let Tom turn off my air supply so that I could tug an alternate regulator off the front of Bret's BC, clear it of water, cram it between my lips, and swim slowly to the surface while holding his air tank, thus saving my own life for what I hoped would be the last time.

Buoyancy, I discovered, is both the crux of a successful dive and a challenging thing to master. If you're breathing too rapidly (because you're nervous), your overinflated lungs will prevent you from sinking to your desired depth, no matter how much extra weight you have strapped to your hips—I wore mine low: "Like a gunslinger," Tom said—or how vigorously you flap your fins. Of course, there is comedy in this: as your fellow divers drift gently to the bottom, you will hover approximately ten inches below the surface of the water, humiliated and alone, like a pimply teenager pinned to his own locker via wedgie. Scuba, then, becomes a kind of Buddhist ideal—to properly fall, you need to relax your whole body and mind, exhale deeply (and if there is anything more counterintuitive than inhaling underwater, it's emptying your lungs), and submit to the weight of the water. Submission is a thing I am working on, but eventually, I got there. By the end of the third night, I had somehow completed all the necessary tasks to pass—including the particularly insane bit where someone rips your mask from your face and you flail around in the water, blind and panicked, trying to find it, strap it back on, and clear it of liquid without accidentally inhaling through your nose, choking, and perishing in three feet of chlorinated water.

Our class started with four students, but it finished with three (Bill, a skydiver who worked in finance and consumed an impressive number of PowerBars, couldn't equalize his ears underwater, which divers attempt to do by holding their noses and blowing until the pressure in their ear canal stops), and at the end of the final night, after we had taken a comprehensive written exam, completed all five confined water dives, and congratulated our classmate Alexia, Bret and I splurged on a cab ride home, threw our flippers into a closet, and consumed an entire bottle of champagne. I'm positive that we deserved it. I passed out in a damp bikini. I still don't know what happened to my textbook.

We decided to complete our open water dives a few weeks later in Beaufort, North Carolina, a sleepy three-hundred-year-old seaside town where Bret's parents keep a vacation home. At the Raleigh-Durham airport, I barely recognized the person plucking a bulky bag of brightly colored scuba equipment off the luggage carousel.

Historically, the southern coast of North Carolina is an especially treacherous stretch of water for boats—it's nicknamed the Graveyard of the Atlantic—and there are an ungodly number of shipwrecks for intrepid divers to explore. I balked at this particular prospect, which seemed karmically incongruous, like laughing at an alcoholic while chugging a scotch. Instead, we booked a private session for Monday morning; we would be diving off Radio Island, between Beaufort and Morehead City, and we'd be looking mostly for soft and hard corals, crabs, urchins, and something called a sea squirt. I was relieved to discover it would be a walk-in dive, which meant we would be waddling into the water straight from the beach, rather than stepping or rolling in off a chartered boat. I convinced myself that walk-in dives were relatively tame, as far as maritime adventures go—really, it was practically snorkeling.

Beaufort, incidentally, is something of a beacon for treasure hunters. The pirate Edward "Blackbeard" Teach ran his ship (a captured French slave vessel he rechristened the *Queen Anne's Revenge*) aground here in 1718, lodging it in a sandbar and cracking its primary mast. The wreck was first discovered in 1996 in relatively shallow water off nearby Atlantic Beach; a few weeks before we arrived, marine archaeologists had helped raise one of the ship's 3,000-pound anchors for the very first time. For hundreds of years, rumors that Blackbeard had buried part of his fortune somewhere in or around Beaufort persisted, and the city still draws bounty hunters with vivid, *Goonies*-inspired dreams of gold doubloons. I felt a certain kinship with these oddball entrepreneurs, who seemed both delusional and pleasantly optimistic—really, in terms of effort to financial reward, record collectors are a far loonier breed—and I convinced myself that Beaufort was an appropriate place to kick off my own underwater treasure-hunting pursuits.

I figured a little sea-level digging couldn't hurt, either. All weekend, Bret and his parents waited patiently while I pawed through every antique and junk shop in the general area. I smiled apologetically—my now-patented shame grin—while they stood outside, holding their two golden retrievers and likely discussing my lunacy. Luckily, I'd started to develop a pretty sensitive radar for old shellac: I could scan an overstuffed room and locate the lone box of records almost instantaneously. First, as Chris King had taught me, I looked for any old home-audio equipment, like a portable Victrola or a full-size phonograph—78s are frequently tucked into the speaker cabinet, a doored cubby that most people mistake for a storage area.

If a phonograph sweep didn't produce any results, I would start staring directly at the floor, searching for sagging, untended cardboard boxes. Because 78s are so heavy when stacked (and, subsequently, difficult to lift), they're typically tossed into small containers and left low, crammed in a cobwebbed corner or shoved under a piece of furniture. Somewhat counterintuitively, asking an employee for help is often a dead end. Cashiers might point you toward a rack of overpriced Beatles LPs, or—and this is more often the case—just shrug, wholly unaware that there are any 78s in stock at all. To the uninitiated, they are uniquely innocuous things.

In nearby Morehead City, I found a hatbox stuffed with 78s—carefully layered in the pages of a local newspaper from 1951—in the back corner of an SPCA rummage store, and in downtown Beaufort I found a Victor record album (a book, similar to a picture album, that holds 78s in paper sleeves) full of old Hawaiian guitar records sitting on the floor of a consignment shop a block from the waterfront. It contained twenty songs I'd never heard before, including six sides by Pale K. Lua and David Kaili, a Hawaiian guitar duet who performed for Victor in the mid-1910s. According to the Library of Congress, they recorded mostly in the winters of 1914 and 1915 in Camden, New Jersey, a fact that exists in marked contrast to the songs themselves, which blow and bend like Hawaiian palms—intoxicating, warm, and forgiving. I bought the whole book for two dollars.

At an antique shop on Front Street, I found a curious assortment—including a record titled *Folk Songs Accompanied by Nightingales and Canaries from Karl Reich's Aviary*, a Columbia musical-comedy album by Van and Schneck, and a copy of "Black Bottom," a high-charting fox-trot from 1926 performed by Johnny Hamp's Kentucky Serenaders—under an oil painting in a half-empty room on the second floor. The Black Bottom was a wildly popular dance (an iteration of the Charleston) in the 1920s, although it supposedly originated in New Orleans closer to the turn of the twentieth century. According to instructions printed on the 1919 sheet music, it required you to "Hop down front then Doodle back, Mooch to your left then Mooch to the right, Hands on your hips and do the Mess Around, Break a Leg until you're near the ground." I surveyed my new purchases with novice pride.

As anyone who's lugged a suitcase full of shellac through a crowded airport terminal knows, 78s are not very fun to travel with. In fact, most serious collectors, all of whom have their own particular methods for packing and shipping, would scoff at the notion of ever stuffing them inside a piece of luggage. But I'd remembered to leave a good portion of my suitcase empty for new acquisitions, and later that night, I wrapped each individual record in bubble wrap and carefully layered them in my bag, folding my softest T-shirts in between. I hadn't found anything rare or of historical consequence, but I still liked the way the records looked, tucked amid my things.

On Monday morning I woke up nervous. I put on my bathing suit and choked down a bowl of Raisin Bran, glugging a bit of coffee from a giant novelty mug in the shape of a pirate's boot. We had one day to dive, which meant two trips to the bottom and back, per PADI (the Professional Association of Diving Instructors) rules. The high-pressure breathing gas in a scuba cylinder is essentially the same air we breathe every day: roughly 80 percent nitrogen and 20 percent oxygen. But because that air is so compressed underwater—at thirty feet, you're breathing air that's been condensed twofold—the excess nitrogen that gathers in your tissues and is released, during and after ascension, into your bloodstream can cause decompression sickness if you don't allow the body enough time to recover between dives.

Bret and I packed up our gear, walked to Discovery Diving, and signed a stack of papers absolving our instructors of all liability should we somehow fail to return. Because the current in Beaufort can be strong, tugging swimmers away from the shore and into the channel, divers are required to wait until slack tide, a fleeting window between high and low tides when the current is reversing and the water is relatively still; if you're lucky, you get thirty or forty minutes of calm surf. After floating a pair of red-and-white dive flags—little buoys to alert passing boats that divers are down, so we don't accidentally surface and get decapitated by a skiff full of dudes chugging Coors Light—we strapped on our equipment and ran through a few drills (clearing our masks of water, towing each other's fake-lifeless bodies to shore, checking our compass bearings, sweeping for lost regulators) in shallow water before swimming out past a rock jetty (home to stone crabs, flounder, black bass, urchins, sea spiders, and a terrifying, toothy thing called an oyster toadfish) and powering down to thirty-five feet. There, we sat on the sandy bottom, equalizing our ears and checking our gauges.

One thing I hadn't expected about scuba diving in an actual body of water is how peaceful it is, particularly for someone so accustomed to the high, incessant drone of New York: you are granted access to an entire portion of the globe that was previously forbidden to you, and it turns out that it's also the softest, quietest part. Despite all my anxiety about diving, I felt like I could sit there forever, weightless and lost in the rhythm of my own breath, watching schools of blennies dodge in and out of dark crevices in the rock. My neurotic, city-dweller fears about being "touched by fish" dissipated, and for the first time in weeks—or at least since I'd gotten grand ideas about recovering Paramount 78s from a river in Wisconsin—I felt calm. I stopped thinking about regulators and air tanks and the adverse effects of increased pressure on the human body. I stopped thinking about records.

We swam to the surface together, ran a few more drills, and went back down, again following the wide angle of the jetty. I paid a little more attention this time, noting that the more sand we accidentally displaced on the bottom, the harder it was to see anything at all—meaning that purposefully digging in river silt was going to pose even more challenges than I'd anticipated (and really, I'd anticipated a lot). Our instructor for the day, a veteran diver named Debbie, suggested that I look into an underwater metal detector, which might at least help with locating any lost masters. (After I learned how much that might cost to buy—anywhere from $400 to $1,000—I crossed my fingers that we could rent or borrow one.) Still, I was worried about getting lost in some abysslike blackness, blind and disoriented, bested by wet dirt. Unlike the clear, sparkling water surrounding most Caribbean islands—like the pictures in my scuba textbook—the Milwaukee River appeared brown and nearly opaque in photographs. I imagined it would be like floating in a Yoo-hoo chocolate-flavored drink, but with pulp.

We surfaced again, practiced swimming using only our compasses for orientation, and then it was done. I squirmed out of my wet suit and disassembled and washed my gear. It was barely past noon. Debbie signed our diver logs and shook our hands.

Walking back down the beach to our borrowed Jeep, I felt almost like a champion.

○

A few weeks before our scheduled departure, Lenny stopped answering his cell phone. I found this disconcerting. Aside from the fact that we needed a guide and a watchdog, I'd been told that diving in the river might require a special license. He had one. I did not. After a day or two, I began wondering how many pretending-to-be-calm voicemails I could theoretically leave him; I hadn't experienced this particular concern since I was maniacally phoning up fourteen-year-old boys in 1995.

When I finally got Lenny on the phone, I was sitting in my living room, eating Swedish Fish and staring at the wall. It was a Wednesday afternoon, and I had dialed without actually expecting him to pick up. I gagged down a wad of candy and started speed-talking. He had a slew of legitimate concerns—Grafton was thirty miles north of his base in Milwaukee, the river was shallow up there ("You can walk across it!"), and anyway, what if I needed permission from the city or county to dive? In addition, planning the dive would require some sense of where the deepest pockets are, which, logically, would be where these records would have gotten stuck (a pit full of records! I felt giddy just thinking about it: an endless chasm, deep in the earth, where dead voices gathered!), and neither he nor I knew how to acquire that kind of map.

Lenny was letting me down easy. I could tell he thought I should find someone local with a working knowledge of that section of the river and maybe a contact or two in the Grafton Fire Department.

He politely told me to keep him posted—but I knew it was a let's-be-friends type of farewell.

Miraculously, I didn't fall apart. Earlier that day, I'd serendipitously Googled my way to Steve Sand, a guy who owned a scuba shop called Sea n' Sand Scuba in Thiensville, about six miles south of Grafton. Given that suburban Wisconsin is not a beacon for scuba specialists, this felt like a gift. It hadn't previously occurred to me to even look for a dive shop outside of the Milwaukee city limits. I filled out the automated "Contact Us" form on the shop's vaguely outdated-looking website and tried not to think about whether it would yield a reply. Two hours later, an e-mail appeared in my inbox. I held my breath and clicked: "Yes, I am sure that I can assist you with your project. Please call me and we will chat."

If you are in something of a desperate state—because, say, you need someone to accompany you on a bizarre underwater adventure in suburban Wisconsin on relatively short notice—it turns out there is no better person to call than Steve Sand. Steve worked as a sign-language interpreter for thirty years before opening a dive shop in 2006, and he remains a remarkable listener. Like Lenny, he had concerns about visibility—"You stir up the muck and you cannot see anything—even on a bright, sunny day, nothing," he warned—and about the legality of hopping into the river, but he was game. Steve worked part-time rescuing golf balls from the bottoms of nearby lakes; he knew a little about blindly digging around in mud. He did warn me about the claustrophobia and disorientation of so-called dark dives, uttering what might be the most terrifying words I have ever heard regarding scuba diving: "I keep a tablespoon of water in my mask so that I can tell which way is up." I gulped. Diving in a river requires negative buoyancy— usually scuba divers aspire to neutral buoyancy, which means you float at around eye level at the surface—and divers are weighted to sink. Add zero visibility, and you've got something resembling a sensory deprivation tank. Only with fish. And snakes. Oh.

Steve promised to look around and to check in with local authorities.

We agreed to meet at his shop early on the morning of the dive. In the meantime, I contacted Jim Brunnquell, the Grafton village president. He told me he didn't believe there were any special requirements for diving in the river and recommended looking north of Falls Road, because the water in the area directly to the south had been dramatically reduced due to the recent removal of a dam. "You may get lucky there as it is still fairly unexplored," he wrote. "Good luck."

Seven

I Like to Get into the Field and Hunt Them Down in the Wild, So to Speak

○

John Tefteller, King Solomon Hill, Angela Mack, Grafton,
Orange Drink, "Shakin' Down That Town"

○

Grafton, Wisconsin, is mild and bucolic in the manner of most Midwestern suburbs: the streets are clean and wide, the houses are modest and well maintained, and an American flag always blows high and proud above the high school parking lot. The first time I drove into Grafton from my hotel in downtown Milwaukee, I tried to imagine which parts of the landscape might look familiar to a blues singer trekking north from the Mississippi Delta in 1929. Central Wisconsin being atmospherically cool, culturally stoic, and overwhelmingly white, here's what I came up with: both places are pretty flat. Mostly, it's hard to think of another American city less cosmically suited to the creation of country blues, or less recognizable to its progenitors.

Angela Mack had agreed to meet me on the corner of Falls Road and Twelfth Avenue at eleven A.M., a few hours before she was due at the North Shore Academy of the Arts, the community arts center where she gave private music lessons. I'd been duly warned—by John Tefteller and others—that there wasn't much of Paramount left to see in Grafton, but when I parked my rented Toyota Corolla near the Falls Road bridge, climbed out, and carried a cup of hotel coffee over to the pressing plant's crumbling foundation, I felt disembodied, spooked. I sat on a cold concrete slab and pulled my bare legs to my chest. I am not always susceptible to the magnetism of sacred ground—I generally find monuments exhausting—but I was entranced by the hard, gray remnants of this place, by its concrete platforms and half-brick, half-stone half walls. The pressing plant was razed in the 1940s, and a private home was built on the north end of the lot; on the south side, flora had intervened, and weeds poked up through every crack in the remaining foundation. I stared at their tiny green leaves, trying to conceive of all the records manufactured here, all the songs that had inextricably altered the course of my life nine hundred miles east. I sniffed the air for the scent of shellac: no trace.

While I waited, I read the historical marker placed a few yards away by the village of Grafton, a tribute Alex van der Tuuk—working in conjunction with the Historic Preservation Committee—had spear-headed. For years, it was the only public mention of Paramount Records anywhere in Grafton. Mack has since worked tirelessly to preserve and commemorate the city's musical legacy, even when its denizens have responded with apathy (or, occasionally, distaste). She moved to Grafton in 1996, but it wasn't until 2002, when John Tefteller mailed Mack and every other citizen of Grafton a postcard with photographs of Paramount 78s plastered across the front, that she learned about the town's odd role in blues history and became dedicated to protecting its presence here.

It's hard to talk about Paramount Records without talking about John Tefteller, the preeminent collector of Paramount 78s in the world. His private stash contains about five thousand records, divided between prewar and postwar blues, with Paramount blues comprising about eight hundred of those, maybe a few more. Although I was certain he would be, at fifty-three, just as feisty and maniacal as his younger counterparts (you'd have to be, to get some of the records he has), he presented an undeniable air of calmness the first few times we spoke on the telephone, and even more so when we met for lunch in Brooklyn a few months later, while he was passing through New York on a record-hunting trip from his home in Grants Pass, Oregon. I'd already heard plenty of stories about Tefteller's collection. His competitors regarded it with a mix of envy and disgust.

Unlike most of his peers, Tefteller made a living buying and reselling rare 78s, LPs, and 45s (his Paramounts were not for sale), meaning his collecting was as much a business as a hobby, and it could be all-encompassing. While most collectors were content to engage in passive trade (bartering with other collectors, setting up saved eBay searches, leaving their cards with junk-shop owners), Tefteller wasn't intimidated by complicated primary research, or by getting on an airplane, or by doling out a significant amount of cash to get what he wanted. That aggression had made him a contentious figure in the community. "I like to get into the field and hunt them down in the wild, so to speak," he said.

While we ate lunch, Tefteller told me he believed that amassing a serious collection of prewar blues 78s was basically impossible for a newcomer—for someone like me. "I don't know how you could do it today," he said, waving a french fry in the air, his big white mustache twitching. "How you could wake up this morning and say, 'Gee, I think I wanna collect prewar blues records and I wanna build a world-class collection of them.' I don't know how you could do that, even if you had millions of dollars to spend. There's only a finite amount of these things available and most of the people who have them have no interest in selling them. So you have to be extremely patient—it's a long process, and a lot of people who start the process get discouraged real quick."

Even for a full-time record hunter with copious cash to spend, Paramount blues are not particularly easy to locate. Tefteller, at least, was willing to put in the legwork, chasing the nominal paper trail as far as it would go. "You find, say, whoever had the Paramount distributor shift in Lynchburg, Virginia, in 1930," he explained. "You find that person's name, and you find out where they died, who their relatives and survivors might be. And do those relatives and survivors have any of that material, or was it all discarded or given away when the person stopped being a Paramount Records distributor?"

My eyes bugged. This was journalism, sort of—it was certainly more than just pawing through moldy records on the greasy linoleum floor of a Goodwill. Tefteller was pursuing his prey with the kind of vehemence typically employed by a PI stalking a client's ex-wife, or a cop chasing a kingpin. It felt calculated and thorough. It also felt thankless. As any beat reporter could testify, not every investigation yields compelling results. How far can you go before you risk losing the plot entirely? How can you solve a murder without a body?

"[78s] can come from anywhere," Tefteller admitted. "There's not any one particular source. Records have a way of hiding. People bought them years and years ago, they took 'em to parties, they played them at home, they beat them to death. Some got thrown away, yeah, but a lot of stuff got shuffled off into a corner, put in an attic, put in a basement, put in a garage, given to a neighbor, given to a friend." As such, Paramount 78s "very rarely" show up at yard sales or flea markets or in thrift stores. For the most part, they're languishing in private homes, entirely out of sight. "Most of the time now, they come from estates where somebody has died and the relatives come in and start hunting through their things and find a little stack of records buried in a house or a basement," Tefteller continued. "The new generation comes in and says, 'Well, we don't need these,' and they start to look for how they can create some money out of the situation. A lot of times the people that have these are not aware that they might have something that has not been heard since 1928 by anybody other than their family—they're just aware that they have a stack of old records."

Tefteller, it turns out, has a singular knack for turning a benign tip into a jackpot. He'll pull on a thread until the whole sweater unravels. For example: in late 2001, Tefteller got a call from a collecting pal, alerting him to a recent eBay auction of interest—a large, full-color poster of Blind Lemon Jefferson in the style of Paramount's *Chicago Defender* ads (it had likely hung in a furniture shop). The auction had ended, but Tefteller e-mailed the seller, who was located in Port Washington, to see if he or she might have any more Paramount-related goodies to unload. When Tefteller finally got the guy—a local reporter named Steve Ostermann—on the phone, he learned that Ostermann and a friend had been tasked with emptying out an old newspaper building in the early 1980s and had accidentally uncovered a slew of Paramount advertising material: hundreds of old publicity posters, photographs, bits of artwork, letterhead and other ephemera, all crammed in the back of an abandoned filing cabinet. Although the reporters weren't blues fans, exactly, they thought the stuff looked compelling enough to save and loaded a few boxes into the trunks of their cars.

Tefteller was giddy but tried to keep his cool. As he wrote in an essay for *78 Quarterly*, Ostermann "listened politely (our phone conversation was punctuated by long silences). I got the impression he thought I was a bit of a nut, and that maybe I was talking too much." Tefteller interrogated Ostermann as gently as possible, ultimately discovering that his partner—a woman from Colorado named Janet—had a bunch of Charley Patton material, including, he thought, a photograph. At this point, only a tiny, cropped picture of Patton's head and neck had ever been uncovered. Patton, for all we knew, could have had three arms and a peg leg. Tefteller was ecstatic.

Ostermann promised to try to get in touch with Janet, who had left Wisconsin following a complicated divorce, to see if she still had the boxes and if she'd be willing to sell them. A few days later, he called Tefteller back. Janet still owned the Patton material, including the photograph. She was reluctant, but finally acquiesced to Tefteller's "generous offer." All three agreed to meet in Port Washington in May to complete the deal in person. Tefteller had promised to pay what he would only describe as "a fortune" for the material. He had to take out a small loan to cover the expense.

The trade was settled, but Tefteller wasn't done searching: if there was more preserved Paramount material decaying in central Wisconsin, he was going to recover it, and soon. He planned to camp out at a Best Western in Port Washington for twelve days, fully canvasing the area for remnants.

"For years—and I mean since the sixties—people had been going to Grafton and Port Washington looking for Paramount 78s, figuring, 'Okay, they were made there, they should be there,'" he said. "And they were right, but even back then and all the way up until I did it, nobody, not one single researcher or collector, was aggressive in—I guess you could use the phrase 'shakin' down that town,'" he continued. "They would wander around the junk stores in the area, they would talk to a few people here and there, but they didn't really go nutty like I did. If I'm gonna do something, I'm gonna do it right—I won't just go in there and halfheartedly do it, I'll do it as best I can. I spent a bunch of money advertising with the local newspapers, generated publicity by talking to reporters, and then mailed out flyers and postcards to every single resident within a hundred miles of where that company was back then. I created a real nice-looking flyer and postcard with pictures of Paramount labels and talked about how some of these records are worth thousands of dollars, and if you have any in your attics or your basements or if any of your relatives worked at the company, or if you have anything else related to the company, I need to talk to you. And I flooded the area with this and then I sat at the Best Western in Port Washington and fielded phone calls at the hotel for days from people who had relatives who had worked there."

What happened for Tefteller in Grafton is the kind of thing collectors dream about at night, their blankets pulled up to their stubbly chins, their hands curled into little fists. Shortly after he checked into his hotel, Tefteller drove to Ostermann's house, where he and Janet were waiting with their scavenged bounty. Sorting through the material spread out on the kitchen table, Tefteller spotted a pile of rare photographs (including pictures of Blind Lemon Jefferson, Blind Blake, and the Norfolk Quartette), flipped through it, and pulled out the now-iconic shot of Charley Patton, seated in a wooden chair, wearing white flannel spats, shiny shoes, and a pinky ring, and holding a battered Stella guitar.

Patton was light-skinned (he was presumed to be African-American by most of his peers, but for years, scholars have wondered whether Patton was, in fact, part Cherokee, part Mexican, part Caucasian, or some combination thereof), and his dark hair is parted on the left side and combed neatly over his forehead. He's wearing a comically over-size suit. His head looks tiny and strange, popping up through his shirt collar as if it had been tied on with his bow tie. He stares blankly at the camera. His ears are bigger than I'd imagined, and more pronounced—I have thought, from time to time, that he resembles a darker-skinned, more serious Alfred E. Neuman—but the oddest thing about the picture is the way Patton's left hand is situated on his guitar: his fingers almost look deformed, spread out on the fret board as if to form some kind of Vulcan hand signal, his index finger and middle finger stretching far apart and pointing straight down. Even now I find it perplexing: who holds a guitar like that?

Although a small picture of Patton's head, cropped from this exact shot, had been uncovered decades earlier, getting a glimpse of Patton's whole body was still exhilarating. He likely didn't choose the clothes he was wearing (the suit was so ill fitting it was almost certainly borrowed), but seeing that old Stella guitar balanced in his lap, seeing the way he held himself—it was like looking up from a campfire, tugging a marshmallow off a stick, and spotting Bigfoot casually leaning on a pine tree outside your tent, waiting for a s'more. It didn't feel quite real. Ghosts and legends weren't supposed to have pinky rings. They didn't sit stiffly in wooden chairs.

Tefteller was freaked out, too, although he held it together for the sake of the sale. "I just looked at it and said, 'Oh, wow, this is great,'" he remembered. "I didn't want to be like, 'This is the Holy Grail of everything!'"

But it was, in a way. Later, writing in 78 Quarterly, Tefteller admitted "I felt as if I had discovered some lost amendments to the Constitution in Thomas Jefferson's own handwriting . . . I knew that photo would have a place in blues history." As anticipated, he bought nearly everything the reporters had for sale, including the Patton picture.

A few days later, Tefteller got a call from a woman who claimed that her grandmother had worked at the pressing plant in Grafton. She had inherited a trunk full of Paramount 78s and recognized the labels on his postcard. Tefteller was tired, at this point, of digging through box after box of terrible records, so he asked her if there were any blues songs in the batch, rather than the standard polkas, marches, country, and dance numbers typically stockpiled by Germanic Wisconsinites. The woman didn't really know, she said, but there was one record with a funny-sounding name: "My Buddy Blind Papa Lemon." Tefteller froze.

"My Buddy Blind Papa Lemon" was recorded in 1932 by King Solomon Hill, a five-foot-three, 130-pound blues singer born in 1897 near McComb, Mississippi. "King Solomon Hill" is a colloquial name for a small neighborhood in Yellow Pine, Louisiana; Hill's real name was likely Joe Holmes (a notion first introduced by the blues researcher and collector Gayle Dean Wardlow in the 1960s and debated, furiously, by collectors for years after). Holmes was probably recommended to Paramount by Blind Lemon Jefferson, whom Holmes had met and traveled with in 1928. In 1932, a Paramount scout named Henry Stephany accompanied Holmes to Birmingham, where they met with a few other bluesmen (Ben Curry, Marshall Owens, and the Famous Blue Jay Singers) before traveling north together to Grafton to record. When they got there, Holmes made six sides for Paramount. He returned to the South shortly thereafter and died, in 1949, in Sibley, Louisiana, likely due to complications from alcoholism. Prior to Tefteller's arrival, only two of Holmes's three records had been recovered and heard by modern ears—no copies of the remaining sides had ever been found.

Tefteller, wheezing, told the woman to carefully place the record somewhere it wouldn't be broken, and asked when he could come over to see it. She told him she preferred to meet somewhere public (I empathized with her impulse). They settled on the parking lot of the Sentry Market in Grafton, and by 10:15 the next morning, Tefteller was the proud new owner of a pristine copy of "My Buddy Blind Papa Lemon" / "Times Has Done Got Hard" (Paramount 13125), the only known copy in the world. "The hundred dollar bills came spilling out of my wallet," he wrote of the transaction in *78 Quarterly*.

Whenever I get frustrated by collectors—by their hostility, their exclusivity, their infuriating single-mindedness—I think about "My Buddy Blind Papa Lemon" and how crazy old John Tefteller saved that wild, miraculous song from rotting away in a trunk in Wisconsin. It's the sort of thing that makes you want to buy a man a cheeseburger, or at least tell him thanks.

"My Buddy Blind Papa Lemon" is a remarkable record; it changes shape almost every time I hear it. The song opens, unexpectedly, with a high, sweet howl: Holmes was slight and his voice is appropriately compact, but that "Ooooowaooooh!" cuts through everything else in the room, including his somewhat spastic guitar playing.

The song itself is a eulogy of sorts for Blind Lemon Jefferson, who died mysteriously, at age thirty-six, in Chicago on December 19, 1929. Jefferson's death certificate, finally unearthed in 2010, lists "probably acute myocarditis" (or inflammation of the heart) as the thing that nixed him, although theories, some apocryphal, abound: Jefferson might have been mugged, or maybe a spurned lover slipped something unpleasant into his coffee, or maybe a gnashing dog attacked him in the middle of the night. Even the reigning assumption—that he became disoriented during a snowstorm and froze to death—is peculiar. But Jefferson's name reflected his rotund, pinched shape, and since it's likely that he wasn't in tip-top condition at the time of his passing, almost anything could have done him in. Myocarditis can be incited by a virus or by trauma (like an allergic reaction, electric shock, or radiation), but often its root cause remains unknown. Paramount paid to have his body returned to Texas by train, and Jefferson was eventually buried in an African-American cemetery in Wortham.

According to "My Buddy Blind Papa Lemon," Holmes learned about his friend's death via mailman: "I received the letter that my friend Lemon was dead," he sings, and although at the time of its recording Jefferson had already been gone for a few years, Holmes sounds as if he just found out about it that morning. The narrative is oddly literal for a blues song: "Everybody got to go, but it's still sad when you lose one of your best friends," he admits. In my darker moments, it is the kind of thing that I secretly hope someone might sing about me after I'm gone—Holmes sounds devastated, enraged. The song ends unexpectedly, three minutes in, after a jerky, extended slide-guitar bit. I almost always start it over again immediately after it finishes, certain that I've missed something (I usually have). Tefteller released the track publicly in the summer of 2004 on the CD that accompanies his annual Blues Calendar, a collection of blues-related images from the 1920s that he usually sells online for twenty dollars. He later allowed Shanachie Records to include it on their *Times Ain't Like They Used to Be* compilation. Today you can buy it, as I did, on iTunes for ninety-nine cents.

There are around thirty missing Paramount race records—including Marshall Owens's "Texas Blues Part Two" / "Seventh Street Alley Strut" and Willie Brown's "Grandma Blues" / "Sorry Blues"—still waiting to be uncovered, which means John Tefteller's mission hardly ended that morning in Grafton. He remains in hot pursuit of the missing shellac, and he wants everyone to know it. When I interviewed him for a *New York Times* story in 2008, he suggested that I print his standing offer of $25,000 for each of the missing Willie Brown records. I did, thinking that someone somewhere might see it—might climb up to the attic, might dig through some records, might make a call. We're both still waiting to hear.

●

I was thinking about records—about fresh, unplayed copies of "My Buddy Blind Papa Lemon" popping hot off a Paramount stamper, about fishing a mysteriously preserved Willie Brown 78 out of the river—when I heard someone calling my name. I looked up, and Angela Mack, wearing an electric blue top, her face beset by a cloud of blonde curls, was waving from across the street.

Mack is the closest thing Grafton has to a local blues historian (a few months after my visit, she was part of a team of researchers who uncovered both Blind Blake's death certificate and his unmarked grave, nearly seventy-seven years after he died of pulmonary tuberculosis, in nearby Glendale), and she had promised to lead me on the Paramount Walking Tour, a normally self-guided journey that begins at the marker and ends about half a mile down Twelfth Avenue, at a photography studio called Photography by Michael. Mack was an enthusiastic and knowledgeable guide, speaking freely and eagerly about various Paramount landmarks; as we walked, she answered every one of my oddball questions about where, say, someone might have tossed a bunch of records into the river. ("Just curious!") From the marker, we wandered halfway over the bridge and paused, staring at a long foundational wall of the factory that's visible only from the east side of the river. Mack pointed out the rusted power wheel that once fueled the presses, barely perceptible through the thick summer overgrowth. We doubled back, past the land where the studio was constructed and connected to the plant via viaduct (it was torn down in 1938; a yellow brick house with red shutters and a for-sale sign sits there now) and past the former home of Alfred Schultz, the chief recording engineer and pressing-plant foreman. Mack told me that his daughter Janet, upon meeting Ma Rainey, mistakenly called her Grandma.

We paused outside the Grafton post office, where records were sometimes shipped to eager buyers, and the Hotel Grafton, where musicians may or may not have stayed while recording for Paramount. (In a 1965 interview, Son House said, "There was a hotel, small hotel, two-story, that was special for all the recorders," but it seems more

likely that visiting blues singers stayed in comparably diverse Milwaukee.) We finally reached the Paramount Walk of Fame, a deserted stone
plaza with a walkway that resembles a piano keyboard. Different keys
are dedicated to different Paramount performers, and the whole thing
is anchored by a fountain featuring three bronzed musicians standing
back to back to back. Mack told me that the village couldn't afford to
pay for the rights to the likenesses of actual Paramount performers, so
the statues are bizarre approximations. A few feet from me, a rendering
of a small man with an acoustic guitar, a mustache, and a wide-brimmed
hat (Son House?) stared blissfully at the clouds while thin beams of
water squirted into the air and splashed at his feet.

I was glad that the village was acknowledging its history—and really,
it was a noble salute—but something about the Paramount Walk of Fame
also felt vaguely tragic. The commercial presentation of "the blues" is
often disastrously corny, wholly divorced from—even antithetical to—
the grimness of the songs themselves. It's a young woman at an open
mic night, oversinging "Chain of Fools" with her hands in the air. It's a
guy with a T-shirt tucked into his shorts, nodding appreciatively at a bar
band with three shrieking electric guitars. It's bright colors and branded
guitar slides and old, pinkish-white guys bellowing about women. It's
three squat, wonky statues in a fountain in Wisconsin.

We finished the tour at Photography by Michael, an unremarkable
two-story white house with an old-timey sign and a small brown awning.
Joseph Cramer, a Civil War veteran, had purchased the lot in 1872 for
eleven dollars and opened a daguerreotype studio sometime thereafter.
The business changed ownership many times, but it's always been a
photo studio of one sort or another. In 2002, John Tefteller, convinced
that his Patton portrait had likely been staged and shot there, pestered
the current owner into letting him spend a day clawing through boxes
of glass negatives in the basement and attic. Unfortunately, as Tefteller
ultimately learned, all the nitrate negatives once stored in the building—photographers stopped using breakable glass negatives around
1924—had been destroyed in 1975 by then-owner Walter Burhop, who

rightfully believed they were a fire hazard; the spontaneous combustion of deteriorated nitrate film has been documented at temperatures as low as 106 degrees Fahrenheit. Most portrait subjects were shot from twelve different angles or poses, but Tefteller's hope of churning up more Patton pictures promptly fizzled. I can almost see him dropping his heavy head into two dusty palms. I can almost hear his exasperated sigh.

Mack invited me back to her home for a cold drink on her porch. She jokingly admitted she'd initially found Tefteller's postcard "creepy." She brought out a few of her scrapbooks of Grafton and Paramount-related material, which were both comprehensive and fascinating: the story of a clean town reckoning with its dirty past. I sheepishly told her about my half-baked scuba aspirations, and she was sympathetic, even supportive. "I bet you'll find something," she smiled. "Call me if you have to." I wanted to hug her.

Instead I spent the rest of the day trawling every antique store in greater Milwaukee, including one that doubled as a paintball studio, looking for Paramount labels—that black-and-gold circle, that eagle with its mighty wings outstretched, clutching the earth in its talons. I didn't find shit.

o

The morning of the dive, I woke up thinking about Jeff Buckley, who drowned in a placid slack-water stretch of the Mississippi River in 1997; his death is one of those morbid rock 'n' roll mysteries that's periodically trotted out and dissected on VH1 clip shows. If I die in a river today, I thought, it won't be mysterious at all. It will be so, so stupid.

I tried to psych myself up by reading passages from an autographed copy of Bill Rancic's *You're Hired: How to Succeed in Business and Life*, an inspirational tome someone had plucked from the hotel library and left on the nightstand in our room. Rancic looked so confident on the dust jacket: his pointer finger was massaging one temple, his other hand was resting casually on his thigh, and his grin was as white and as wide as his shirt collar. He was mostly selling platitudes, which I committed to memory. Reject conventional wisdom. Look back to look ahead. Do what you can. Seal the deal. Be reasonable.

Bret brewed us a tiny pot of coffee, and I tied on my swimsuit, brushed my hair back into a ponytail, and swallowed two big multivitamins. Neither of us was very interested in breakfast, so we shoved our gear into the trunk and drove north to Thiensville, arriving at the shop by 7:45 A.M. While New York City summers test the human capacity for swelter, late July in Wisconsin is crisp and clean. It was sixty degrees and sunny. I was wearing a sweater and jeans over my bikini.

Steve met us at the door. Because I was so jumpy, I asked him approximately nine hundred questions about golf-ball diving, which he patiently answered (he collects five hundred to seven hundred per hour, he rarely wears gloves, and black walnuts feel an awful lot like golf balls). After filling out some paperwork, Steve sized us up for full-body wet suits (there's only a small window of time each year in which Wisconsin-based divers are not required to wear dry suits, the expensive, insulated outfits that protect against cold water and require additional training to use) and collected the rest of our equipment from the back of the store, testing our air tanks and regulators. I told Steve about my three primary concerns—the current, visibility, wildlife—and he nodded. Yes. Yes. Yes.

Bret, being the reasonable sort, decided not to actually dive but to snorkel next to me, making sure that I didn't get caught in any rocks or riptides. (If you get stuck on something and lose your oxygen regulator in zero visibility, and then don't have the space or wherewithal to perform a proper sweep, you'll drown, even in a just a foot or two of water.) Following advice from Mack, we'd brought a small shovel and gloves, and when he wasn't acting as my own personal lifeguard, Bret planned on snorkeling near the banks, digging around for buried goods. Steve was mercifully nonjudgmental about my lack of preparedness—a real archaeological exploration would have required methodically relocating all the rocks from the bottom of a section of the river, blocking it off, and slowly sifting through the silt, repeating the process while moving downriver, as opposed to my plan of blindly clawing through the muck, then doing it again somewhere else. We decided to look for deep pockets, paying special attention to the banks, where errant artifacts may have gotten wedged. Steve got in his van, we got back into the Toyota, and we all headed north to Grafton, pulling over and parking near the chair-factory marker.

Changing into a wet suit on the side of a busy road in a residential community in suburban Wisconsin is a uniquely humiliating experience. While I was frantically trying to yank mine up and over my hip bones, a man from a nearby construction crew trotted over, his striped orange vest lustrous in the sun. I was afraid he was going to tell us we couldn't dive here or place all three of us under citizen's arrest, but instead he just grinned, held up his hands, and said, "Okay, I gotta ask." I reluctantly recited my spiel while staring at the ground. The man hooted and wished us luck.

A few minutes later, while I was zipping up my booties, a young kid in a black T-shirt came running out of the building across the street—the yellow brick house on the land where the old recording studio had been. He seemed to know what we were there for. "You guys looking for records?" he shouted. We nodded. "Go north. They blasted the dam so you need to look north." We waved. "Good luck!" he yelled.

I heard the river before I saw it. We had planned to enter the water at a particularly knotty stretch just south of the pressing-plant foundation, and it was hard, at first, to even figure out which way the water was tugging us. Although the river is shallow here—anyone over five-and-a-half-feet tall could probably amble from bank to bank without getting their hair wet—the current was aggressive, and I hollered at Bret to stop pushing me before I realized he was standing a foot and a half away. Accidentally lunge into the wrong spot and the river will knock you down; if you drop something, you'll see it rocket downstream before you can wave a helpless good-bye. We trudged under and past the Falls Road bridge, trying to situate ourselves a good distance from where the first dam was removed in 2000. Steve loaded my buoyancy-control device with extra weight to compensate for the current, and while the added pounds made it awkward to walk—I kept losing my balance and banging my air cylinder on rocks, then waiting for Steve to help wrench me upright again—it had a grounding effect once I stopped moving. Staying in one place felt like a victory.

The current may have been strong, but the river was also shallow enough that all my dramatic posturing had started to feel silly. I was probably not going to die here, I conceded, and it is possible that I had been acting like a bit of a baby regarding scuba diving in general. I waddled back and forth between the banks as best I could. I was trying to locate the deepest pockets, which I discovered by falling into them. Eventually, I settled on a small area near the west bank, popped my regulator into my mouth, signaled to Bret, and sank into a dark hole. It felt like a baptism.

Lying flat on my belly, I could barely see more than six inches in front of me, and my visibility became more compromised each time I turned over a rock and started pawing through silt: I was blind and flailing, splayed in a green, blurry abyss. I repeated this as often as I could, moving north, finding cavities, checking for snapping turtles, digging, flicking crayfish off my wet suit, resurfacing when I ran into rocks. Several times I spotted a flash of silver—a master?—and my stomach lurched, but more digging would just reveal another pearled bit of shell, or a piece of a tossed CB radio (with a few exceptions, I found the Milwaukee River to be curiously free of garbage, which was either a testament to Wisconsin's citizens or an indication of just how quickly the water moved). Bret, raking through the trees on the west bank, was pulling up rusty, ancient-looking bits of machinery that may or may not have been parts from the pressing plant, but my hands were still empty. After a few hours, I noticed Steve giving me sympathetic looks. I was tired, and running out of ideas.

I surfaced and scanned the shore for Bret, who was still picking through mounds of dirt near the riverbank. While trying to get his attention, I had a brief out-of-body experience: it is incredibly strange to see someone wearing a full wet suit and a pair of leather-and-canvas gardening gloves, with a yellow mask and snorkel perched atop his head, digging through dead branches with a tiny shovel, looking for possibly nonexistent records on the side of a river in Wisconsin. I spit my regulator out, cocked my head, and pushed my mask back: he looked like a gangly, neoprene-clad insect scavenging for grubs.

I could tell Bret and Steve were both waiting for me to say we could all go home now, that I'd tried my best and I was ready to spin the entire fiasco as a character-building experience, the kind Bill Rancic might consider transformative. I slowly pulled myself to shore and hobbled up the bank. I unhooked my BC and tank. I drank some water. I took a look at the rusted, mechanical-looking gears Bret had pulled out of the earth and snapped a few photographs to e-mail to Angela Mack and Alex van der Tuuk. I unzipped the top half of my wet suit and pulled on a sweatshirt. I talked for a while with Steve while he changed out of his gear and pulled a plaid button-down shirt on over his Speedo. With each passing car I became increasingly aware that to drivers, it almost certainly appeared that I was chatting casually with a man wearing no pants at all. Someone honked.

We were done.

●

The day after the dive I came down with a stomach flu, which I loudly and deliriously credited to "river sickness" when Bret tried to coax my bruised, exhausted body off the hotel room floor. I was convinced that the river was trying to kill me, and that whatever water I had accidentally ingested while diving for 78s was loaded with debilitating foreign bacteria (this part may have been true), and that my present ailment was something I deserved for my hubris, and also for my stupidity. It felt like a warning: stop, go home, who are you kidding. All night I whined to Bret about the river's cruelty when I wasn't demanding that he fetch me a cup of orange drink from McDonald's, a beverage I had not consumed since I was seven years old. He patted my head. When I closed my eyes I saw spinning 78s, spiraling into oblivion, like the hypnotic black-and-white swirl from the *Twilight Zone* opening. I dreamed of unhinged turntables, soaring through the sky like Frisbees, high and free. I awoke and kicked all the blankets off.

The following morning I felt better, at least physically. I requested that we drive immediately to the closest Kopp's Custard so I could soothe the sting of defeat with a giant cherry milkshake. The entire debacle was starting to seem funny.

A day later we steered the Toyota south to Chicago for the Pitchfork Music Festival, where I joked easily and endlessly to my fellow Pitchfork staffers about what I'd just done. I laughed. They laughed. I hollered along to No Age. I slept in a Hard Rock Hotel. I ate gooey deep-dish pizza at two thirty in the morning and drank several dozen free cups of Heineken. It was fine, I repeated. After all, I had given it a pretty good shot. I'd tried.

Later, at the airport, while reading a *Wired* article about the retrieval of black-box recorders from airplane crash sites (not the best preflight reading, maybe), I encountered a quote from Dave Gallo of the Woods Hole Oceanographic Institution, a research-based nonprofit that often aids in the location of sunken wreckage. "You can find a needle in a haystack," Gallo told the reporter. "But you have to find the haystack first." I set the magazine down. I put my headphones on and took them off. I did an anxious lap around the terminal, fidgeting for a while in an empty Hudson News. In the search for rare 78s, there was no haystack. The whole world was the goddamn haystack.

What I had learned was how intoxicating—how overwhelming and how crushing—the search could be, even (or especially) when it didn't yield any results. I hadn't found a rare Paramount 78, but, just the act of looking had provided an instant remedy to the oversaturation of contemporary life. I could have it all whenever I wanted, but I couldn't have this, or at least not right away, and I savored every moment of that ache—it was no longer about what I could do. It was about what I could find. It was about what I could own.

Eight

All I'm Saying Is There's No Way You Can Game This Kind of System

○

Marshall Wyatt, Blind Blake, the Man from Raleigh, Devastation

○

I hadn't thought much about the Hillsville flea market since Chris King and I had rolled out of that dusty field, the acrid stench of junking still emanating from our overheated bodies. Then, one morning, I was idly scrolling through Facebook when I noticed a posting from a blues collector I'd talked to a few times. It concerned a previously undiscovered Paramount 78 that had turned up suddenly in North Carolina. I felt the contents of my stomach shift, then curdle. I clicked through to the website for Old Hat Records, a reissue label based out of Raleigh and operated by the collector Marshall Wyatt, where I found forty-five-second streams of Blind Blake's "Miss Emma Liza" and its flip side, "Dissatisfied Blues." Both songs had been recorded at Paramount's Grafton studio in January 1932. I had never heard either one before—this was the last of Blind Blake's forty-two 78s to be found, and, apparently, the only known copy in existence. Wyatt didn't own it; he was just hosting the audio clips on his site. According to the few lines of text posted alongside the streams, the record was unearthed "at a flea market in Virginia in August of 2012 by a collector who wishes to remain anonymous."

Shit, I thought.

My first phone call was to John Tefteller. He was in a rental car, en route to Florida for a record-scouting mission. He confirmed that he'd bought the record within a week of it being found. He wasn't sure where it had come from, exactly, but he'd paid a lot of cash ("a silly amount") for it. Whoever found it had known exactly what they had and who to call about it: "He just wanted to get it to the right person to get the most money for what he had, and of course that's me," Tefteller said.

The samples posted on Old Hat's website were garbled, and it was hard to tell exactly what the songs were like, although the snippets were playful, jazzy, and almost improvised sounding. Tefteller had plans to release the tracks commercially, but not until the following year, on the CD that would accompany his annual Blues Calendar—just as he'd done with the missing King Solomon Hill sides. He admitted that the record was in pretty terrible shape. "You can hear it all the way through, it doesn't skip, but it was basically played with a nail, and so it's ground down to the point where it's very hard to make out the lyrics because there's so much distortion," he said. Tefteller had already sent it to Richard Nevins for remastering. Only a handful of people had heard it in full.

"You can't really tell from the clips, but it's dramatically different from his normal stuff," Tefteller went on. "At that point in time, Paramount was basically done. They knew they were going out of business shortly. They were grasping at straws to find any hope of raising money through record sales, and so they were telling the few people who were still recording for them to experiment a little bit and try to come up with something that would sell. The clips you hear—which, again, are some of the clearest portions of the record—are of standard Blind Blake runs on the guitar and they're good, but when you hear the whole thing, there are a couple things that stand out. I believe 'Emma Liza' is a reworking of a Clarence Williams jazz record, but what [Blake] does in the song is, he tries to sound like Louis Armstrong—he's trying to do it in a jazz fashion. There's a part on the record where he does scat singing and changes his voice to a little bit of a falsetto, and it's quite different. What you heard on that clip is a pretty standard Blake run. But the record, it's a bit different."

Tefteller kept talking—"And the other side of it, 'Dissatisfied Blues,' is more along the lines of a traditional Blind Blake record, but again he's using a variant in his voice and he's actually doing a whole lot of rapping on the guitar, which he never did in any record before that . . ."—but I had stopped listening entirely by then. I was certain the record had been found at Hillsville. That King and I had been close to it.

When we finally hung up, I immediately dialed Marshall Wyatt, who confirmed what I'd figured. It had been bought at Hillsville, from Rodger Hicks, and the collector who found it wanted to remain anonymous. "What he told me is this," Wyatt said. " 'If they'—they—'know my name, they might break into my house and steal all my records.' Typical record collector's paranoia at work. There could be other reasons, but that's what he actually said to me."

Wyatt also said the guy had driven to Hillsville from Raleigh a few days before the flea market officially opened, and that was when he found it amid Hicks's boxes. When he brought it to Wyatt, he was asking $10,000. "I made him a very serious cash offer for the disc, but he had already called Tefteller, and he knew Tefteller had more money than anybody else. He turned down my offer immediately. It was serious. But once I played the record and realized the condition problems, I was just as happy he had turned me down because it would have been a lot of money for a record that's very important and very significant and obviously very rare, but I couldn't enjoy sitting in my music room and playing it. The noise and the stripping would just be so aggravating. It turned out fine from my perspective, because I did at least get to hear the record and hold it and play it and announce it. And then I guess Tefteller came through town a few days later and negotiated with him and bought it."

I felt a palpable sense of loss. I knew how hard it was to find a 78 like that; I hadn't ever even expected to get that close. But it was still invigorating, wanting something so badly, even as I was being told (again) I couldn't have it. I could see, then, that my sense of what music was worth (even contemporary music, even the CDs accumulating in my mailbox) was shifting. I was remembering how precious a song could be.

Later that night, I finally spoke to King. He'd sent me an e-mail earlier in the day, saying that he'd call around nine, after he put his daughter to bed. "Perfect . . . actually, pitch-perfect twist, if you ask me," he wrote. "You were within days of witnessing something that would have been beautiful in your book, and it was done stole from you. Sort of like being on the road to witness the landing of the Hindenburg and seeing the smoke a mile away . . . *Oh, the Paramounts!*"

King spent most of the call laughing at me. He was being annoyingly reasonable about everything. There was no way we would have ever gotten there early enough, he insisted. "All I'm saying is there's no way you can game this kind of system! This is beautiful," he kept saying. "It almost fell into your hands. That would have been really beautiful. But it didn't. *This* is beautiful."

I took a deep breath. "Chris," I said. "Shut up."

The collector John Heneghan with his 78s in 2009. *Photo by Theo Morrison.*

An early advertisement for Edison's phonograph Tone Tests, printed circa 1906.

78 *Quarterly*, volume 11, published in 2000 and featuring a story on the elusive Black Patti label. *Courtesy of Pete Whelan.*

The collector Chris King in 2012. *Photo by Dave Anderson, dbanderson.com.*

Portrait of Les and Anne Andrews King, Chris King's parents, among Les King's phonograph collection in Bath County, Virginia, in 1957. *Courtesy of Chris King.*

Blind Uncle Gaspard's "Sur le Borde de l'Eau," Vocalion Records, 1929. *From the collection of Chris King.*

Geeshie Wiley's "Last Kind Words Blues," Paramount Records, 1930. *From the collection of Chris King.*

The Paramount talent scout H. C. Speir in Jackson, Mississippi, in 1966.
Photo by Marina Bokelman, courtesy of David Evans.

A promotional portrait and the only extant photo of the blues singer Blind Lemon Jefferson, taken circa 1926.

A promotional portrait and the only extant photo of the blues singer Charley Patton, taken circa 1929.
Photo copyright © 2003 by John Tefteller and Blues Images, www.bluesimages.com. Used with full permission.

To promote the release of Charley Patton's second release, "Screamin' and Hollerin' the Blues," Paramount Records devised a contest wherein readers of the *Chicago Defender* were invited to guess the identity of the artist, named in advertisements like this one as "The Masked Marvel."

The former Paramount Records pressing plant in Grafton, Wisconsin, likely taken in the mid-1930s. *From the collection of Edward Rappold, courtesy of Angela Mack Reilly and Alex van der Tuuk.*

Postcard view of the Wisconsin Chair Company factory from the Milwaukee River. *Courtesy of Angela Mack Reilly and Alex van der Tuuk.*

The collector Harry Smith, compiler of *The Anthology of American Folk Music*, "transforming milk into milk" in New York City in 1985. *Photo by Allen Ginsberg, courtesy of the Allen Ginsberg Trust.*

Big Joe Clauberg, behind the counter at the Jazz Record Mart in New York City, circa 1945. *Photo by Jack Whistance, courtesy of Bruce Whistance.*

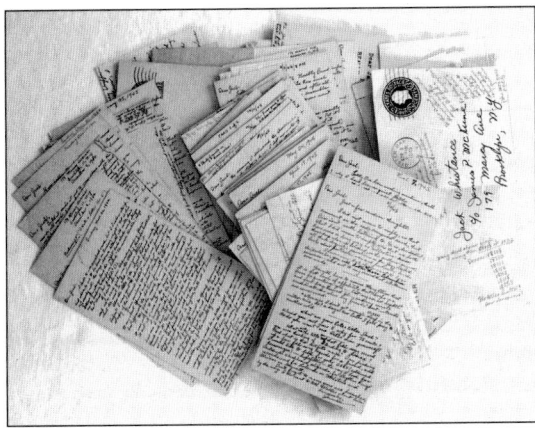

An assortment of letters from the collector James McKune to the collector Jack Whistance in the mid-1940s. *Courtesy of Bruce Whistance.*

A rough draft of one of Don Wahle's "Records Wanted" advertisements, possibly for publication in *Disc Collector* magazine, composed circa 1960. *Courtesy of Nathan Salsburg.*

The collector Jonathan Ward of Excavated Shellac in 2011. *Photo by Chris Casilli, courtesy of Jonathan Ward.*

The collectors Chris King and Joe Bussard in Bussard's basement in Frederick, Maryland. *Photo by Amanda Petrusich.*

Long Cleve Reed and Little Harvey Hull, the Down Home Boys, "Original Stack O'Lee Blues," Black Patti, 1927. *From the collection of Joe Bussard.*

11 1/2″ etched Algerian Pathé disc, circa 1907. *From the collection of Jonathan Ward.*

An advertisement for the Red Fox Chasers new release on Gennett Electrobeam Records, specially commissioned by the banjoist Paul Miles after the group's April 1928 recording session (when they recorded "The Arkansaw Traveler," pictured). This piece was likely printed and displayed in a furniture shop window. *From the collection of Chris King.*

An advertisement for the Vocalion Records catalog, printed in April 1930 and sent to record wholesalers and furniture stores. *From the collection of Chris King.*

An image of a man amid 78s, likely part of a set included with a stereoscopic viewer purchased from Sears, Roebuck & Co., which also operated a handful of record labels (like Silvertone, Supertone, Superior, Champion, and Challenge). *From the collection of Chris King.*

A 1981 advertisement for a monthly 78 swap meet in El Cerrito, California.

Nine

Now There's a Man
on His Way Down

○

*James McKune, the Jazz Record Center, Big Joe Clauberg,
Jack Whistance, the Blues Mafia, "List of American Folk Songs on
Commercial Records," a Suitcase of Pornography*

○

There's a pervasive, romantic notion of the Outsider as Omniscient Loner: preoccupied, brooding, mumbly. He is human—for example, he might read a paperback book that he tugs from the back pocket of his jeans, or gaze intently into a woman's eyes for a beat too long—but he doesn't celebrate holidays or use the toilet. He is usually leaning against a wall. This is one way of thinking about it.

Then there are the men—outsiders, also—who routinely congregated at the Jazz Record Center, a long-defunct music shop that once existed on the north side of West Forty-Seventh Street in midtown Manhattan, a touristy stretch now better known for its approximations of pizza and dubious (if well-lit) electronics shops. In the 1940s, the Jazz Record Center became the default clubhouse for a cabal of distinctive gentlemen: exiles, recluses, characters so outsize in their eccentricities that they feel invented, except better. Here there was not a sense—as with the archetypal Outsider—that a choice had been made. Here, the earliest collectors of 78 rpm records found each other.

The Jazz Record Center was operated by Big Joe Clauberg, a chunk of a man with a deeply creased face (his skin appears to fold back on itself, like the underside of a poorly reupholstered chair) and black eyes that express a deep aversion to certain kinds of nonsense. He came to New York from the southwest, had worked as a circus strongman, and stumbled into the used-record business after being offered a few truckloads of cheap records from a wholesale jukebox operator.

"He was a giant," Pete Whelan told me. "He was very overweight. And he was a full-blooded Indian, I think, from Arizona. And very nice. He would just listen to everybody, hardly saying anything. And he was very generous in his prices. Records that were really worth ten dollars or fifteen dollars then and that would be worth hundreds or maybe thousands now, he would sell for one dollar," Whelan said.

Clauberg settled at the Forty-Seventh Street location in 1941, bolstering his jukebox supply by selling new stock from small coastal jazz labels. (He couldn't afford to buy records from the majors, who then refused credit to independent shops.) The store was originally called Joe's Juke Box, then the Jazz Record Corner, then the Jazz Record Center. Its inventory was jazz heavy but eclectic, including "Everything from Bunk to Monk," as a 1949 ad in the *Record Changer*, an early jazz-collecting magazine, read. (The "Bunk" in question was almost certainly Bunk Johnson, the beloved New Orleans jazzman who lost both his trumpet and his two front teeth in a bar fight in Louisiana in 1931, but it's tempting to consider its more colloquial use—one collector's bunk being another's prize, after all.)

Collectors flocked to Big Joe's—or Indian Joe's, as it was occasionally called—with a savage servility. Although he was part deaf (and emotionally ambivalent to the bulk of his stock), Clauberg, working in conjunction with his onetime partner, the collector and dealer Bob Weinstock, helped coalesce a community that was only beginning to establish itself as such. "Collectors are invited to come up—play records—and chew the fat," another ad read. They also received 20 percent off current releases, itself no small draw.

It's hard to say when, exactly, record collecting got its feet as a hobby—probably the day the first Edison cylinder was packaged and sold to a person in ill-fitting trousers. 78 collecting certainly blossomed in the 1940s, in part because radio had begun to supplant home audio as the preferred method of song delivery (meaning secondhand stores were suddenly flooded with abandoned 78s, sold in bulk and for cheap), and in part because the war had required the clearing of warehouses for storage (meaning discounted back stock was suddenly omnipresent).

Collecting itself is an ancient practice, and not an exclusively human one. Critters—squirrels, crows, rats—often hunt down and hoard shiny objects for no immediately discernible evolutionary reason. In their introduction to the anthology *The Cultures of Collecting*, John Elsner and Roger Cardinal place collecting in a biblical context, declaring Noah the first collector: charged with corralling, classifying, and sustaining entire species of life, Noah was comprehensive by default. "Noah, perhaps alone of all collectors, achieved the complete set, or at least the Bible would have us believe," they wrote. The ramifications of acquiring a perfect series of Grimace drinking glasses or every last Betty Boop key chain manufactured in 1934 are considerably less urgent, perhaps, than Noah's purported mission, but the scholars still see Noah as the embodiment of the entire enterprise: "In the myth of Noah as ur-collector resonate all the themes of collecting itself: desire and nostalgia, saving and loss, the urge to erect a permanent and complete system against the destructiveness of time . . . [Modern collectors exist] at the margin of the human adventure, that pivotal point where man finds himself rivaling God and teeters between mastery and madness."

The crowd at Big Joe's, at least, confirmed that bit about madness: Clauberg had courted (and indulged) a perfect outcast harem. Many of the shop's most beloved denizens weren't even patrons, or at least not in the traditional sense. A Greek dishwasher and janitor named Popeye helped keep the place clean, rubbing oil into the floorboards as necessary. According to the collector (and former employee) Henry Rinard, who chronicled his experience working with Big Joe for 78 *Quarterly*, Popeye was a short, well-muscled man with no teeth, hair, or eyebrows, prone to mumbling to himself for hours "in gibberish not even another Greek could understand." Clauberg let Popeye crash on the floor at night, and in exchange, Popeye performed additional odd jobs, like bringing Clauberg food from the joint where he washed dishes, cutting his hair, and helping him yank a rotten tooth from his gums using a pair of pliers (that's what friends are for). Another regular, Abbie the Agent, wore "thick-lensed eyeglasses, smoked continuously, and was seldom sober." An outcast from a wealthy Connecticut family, Abbie fetched cigarettes and wine for Clauberg, and periodically became so inebriated himself that he passed out on the Popeye-oiled floor. (His other nickname—and I think it's the better of the two—was Horizontal Abe.) Rinard also wrote about one of Clauberg's old hobo friends, a guy known mostly as the Sea Captain, who wore a wool hat, raincoat, and heavy, too-big, laceless boots, even in June. The Captain was something of an enigma, even to Rinard: "He was either Swedish or Norwegian; he understood English, but never spoke," he wrote.

The clientele was no less unique. "It was very interesting," Whelan recalled. "It was a stop on the way. There would be these characters that would be there. Specialists. One guy who just collected European jazz, named Hal Flaxer. He's probably still around. I think he went through three or four wives and they all looked identical. I couldn't tell the difference. They looked like twins of each other." In her book *In Search of the Blues*, the scholar Marybeth Hamilton includes what might be the single greatest description of early record collectors flourishing in their natural habitat: "Saturday afternoons they met at Indian Joe's, where they thumbed through the bins in between swigs from the bottles of muscatel that Pete Kaufman brought along from his store, suspending their searches briefly at three, when a man called Bob turned up with a suitcase of pornographic books."

My favorite published photo of the shop first appeared in *Jazzways* and was later reprinted in *78 Quarterly*; it's not even of the interior, it's of the rickety wooden stairs leading to the door. The face of each step is painted with an incitement (RECORDS, HOT JAZZ RECORDS, RECORDS 4 SALE, STEP UP SAVE A BUCK, POPULAR BANDS, HOT JAZZ RECORDS), and I can only imagine the half-furious, half-wheezy sounds eager collectors made clomping up them, balls of cash wadded up in their pockets. Regardless of what the inside of the shop actually looked like, I like to imagine it crammed with weirdos bickering in high-pitched voices, nostrils expanding, slowly swarming Bob and his suitcase. I like to imagine myself there, with a record or two tucked under my arm.

●

James McKune showed up at Big Joe's nearly every Saturday night at six and stayed until the store closed at nine, wandering off, on occasion, to eat supper at the Automat around the corner on Sixth Avenue. McKune was likely born somewhere on the East Coast in or near 1910, although no one knows precisely when or where (depending on whom you ask, he was from Baltimore, or North Carolina, or upstate New York). That McKune has no clear origin story—and that his end was equally inscrutable—only amplifies the mythic place he occupies in collecting lore. Maybe more than any other collector, James McKune was defined by his records.

McKune wasn't the first 78 collector, but he was one of the earliest to single out rural blues records as worthy of preservation and is arguably the field's most archetypal figure. At the very least, he established the physical standard. He was flagpole skinny and otherwise nondescript (medium height, tapering hair), prone to wearing the same outfit nearly every day (a white shirt with rolled sleeves, black pants, white socks, black shoes). He had a tough time holding a steady job, and during his time in New York, he worked briefly as a subeditor for the *New York Times*, a desk clerk at the YMCA, a checker at a South Brooklyn beer distributor, and a mail sorter in a Brooklyn post office.

He seemed generally irritated by the necessity of employment, and in a June 1944 letter to the collector Jack Whistance, wrote: "During the day (when it doesn't rain) I continue my quest for a suitable job in [an] essential industry. In N.Y.C., be it said—not in Newark. I am a particular guy, perhaps alas. The jobs I can have I don't want. And those I want I can't get." (Ironically, US unemployment was at an all-time low in 1944, at just 1.2 percent—about as close to "full employment" as economists believe is possible.) According to all reports, he drank like a pro. In his letters to other collectors, he was exacting but not unlikable; his missives are impeccably punctuated and endlessly readable, packed with peculiar asides and unexpected jokes. Although he was constitutionally private—a loner in the most nonromantic sense possible—and wrote almost exclusively about which records he wanted or had recently acquired, McKune did seem to savor his correspondence. In a 1951 letter to Henry Rinard, he even mentioned his glee about receiving an Easter card from a pal for Christmas. "A delightful variation, which I would have copied but for the lateness of this melancholy December," he wrote in neat, minuscule script. (He was also prone to hastily changing tone by writing NEW SUBJECT midletter, an underused literary device I aspire to someday employ.)

"Not that it means anything particularly, but he was gay, and I didn't know that at the time," Whelan explained to me one night. He and McKune met at Big Joe's. "I was at the time interested in getting blues on this particular label called Gennett. There was this guy Sam Collins on Electrobeam Gennett that I liked very much—he was an impassioned tenor. So I met this guy McKune," he continued. "I was like twenty-three or twenty-four and he was fifty. He had been collecting since probably the late thirties. Blues. One of the very few. He looked like a scarecrow. He would gesticulate when he talked, very excitedly. You'd find these elbows coming at you, and you kept backing up. I think in the late 1930s he was a reporter for the *Long Island Star*, and then became, I think, city editor. And then he gave it up and worked for the post office. And then he became an alcoholic."

Unsurprisingly, McKune was also a bit of a crank. He was wildly discerning, even by collector standards, and owned just three hundred records, all tucked into cardboard boxes and stored underneath his single bed at the YMCA on Marcy Street in Williamsburg, Brooklyn. He often referred to his listening sessions as "séances" and was required to play records at a low volume so as not to enrage unsympathetic neighbors (thin walls). He fretted endlessly about his own taste. McKune's desires were expansive, and he didn't just want to collect the music he loved the most, he wanted to collect the best possible permutations of sound and for those decrees to be definitive. In an October 1944 letter to Whistance, he wrote of his ongoing struggle for objective judgment, that impossible critical ideal:

"Which one of a dozen such is THE standout depends it seems to me, upon the individual likings in jazz of the rater. Hayes's Stompers soothe me wonderfully, for instance. Yet I ought to hesitate to declare that this band, or even the best of its records, is any better than the other great hot bands or their respective best recordings. Hayes's band is nearer to my taste than Armstrong is, or Moten, or Henderson (on 9 of 10 of H's records, that is) or Oliver or Goldbetter or good Goodman . . . or Ellington. H's DS records are similarly close to my taste. So are Austin's Serenaders and some of J. R. Morton (that Trio record I own, for instance) and McKinney's C.P.s and the Washboard Rhythm Kings. The Washboard Rhythm Kings rock me always, without exception. Yet the thrill I get out of hearing them shout the world down is different again from the thrill I get out of hearing the breathless melancholy that Hayes's jug blowers and Washington's Six Aces manage to put across. That is all I can say. That is all I ought dare to say—assuming that I have respect for accuracy and truth."

It's the exact kind of record review I've always wanted—but never dared—to file.

McKune supposedly never gave up more than ten bucks for a 78 (and often offered less than three dollars), and was deeply offended—outraged, even—by collectors willing to pay out large sums of money, a practice he found garish, irresponsible, and in basic opposition to what he understood as the moral foundation of the trade. He didn't like the notion that records could generate profit for their handlers: in the fall of 1963, in another letter to Rinard, he referenced his skepticism of a fellow collector, writing, "Somehow, I distrust him. He bought some records from the Negroes in Charleston, S.C. He spent $19 or $20 and sold the records for more than $500." For McKune, collecting was a sacred pursuit—a way of salvaging and anointing songs and artists that had been unjustly marginalized. It was about training yourself to act as a gatekeeper, a savior; in that sense, it was also very much about being better (knowing better, listening better) than everyone else. Even in the 1940s and '50s, 78 collectors were positioning themselves as opponents of mass culture, and McKune cultivated a fantastic disdain for pop stars as well as the so-called protest singers of the era. He thought, for example, that Woody Guthrie was bullshit, although by 1950 he'd come back around on folk music as a genre, a shift he attributed to getting older. (The career of Glenn Miller, though, was a constant source of jokes.)

I'm not sure what McKune was looking for, exactly. Maybe the same thing we all look for in music: some flawlessly articulated truth. But I know for sure when he found it.

In the 1940s, 78 collecting meant jazz collecting, and specifically Dixieland or hot jazz, which developed in New Orleans around the turn of the twentieth century and was defined by its warm, deeply playful polyphony (typically, the front line—a trumpet, trombone, or clarinet—took the melody, while the rhythm section—banjo, guitar, drums, upright bass, piano, and maybe a tuba—supported or improvised around it). Because of its origins, collecting rare Dixieland records in 1942 was not entirely unlike collecting Robert Johnson records in 1968, or, incidentally, now: deifying indigent, local music was a political act, a passive protest against its sudden co-optation by popular white artists. As Hamilton wrote, "it meant training the spotlight on a distinctly black, definitely proletarian art form in an era when, as they saw it, jazz had been tamed, sweetened, and commodified, with white performers like Benny Goodman and Paul Whiteman praised as its consummate practitioners." But for whatever reason, blues records weren't of any particular interest to early collectors. "The original 78 collectors despised country blues. They just liked jazz, and there were few exceptions," Whelan explained. "It was a sharp divide. They thought it was less artistic. They were intellectuals."

According to Hamilton, in January 1944 McKune took a routine trip to Big Joe's and began pawing through a crate labeled "Miscellany," where he found a record with "a sleeve so tattered he almost flicked past it." It was a battered, nearly unplayable copy of Paramount 13110, Charley Patton's "Some These Days I'll Be Gone." Patton had recorded the track in Grafton fifteen years earlier, and he'd been dead for less than ten when McKune first picked it up. Patton was almost entirely unknown to modern listeners; certainly McKune had never heard him before. He tossed a buck at a snoozing Clauberg and carted the record back to Brooklyn. As Hamilton wrote, "even before he replaced the tonearm and turned up the volume and his neighbor began to pound on the walls, he realized that he had found it, the voice he'd been searching for all along."

"Some These Days I'll Be Gone" is one of Charley Patton's more staid tracks, in both rhythm and narrative. According to Gayle Dean Wardlow and Stephen Calt's *King of the Delta Blues: The Life and Music of Charley Patton*, "Some These Days I'll Be Gone" was "likely conceived for white presentation: it used diatonic intervals and featured the keynote as its lowest vocal tone, a technique Patton usually avoided in singing blues and gospel material." Wardlow and Calt suspect the tune was conceived for "white square dances and sociables," where Patton was likely accompanied by a fiddler who'd been tasked with playing lead over his strums. Lyrically, it's a sweet imploration: Don't take me for granted, Patton warns. "Some these days, I'm going to be leaving / Some these days, I'll be going away," he slurs, strumming a faint, bouncing guitar line. For once, he sounds more bemused than angry. You'll see, he seems to grin. Just wait.

McKune wasn't entirely unfamiliar with blues music before he brought "Some These Days I'll Be Gone" home. As Hamilton tells it, McKune had worked at a record store in a black neighborhood the summer after he graduated from high school, where he sold copy after copy of popular 78s by Ma Rainey and Bessie Smith and developed a "gut-level aversion" to race records, which he considered cheap and tawdry. For years, he eschewed any record with "blues" in the title, although he did come around eventually. (In May 1944, in another letter to Whistance, he wrote: "Please play 'Downhearted Blues,' first by Bessie Smith, then by Eva Taylor, then by Alberta Hunter. Don't let the difference in recording fidelity fool you, though; Bessie Smith has much more melancholy in her voice than any of her contemporaries. They had melancholy, too, but in lesser degree.") According to Hamilton, in 1942 McKune was contacted by the owner of the Central General Store on Long Island and offered two unopened boxes of mint-condition Paramount blues 78s, which the proprietor had recently discovered buried in the back of his store and was hoping to unload for a buck apiece. McKune, the legend goes, passed without pause.

It was Charley Patton who changed everything for McKune. I can run an assortment of scenarios—recounting all the fireworks-type stuff I imagine happened when he first dropped a needle to "Some These Days I'll Be Gone"—but those particular moments of catharsis are too weird and too personal to translate. What's important is that McKune's discovery of Patton set off an avalanche of cultural events, a revolution that's still in progress: blues records became coveted by collectors, who then fought to preserve and disseminate them. In the liner notes to *The Return of the Stuff That Dreams Are Made Of*, a collection of 78 rarities released by Yazoo in 2012, Richard Nevins called McKune " 'the man' who set it all in motion, who led blues collectors away from the errors of their wayward tastes . . . a fantastic, brilliant young man . . . [his] perspectives had profound influence and resound even today." In the same notes, Dick Spottswood—in conversation with Nevins and Whelan—spoke about how McKune raised the stakes for everyone, about how things changed: "All I'm saying is that the records themselves as collectible artifacts were not buy or die [before]. They were desirable records but they weren't life or death. You know, the way they have since turned into." After McKune, collectors became invested in rural blues. They sought those records with fury, the music was preserved and reissued, and the entire trajectory of popular music shifted to reflect the genre's influence.

While it seems egregious to suggest that someone wouldn't have eventually taken a chance on a Patton record (or, say, one by Son House) and absurd to discount the faith of the performers themselves (who believed fiercely in their own work), McKune was the first collector to realize how powerful these artists could be outside of their original contexts, inadvertently spurring the creation of what would later be called the Blues Mafia—a coterie of frantic, competitive blues collectors (McKune, Whelan, Spottswood, Wardlow, Nevins, Bernie Klatzko, Pete Kaufman, Nick Perls, Stephen Calt, Max Vreede, and others) who, as Hamilton explained, "set up record labels, issued LP anthologies, and wrote liner notes, articles, and books of blues history that framed the blues as we now know it, a music of pain and alienation, a cry of African-American despair."

Hamilton boldly charged the Blues Mafia with creating that specific narrative of the blues, which she understood as a collectively conjured fantasy that cast underappreciated outcasts as heroes—a portrayal that, unsurprisingly, appealed to 78 collectors. (She also accused them of feeding on a "faintly colonialist romance with black suffering.") I believe prewar acoustic blues music was coveted by these men for a variety of reasons—its rareness, its artistic worth—but the notion that collectors might empathize with its creators, or have some vested, self-aggrandizing interest in reconfiguring them as stars, is compelling. Hamilton even went so far as to compare McKune's arc to Robert Johnson's, noting that both men were "homeless, friendless" wanderers.

Although I think the average 78 collector lives the sort of life—quiet, studious, steady—a country blues singer circa 1929 would find unrecognizable, it's still easy to linger on the parallel. The performers most revered by early collectors did tend to be unpopular, alienated interlopers with a penchant for cheap liquor; men like McKune seized upon outsider records, not the high-selling sides peddled by more palatable artists like Lonnie Johnson and purchased with abandon by early black blues fans. It is undeniably strange that an idiosyncratic, outcast performer like Skip James would ever come to represent prewar blues, because no one was buying Skip James records in 1931; it is the equivalent of plucking some obscure, small-label psych-folk act from the late 1960s and declaring it the epitome of rock 'n' roll. There is a severe and startling time-place disconnect. What concerned me, though, was Hamilton's veiled assertion that collectors projected their own sorrow onto these records: few things are more obvious to me than the devastation of early country blues songs. Collectors may have been responding to that anguish, but they did not invent it.

Since 1944, collectors have managed to amass a complete discography of Patton, and there aren't any known recorded sides that haven't been resurrected, although that doesn't necessarily mean they don't exist. The Blues Mafia eventually turned its collective attention to other marginalized performers. By the mid-1940s, collectors had discovered a nineteen-page Library of Congress monograph, first published in *Report of the Committee of the Conference on Inter-American Relations in the Field of Music* and called "List of American Folk Songs on Commercial Records." The document eventually became a kind of buyers' guide for 78 fanatics and a default seed for the folk and blues canon as we understand it today.

The annotated list was created by the musicologist Alan Lomax in September 1940, with help from his sister Bess and the musician Pete Seeger, who was then just nineteen years old and working as Lomax's assistant for fifteen dollars a week. In the document's introduction, Lomax explains how he listened to "three thousand odd commercial records of white and negro songs and tunes from the South" and compiled a list of 350 representative titles "in order that the interested musician or student of American society may explore this unknown body of Americana with readiness. The choices have been personal and have been made for all sorts of reasons." The list covered a dozen labels (Gennett was noticeably absent) and could be acquired by writing to the Library of Congress and requesting a copy. It's a strange and captivating read, in part because Lomax was not yet besmirched by all the blues mythologizing that would come later; in 1940, this was uncharted terrain. His notes are riddled with abbreviations (a key, titled "Code used in condensation," is included: NB for Negro Ballad, WPS for White Prison Song, Pa for Paramount Records, f for fine, vf for very fine, imp for important, r for remarkable, et cetera), and Lomax especially enjoyed calling things "authentic" or "typical," terms which now feel frustratingly vague. Still, he knew, upon hearing Robert Johnson's "Hell Hound on My Trail" ("unusual m[elody], traces of voodoo, beautiful g[uitar]") or Blind Boy Fuller's "Careless Love" ("brilliant folk g[uitar], v[ery] f[ine] ver[sion], one of the earliest blues") that American folk music was "in a healthier condition" than the "folklore specialists [who] have been mourning its decline" believed.

Regardless of what drew James McKune to these types of songs or what sustained his interest, I still believe he's an underheralded figure in the history of American popular music. This may seem like a naïve if not silly contention; it's hard, after all, to visualize a bronzed McKune guarding the entrance to the Rock and Roll Hall of Fame, curved at the midsection, clutching a 78 and a bottle of something brown, squinting nervously at passersby. But while collecting is inherently passive—McKune didn't make anything; these songs weren't his; he didn't do anything except listen well, and besides, early fans (if not collectors) were buying and playing at least some of these blues records in the 1930s—I also can't conceive of the American pop canon without the music he so purposefully sought and lionized. A guy from no place, saving music from the same.

●

James McKune's naked, strangled body was found, bound and gagged, in a grimy welfare hotel—the Broadway Central—on the Lower East

Side of Manhattan in September 1971. Detectives concluded that he had likely been murdered by a man he had solicited for sex; Whelan later called the perpetrator a "homosexual serial killer" with, he thought, five or six other homicides on his record. By then McKune had moved out of the YMCA and was living primarily on the streets of the Bowery, among prostitutes and thieves. For those on the lookout for such parallels, McKune's death did ultimately mirror Robert Johnson's—who, as Hamilton pointed out, also died under "violent, mysterious, and sexually charged" circumstances. (The itinerant Johnson supposedly keeled over after taking a slug of poisoned whiskey, provided by a man whose wife he'd been eyeing or maybe worse.) Nobody knows for sure what happened to McKune's record collection, although rumors still flutter up from time to time. It was likely sold, or stolen, or maybe given away bit by bit.

By the late 1960s, things hadn't been looking particularly rosy for McKune. Work was scarce and drinks were plentiful, that ancient, odious pairing. "I remember [the collector] Bernie [Klatzko], who was an accountant and was doing this accounting for this business guy who was an old-time New York type, with the old-time New York accent, and he said to Bernie, 'Now there's a man on his way down,' " Whelan recalled.

The bulk of what I know about McKune's life—and it's not a whole lot—I learned from his letters to the jazz and blues collector Jack Whistance, who died in 2007. In 2011, Pete Whelan put me in touch with Whistance's daughter-in-law, Gail; she was still sorting through his papers the morning I called. She told me Whistance and McKune likely met at Big Joe's. "He talked about this McKune a lot," she said. "He had this cache of postcards and letters from him, and he always thought they were important enough to save," she continued. "[McKune] would often send postcards because they were cheap. He had tiny, tiny writing that would go upside down at the bottom and over different angles, even on the front a little bit if he ran out of room."

Although McKune's relationship with Whistance was clearly

affectionate—McKune was cowed, at times, by Whistance's considerable knowledge of hot jazz, and his valedictions grew more colloquial
as the years passed, from "Sincerely, James P. McKune" to "Yours
Ever, Jim," to, my favorite, "Hasta la Vista"—it's clear he didn't have
the same yearning for face-to-face communication. He often left records he wanted Whistance to hear with one of Whistance's neighbors, avoiding corporeal interaction altogether. In December 1944,
McKune wrote: "Couldn't make it out to your place with the records
all week. Knew that last Sunday aft, and so, taking a long chance, I
hied me then to Jamaica. But you and MaryEllen were out, or sleeping
and so I came away again. I purposely rang the bell only once so that, if
you were sleeping, you wouldn't be roused needlessly. On top of that
Saturday night jamboree, thought I, sleep might be the only Sunday
desideratum. Well, I'll try again on Friday of the coming week. All I
want to do is leave the records (by the N.O. Five and the N.O. Blue
Nine) for you to assay. So if either of you is home (or if a trustworthy
neighbor is home), my trip will not be in vain. This is not a visit I
contemplate, mind you . . . but only a record-bringing." Then, a few
months later, in February: "You will have to assure MaryEllen that it
is not lack of affability that keeps me from frequenting you . . . but my
so-so health (whenever I don't get enough sleep in the winter-time,
lo! a day or two later I fall prey to another cold). And your long-
houred job . . . and my innate considerations where my friends' best
interests are concerned."

Gail told me MaryEllen—Whistance's wife, then ninety-two—
didn't recall ever meeting McKune. "She does remember visiting the
record shops—[she was] one of the very few women who ever set foot
in those places. She was a good sport about it," she said.

A few days later, Gail e-mailed me a scan of a grainy black-and-white
photo of Big Joe standing at the counter of the Jazz Record Center,
giving side eye to the camera. It's a look that seems to say, "Settle
down." He's squeezing a lit cigar between two thick fingers and wearing a striped button-down shirt. His black hair is slicked back; it looks

Ten

I Saw America Changed Through Music

○

Harry Smith, The Anthology of American Folk Music, *Tinctures, the Celestial Monochord, "Anything Shaped Like a Hamburger," Allen Ginsberg, the New York Public Library, 50 MILES ELBOW ROOM*

○

In 1952, eight years after James McKune ferried "Some These Days I'll Be Gone" back to the Brooklyn YMCA, a twenty-nine-year-old collector named Harry Everett Smith squirreled himself away in a two-room office at 111 West Forty-Seventh Street, chewing on peyote buttons and compiling a six-LP compendium for Folkways Records. *The Anthology of American Folk Music*, which was released by Folkways in 1952 and reissued on CD by the Smithsonian in 1997, was culled exclusively from Smith's 78 collection and contains only songs issued between 1927 and 1932, that fruitful five-year span between the advent of electrical recording and the apex of the Great Depression. Despite its self-imposed parameters, Smith's anthology is generous in its definition of folk music: child ballads, spirituals, Alabamans playing Hawaiian steel guitar, fiddlers, Charley Patton as the Masked Marvel, Appalachian coal miners, Cajun accordionists, the Carter Family, jug stompers, string bands, church congregations, and Uncle Dave Macon—mouth open, banjo wedged behind his knee, hollering "Kill yourself!"—all appear. Taken as a whole (and that's the entire point), the *Anthology* is a wild and instructive portrait of a young country working itself out via song.

It's also deeply confounding. There are times when I have clung to it as a kind of last hope, believing that it's an object that unlocks other objects; there are other times when I have found it solipsistic and nonsensical and inherently ill conceived. Whatever the *Anthology* offers, it's not revealed quickly.

Like most serious collectors, Harry Smith got going early. The arc of his life is both predictable—as if, like a river, it could have only ever led to one place—and meandering. He was born on May 29, 1923, the son of a boat captain and a schoolteacher, theosophists who encouraged his burgeoning interest in ethnography. He spent a good chunk of his high school years studying the tribal ceremonies of the Lummi Indians in his hometown of Bellingham, Washington, and started amassing 78s around the same time. The first one he bought was by Tommy McClennan, a rough-voiced blues singer who recorded in Chicago in the early 1940s. ("It sounded strange and I looked for others," Smith later said of it.)

In his early twenties, Smith was just undersized enough to be able to crawl inside the fuselage of an airplane, and after six months working for Boeing as an engine degreaser, he decamped to San Francisco, then Berkeley, and finally New York City, where, in desperate need of cash for things like food and shelter, he tried to pitch his record collection wholesale to Folkways Records. Instead, cofounder Moe Asch persuaded him to produce a multidisc compilation for the label. Asch's biographer, Peter Goldsmith, suggests that Smith's "appearance and manner" might have reminded Asch of his pal and partner Woody Guthrie, another charmingly arrogant polymath who recorded for Folkways in the 1940s. (Incidentally, Guthrie—who spent a good percentage of 1952 in a state psychiatric ward—adored the *Anthology*, and in a letter to Asch admitted to playing it "several hundreds of times.") In a 1972

Sing Out! interview with Ethel Raim and Bob Norman, Asch confirmed his admiration for Smith's purview, saying "[Smith] understood the content of the records. He knew their relationship to folk music, their relationship to English literature, and their relationship to the world." Smith was paid $200 for his work on the *Anthology* and promised a twenty-cent royalty for each copy sold.

Although he's now equally beloved for his experimental films, paintings, and animations, Smith is about as close as the practice of 78 collecting has ever come to producing a known cult figure. (These days Robert Crumb also qualifies, but his collecting is far more incidental to his legacy.) Smith, who died in 1991 in room 328 of the Chelsea Hotel in New York, a building already infamous for its output of body bags, was the kind of guy who designed his own tarot cards. He was a dedicated mystic, a consecrated bishop in the Ecclesia Gnostica Catholica (a fraternal organization based on Aleister Crowley's *The Book of the Law*), and, supposedly, an initiated Lummi shaman. He palled around with folks like Dizzy Gillespie, Charlie Parker, Allen Ginsberg, and Gregory Corso, and was eventually appointed "Shaman in Residence" at the Naropa Institute in Boulder, Colorado, a Buddhist-inspired university founded by an exiled Tibetan *tulku*. Along with records and rare books, which he arranged on his shelves by height, Smith collected Seminole textiles, hand-decorated Ukrainian Easter eggs, and anything shaped like a hamburger. He lived with a goldfish in a series of tiny apartments crammed with ephemera (quilts, weavings, clay models, mounted string figures, women's dresses). In 1984 he donated "the largest known paper airplane collection in the world"—sourced exclusively from the streets of New York City—to the National Air and Space Museum in Washington, DC. Smith was also an obsessive chronicler of found sound, be it the peyote songs of the Kiowa Indians or the wheezing vagrants of the Lower East Side; one Fourth of July he recorded every single noise he encountered.

In almost all the photos I've seen of Harry Smith, he's wearing plastic-framed, thick-lensed eyeglasses and sporting a robust, scraggly beard. His skin looks papery but his eyes are sharp, narrowed, and alive under two drooping lids. In my favorite shot, taken by Ginsberg in 1985, he's pouring whole milk from a cardboard carton into a glass jar ("transforming milk into milk," Ginsberg noted). His face is approximately 80 percent glasses. Atop his head, little tufts of white hair wisp to the left, the consistency of fresh spiderweb. He appears to be about ten thousand years old.

Cantankerous and exacting in the manner of most collectors, Smith often bickered with his peers about money or objects. He would demand to borrow a book or record and then refuse to give it back. As his archivist and friend Rani Singh told me, he was constantly informing people that their belongings were better off in his collection. ("'It should be in my collection, it shouldn't be in your collection,'" she recalled him saying.) His compulsions were driven by a fierce internal logic; Smith was painstaking in his pursuit of proper serialization, even if it meant pilfering other people's most beloved shit. Things, he believed, belonged next to other things—like sentences in a story, books along a shelf, songs on an LP. "He was looking for undercurrents. He was looking for ideas that were disappearing, nuances that were disappearing, trying to make connections not just among 78s from Georgia or North Carolina versus upper New York State or Canada, but connections between the string figures that he was interested in from all cultures across the world," Singh said. "He was comparing string figures to tarot cards to 78 records to creation myths to all these other things and finding the things that link all of us as humans together."

It's still hard to quantify the cultural impact of the *Anthology*. In the liner notes to its Smithsonian reissue, John Fahey wrote: "Had he never done anything with his life but this *Anthology*, Harry Smith would still have borne the mark of genius across his forehead. I'd match the *Anthology* up against any other single compendium of important information ever assembled. Dead Sea Scrolls? Nah. I'll take the *Anthology*. Make no mistake: there was no 'folk' canon before Smith's work. That he had compiled such a definitive document only became apparent much later, of course. We record-collecting types, sifting through many more records than he did, eventually reached the same conclusions: these were the true goods."

There's also no satisfying term for what Smith did. Both "compiler" and "curator" feel too removed, too impersonal. Smith didn't just corral a bunch of parts, he dreamed a whole. While I'll admit to a tendency toward certain flights of sentimentality—and while I don't want to discount either Smith's intentionality or his authorship—I also don't think it's so preposterous to believe that these records were delivered to Smith for this precise purpose and that he ordered them as a poet orders words on a page, channeling, building meaning from nothing, becoming a physical conduit for a spiritual truth. That Smith understood how to place these records in useful dialogue is a function of his expertise and experience, but there is also a sense, here, of a story that needed telling. That's not an unfamiliar feeling for most 78 collectors.

In *The Old, Weird America*, Greil Marcus calls the *Anthology* "an occult document disguised as an academic treatise on stylistic shifts within an archaic musicology." I think that costume is essential to its premise; although it might seem counterintuitive, the illusion of authority allows the *Anthology* both its insularity and its limitations. Anyone who attempts to use it as an objective textbook—as the definitive, omnipotent document implied by its title—will be devastated by its shortcomings. It's a wonky portrait of America at nearly all stages in its development. It contains no field recordings sourced from the Library of Congress or anywhere else and excludes entire communities of citizens, including Native Americans, immigrants, and (with a few exceptions) people who lived in the northern half of the United States. Per Smith's vision, every track on the *Anthology* was professionally rendered and released, an oddly normative and antiacademic approach to something as intrinsically noncommercial as folk music. Smith clearly wanted to exalt the records people actually hunted down, bought, and cherished, just as he did.

While the *Anthology* isn't comprehensive, it's still a self-wrought universe with its own logic and revelations. It encourages—maybe even requires—its listeners to devise their own (personal, imperfect) explanations for how and why people sing. It's all in here, Smith is saying, and if you can accept the *Anthology* on faith, as the sacred text he clearly envisioned, its world might open up to you, become your own.

Smith divided his eighty-four tracks into three categories, a kind of holy triumvirate: Social Music, Ballads, and Songs. All six records (two for each section) were collected under a cover illustration of a celestial monochord, an ancient, one-stringed instrument that vaguely resembles a mountain dulcimer. Here, the monochord is being tuned by the hand of God, which is stretching down from an illuminated cloud. The picture was drawn by the Belgian engraver Theodor de Bry and first published in Robert Fludd's *The History of the Macrocosm and the Microcosm* sometime between 1617 and 1619. When properly played, the celestial monochord is supposed to unite the base elements of air, water, fire, and earth. The drawing is an allusion, certainly, to Smith and Fludd's shared belief in serialization—in linking everything to everything else.

In the most basic sense, what Smith did with the *Anthology* will be familiar to anyone who has ever crafted or received a fussed-over mix tape from a paramour or a pal. As the rock critic Rob Sheffield wrote in his 2007 memoir, *Love Is a Mix Tape*, "It's a fundamental human need to pass music around." And of the mix tape, specifically: "There is always a reason to make one." The idea, of course, is that music can be arranged in such a way that it communicates something new and vital—something impossible to say in any other way.

"The whole purpose is to have some kind of series of things," Smith himself announced in a 1969 *Sing Out!* interview with John Cohen, and indeed, much of the *Anthology*'s lingering effect has been attributed to Smith's sequencing. Previously, these tracks were islands, isolated platters of shellac that existed independently of anything else: even flipping over a 78 required disruptive action. Shifting the medium from the one-song-per-side 78 to the long-playing vinyl album allowed, finally, for songs to be juxtaposed in deliberate ways. It's possible now, of course, to dump all eighty-four tracks onto one digital playlist and experience the entire *Anthology* uninterrupted, but I still prefer to acknowledge the demarcations between its three sections—to play it as Smith did.

The *Anthology*'s rubric was entirely Smith's own. He deemed extra-musical qualifiers (race, style, chronology) irrelevant, and rarely does the actual content of a song explain or justify its placement. Sometimes tracks by the same artist are lumped together; sometimes they're not. Its blueprint isn't obviously rendered or easily parsed, and the collection's narrative, insomuch as one exists, is deliberately obscured. As such, the *Anthology* can feel like the musical equivalent of shouting *cellar door*, a phrase trumpeted for its ethereal beauty—it's affecting in ways that have nothing to do with literal meaning. It can also be supremely frustrating. Like a good poem, nothing makes sense until everything makes sense.

"To me, what's in plain sight is that the *Anthology* induces you to look for some underlying, organizing principle," Kurt Gegenhuber, the author of my favorite *Anthology*-based website, The Celestial Mono-chord, offered. "To some, it may be natural to seek stories when looking for order, but the *Anthology*'s main effect is to seduce us into all sorts of hard, sense-making work. What I see as important is the way the cuts *refuse* to legibly lead to each other. Discontinuity and the lack of context seem to me crucial to the *Anthology*. Throughout, the MO is for each cut to just materialize out of some dark forest and float before you like a disembodied face, hang there for a few minutes, and then fade to black. And then that memory is dispersed by the next cut, which hypnotizes you all over again. The sequencing gives each cut a context of no context."

That so much of this material is so strange (try to make literal or metaphoric sense of, say, Bascom Lamar Lunsford's "I Wish I Was a Mole in the Ground"), performed wildly and linked together according to some unspoken pedagogy, means the *Anthology* is disorienting long before it's revelatory. I can only imagine what it sounded like sixty years ago. Gegenhuber, for one, believes that Smith inadvertently foresaw— or even created—the way people now listen to long-playing records, devouring them as whole texts and not just indiscriminate strings of songs. "You might say the *Anthology* was the first draft of *Sgt. Pepper's Lonely Hearts Club Band* (or *Highway 61 Revisited*), since 'listening' to albums [now means] falling into very close 'reading,'" he said.

The *Anthology* does contain a few concrete arcs to keep listeners grounded. Over the course of six LPs, for example, Smith slowly builds a not entirely surprising argument about the harshness and futility of work in the face of things like love and home. It culminates, for me, with Mississippi John Hurt's generous, mesmeric performance of "Spike Driver Blues" on the final side of the final LP. Even now, the whole thing (from the Williamson Brothers and Curry's "Gonna Die with a Hammer in My Hand" to the Carolina Tar Heels' "Got the Farm Land Blues" to Uncle Dave Macon's "Buddy Won't You Roll Down the Line") makes me panic that I and every gainfully employed person I know should actually be subscribing to some unsustainable hobo ethos. "Take this hammer and carry it to the captain, tell him I'm gone, tell him I'm gone," Hurt sings, his voice eerily, tellingly placid. It's a declaration of autonomy that also suggests a deep reordering of basic priorities. It's fearless, and I can't think of another musical moment that makes me want to kick my laptop out a window more. When I first heard about a friend who quit her office job via petulant Post-it—"I'm outta here," she scrawled, affixing the note to her computer, a bold if indulgent decree—my first thought was how proud Harry Smith would be.

Elsewhere, there are clear lessons about love and fidelity and re- venge. There is an extraordinary amount of bad behavior. It turns out people have always been doing the same ugly and beautiful things to each other. Nearly any emotion you can imagine feeling—lust, con- tempt, rage, satisfaction, jealousy, love, loneliness, joy, exhaustion, guilt, unbearable sadness—is articulated and slotted onto Smith's continuum.

It's impossible for me to believe that Smith, who fancied himself a bit of an alchemist, didn't engineer this thing specifically for those sorts of reactions. Ultimately, the *Anthology* is about sewing together self-made worlds—establishing a supernarrative of the human condition. I understand how that might sound absurd. An eccentric, possibly hallucinating twenty-nine-year-old pawing through a pile of records and deciding which ones and in what order they should play isn't exactly comparable, say, to Albert Einstein defining relativity. But Smith's role in the creation of the *Anthology* did reposition the collector, rather than the critic or scholar, as an architect of canons, an arbiter, a storyteller. He sussed a narrative from incongruous parts and presented it as an edifying fable. Practically, there is a parallel, certainly, to the songs contained therein, which are often based, at least in part, on other songs—a new work from old work, a tapestry from string.

It's not unusual, then, for the *Anthology* to elicit a dramatic response. "I've met dozens of people who heard the *Anthology* and ran off to join some circus or other," Gegenhuber said. "For [folklorists and musicians like] Mike Seeger, John Cohen, and many others, the response was to learn to play, yourself, its songs and styles, and go looking for Boggs, Ashley, Hurt, et cetera. For still others, the *Anthology* induced the record-collecting response, which seems to be about sense making."

Accordingly, even otherwise-reasonable authors go a little loopy when writing about the *Anthology*'s inexplicable allure. In *When We Were Good*, Robert Cantwell's treatise on the folk revival, he describes it as "strange, even sinister: a closet-like enclosure from which the world is shut out, spangled with occult symbols whose meaning we have not yet learned, fitted to an obscure design or purpose and harboring a vague threat, like the gypsy's tent or the funhouse, that by some unknown force will subject us to an ordeal over which we have no control and which will leave us permanently marked." (Yikes!) Marcus, meanwhile, conjures a place called Smithville, and in describing the first side of *Songs*, writes: "The streets of Smithville have been rolled up, and the town now offers that quintessential American experience, the ultimate, permanent test of the unfinished American, Puritan, or pioneer, loose in a land of pitfalls and surprises: Step right up, Ladies and Gentlemen! Enter the New Sensorium of Old-Time Music, and feel the ground pulled right out from under your feet!"

I understand—deeply—the impulse toward hyperbole, the desire to speak of the *Anthology* as a contained spiritual experience that incites certain epiphanies. It is, after all, a thing you can inhabit if you want to: there are alehouses to drink in and Stetson hats to bicker over and corn to hoe and people to marry and love and betray and maybe murder.

Then there's Smith, a welcome little Virgil, typing his short, all-caps headline-style summaries (they are stylistically reminiscent, at times, of the descriptions included in Lomax's "List of American Folk Songs on Commercial Records") that mostly make me snicker but occasionally make me gulp. Like the synopsis he cobbled together for Rev. F. W. McGee's "Fifty Miles of Elbow Room," a spastic, lyrically unintelligible gospel song that I think is about heaven, or at least some heavenly analog (it appears to be based on the New Jerusalem as seen by John in Revelation 21:9): "WHEN GATES WIDE ON OTHER SIDE ROOM FOR YOU, ME. FOUR SQUARE CITY, JASPER WALLS, LIMITS 1200 MILES. ON RIGHT HAND, ON LEFT HAND 50 MILES ELBOW ROOM." It's Smith reducing a song to its weird essence—to the best, most universal truth contained therein.

At the very least, the *Anthology* contextualized—if not accelerated—the folk revival of the 1950s and '60s, coaching new fans about the genre's recorded precedents. The songs Smith included may have only been twenty to twenty-five years old, but they were hardly accessible (or even known) to noncollectors in 1952. Now, in the second decade of the twenty-first century, it seems deeply bizarre to think that cultural artifacts could become extinct so quickly (for example, in 2011 I heard Journey's "Don't Stop Believin'," a song first released thirty years before, approximately eight thousand times without trying), but the bulk of these tracks were either half forgotten or entirely unheard of by the time Smith polished them up for rerelease. In a 1993 interview with the music producer Hal Willner, Ginsberg called the *Anthology* a "historic bomb in American folk music," claiming that "it turned on Peter Paul and Mary, turned on the whole folk music world at that time, including Ramblin' Jack Elliott and everyone else, because it was this treasure of American blues [and] mountain musics. Happy Traum, everybody, including Dylan, [were] affected by it up to Jerry Garcia, who learned blues from Harry Smith's records."

By the mid-1980s, Smith was living in a flophouse on the Bowery, intermittently boozing himself into comas. He was toothless save a few decayed, abscess-ridden molars, and because of an injury sustained while ripping a feeding tube out of his mouth (after one particularly gnarly drinking binge, he'd ended up in St. Vincent's hospital, connected to a cornucopia of machines), he could eat only pea soup and mashed bananas, and not, apparently, without a good deal of gurgling. Prior to his arrival on the Bowery, he'd been shacked up in a tiny, book-stuffed room at the Hotel Breslin on Twenty-Ninth Street and Broadway, then home to the indigent elderly and the welfare bound, now repurposed as the modish Ace Hotel. (Its popular restaurant—I mean gastropub—presently serves a twenty-one-dollar hamburger; model types with expensive laptops are often draped around the lobby.) According to Ginsberg, the scene there was such: "And in the bathroom he had a little birdie that he fed and talked to and let out of his cage all the time. And when his little birds died he put their bodies in the freezer. He'd keep them for various Alchemical purposes, along with a bottle which he said was several years' deposits of his semen, which he was also using for whatever magic structures."

In 1988, Ginsberg helped bring Smith to the Naropa Institute, where Smith studied and lectured and cleaned up a bit: he quit drinking (he still self-medicated freely, smoking weed and ingesting, as Rani Singh writes in "Harry Smith, an Ethnographic Modernist in America," "whatever combination of Sinequan and Valium he found in his jacket pocket") and began aggressively chronicling found sounds (church bells, children jumping rope, cows). He gained thirty invigorating pounds on an ambitious diet of bee pollen, raw hamburger, ice cream, instant coffee, and Ensure. He lived and worked in a cabin with an index card—DO NOT DISTURB, I AM EITHER SLEEPING OR WORKING— posted semipermanently to the front door. Singh, who first met Smith while she was studying with Ginsberg at Naropa, called his years in Colorado "relatively tranquil."

For someone so invested in interdependencies, there's little evidence of Smith sustaining a significant romantic relationship in his lifetime. Singh described him as asexual. "I just think that he was more of an intellect. He lived in his head more than in his body," she said. He was also a relentless hustler, prone to harrowing fits of rage, and particular about his habits and beliefs. In "The Alchemical Image" (which originally appeared in the catalog for "The Heavenly Tree Grows Downward," a 2002 exhibition of Smith's selected visual works), the curator Raymond Foye wrote: "The cardinal rule in listening to records with Harry was NO TALKING. Absolutely none, whatsoever, until the record was finished. Hanging out with Harry was always characterized by a mixture of pleasure and fear. Several of his visitors were unstable, armed, and dangerous, and Harry's anger could clear a room. A gouache that took three painstaking weeks to complete might be torn up in a flash. There were always his sudden mood swings, and, of course, his drinking."

By the time Smith ended up back at the Chelsea, in 1990, he was living on food stamps and Social Security and a yearly donation from Jerry Garcia, who had publicly declared the *Anthology* the primary source of his understanding of the blues (the Grateful Dead frequently performed songs from the collection). One day, according to Ginsberg, Smith said, "I am dying," threw up blood, and fell over. His body was taken to the morgue at St. Vincent's, where Ginsberg later "pulled him out of the wall on this giant drawer. His face was somewhat twisted up, there was a little blood on his whitish beard. So I sat and did the traditional Tibetan liturgy, refuge liturgy, and then spent an hour meditating."

○

Like James McKune's ill-fated 78s, no one knows exactly what happened to Harry Smith's record collection. At some point Smith donated a good portion of it to the New York Public Library, where it was
eventually integrated into the general collection. Before its absorption,
it was cataloged and stealthily taped by the musicians and folklorists
Ralph Rinzler and Mike Seeger. In *Music from the True Vine*, his biography of Seeger, Bill Malone describes how, in 1956, Rinzler and Seeger
taped "hundreds of 78 rpm records from Harry Smith's unrecorded collection . . . Working as volunteers, Ralph cataloged over 1,000 records
on three-by-five cards while Mike recorded his favorites on his reel-to-
reel recording machine. When told to cease his recording, Mike then
smuggled out scores of records in a suitcase—including many highly
choice items from the Columbia and RCA Victor catalogs—which he
then taped at Ralph's home in Passaic [New Jersey]." In a 2007 interview with Ray Allen, Seeger recalled their caper: "That evening we went
out with my tape recorder and the box [of records]. So the guard at
the door said, 'Oh, I want to look at the box.' So Ralph went into kind
of like a frenzied dance, looking for a card or something to show him.
So he got the guard, who was like this 60-year-old, like a cop doing his
retirement, so flustered and confused, and I just walked out with the
box." The pilfered recordings were dutifully returned the next day, but
their bootlegged tapes were passed around folk circles for years like a
talisman, or a secret.

Moe Asch eventually bought or otherwise obtained whatever records Smith didn't give to the library. They were similarly assimilated
into the Folkways archive and became the property of the Smithsonian
in 1986, after Asch died and his family coordinated the institution's
acquisition of the label (the Smithsonian agreed to keep all 2,168 Folkways titles, including the *Anthology*, in print indefinitely). According to
Folkways archivist Jeff Place, they still have "a few thousand" of Smith's
records "mixed in with the rest of the 78 library," but when they began

work on the reissue in the late 1990s, they could only locate one of the 78s—Bill and Belle Reed's "Old Lady and the Devil"—that Smith had used to source the *Anthology*. "We had to go find the rest," Place said, which meant knocking on collectors' doors (records were borrowed from Joe Bussard, Dick Spottswood, Don Kent, and Dave Freeman) or, in some cases, reusing the original master tapes Asch and Smith made of the *Anthology* prior to its release.

Although that seems pat enough—Smith's collection was broken up and deserialized, sure, but it was relocated to two relatively safe places—the story of what actually happened to his 78s still gets muttered between collectors as a warning, an illuminating parable with a worrying end. Chris King was the first to tell it to me. "By the time [Smith] had basically exhausted his mental faculties or his ability to manage his collection, he had amassed over thirteen thousand 78s, which would be a lot of hillbilly, a lot of blues, and a lot of ethnic music," King explained. At some point, well after Smith had submitted the bulk of his records to the library for safekeeping, Richard Nevins had received a call to purchase a few Fiddlin' John Carson records plucked directly from Smith's collection and marked as such. But how had they become separated from everything else? King heard that the library had junked most of Smith's donation. "Deacquisitioned. It was all put in a Dumpster and destroyed." He shrugged. "So basically thirteen thousand 78s and a man's life—just snuffed away, just like that, in a Dumpster."

When I e-mailed Nevins to see what he knew, he was more optimistic about the collection's fate: "As far as I know, the collection never left the NY library and should still be there—but it was at their Lincoln Center musical branch. I have about four or five 12″ 78s from Harry's collection that I got from [the collector] Eugene Earle—don't know why they were separated. The bottom line, though, is who cares where the collection is at—there's little or anything in it that doesn't reside in many other collections. It was Harry's insight and good taste as an LP compiler that was special, not his actual collection."

Nevins was right, of course, but I was still curious. I figured there was no way anyone could know exactly which records Smith had amassed over all that time, especially if his collection was as monstrous and diverse as many people claimed it was. It seemed plausible that, given Smith's pedigree as a listener, his collection could have contained any number of unheralded masterpieces. My nosiness manifested as a flurry of correspondence: first, I wrote to the folklorist and filmmaker John Cohen to see if he had a list of the records Seeger and Rinzler had recorded and cataloged (I knew he still owned a copy of the reel-to-reel tapes they'd made), so I could at least see if the library had copies of those songs. I sent a similar e-mail to Steve Weiss at the Southern Folklife Collection, which acquired Mike Seeger's papers in 1991 (Seeger died in Lexington, Virginia, in 2009, at age seventy-six), and another to Place at the Folkways office, which holds Rinzler's (Rinzler died in Washington, DC, in 1994, a few days shy of his sixtieth birthday). Although neither collection had been cataloged for research yet, Weiss and Place both told me I was welcome to sort through their physical archives—to look for a list, for a rogue stack of yellowing index cards, for a record—if I thought it might help. I did: I wanted, badly, to know what Seeger and Rinzler knew, to hear what they'd heard. Seeger's widow, Alexia Smith, told me the pair had even considered putting together a companion to the *Anthology* based on the rest of Smith's collection. "Near the end of Ralph's life, he and Mike made a selection of cuts from these tapes—songs and tunes not included in Smith's *Anthology*—for a CD, which never got made," she wrote. "I'm aghast to think Harry Smith's record collection may have been 'integrated' or sold."

I also contacted my source at the New York Public Library, a publicist named Jonathan Pace whom I'd worked with on a few library-related stories for the *New York Times*. Pace referred me to Jonathan Hiam, curator of the American Music Collection at the Library of the Performing Arts at Lincoln Center, who offered to give me a private tour of the recordings archive. Within minutes of receiving his e-mail, I began imagining the grand moral dilemma I'd face when, alone in some unswept corner—having descended an obscured, rickety staircase to an unmarked catacomb deep below Sixty-Fifth Street, insulated from the day tourists thronging Damrosch Park and lit by the orange flush of a single Edison bulb—I discovered a stack of unheard Smith-owned 78s in a crumbling cardboard box. Would I stuff them into my backpack and climb out the bathroom window? It would be a noble reclamation. Possibly even heroic.

I also sent a note to John Mhiripiri, the director of the Anthology Film Archives; I knew they had ended up with a rogue box of Smith's paper airplanes, and I reasoned there might be some other pieces there, too. "Anthology has been storing the bulk of Harry Smith's collections since his materials were packed, labeled, etc., following his death in 1991. This includes one box of his paper airplane collection (in addition to the many books, records, Ukrainian Easter eggs, string figures, etc)," Mhiripiri replied. "The collections are mostly in off-site storage, however I am open to making the airplanes available for you to view, provided that Rani [Singh] agrees, there is no super-urgent deadline, and that it could be done within a specific timeframe, ideally not exceeding an hour." I accepted his conditions and forwarded consent from Singh. Mhiripiri told me to call him again in two weeks.

I had a research stake in untangling Smith's material legacy, but I was also becoming dangerously interested in just getting my hands on some of his stuff, which had started to seem like the most obvious way to discern any useful information about his life and work. Besides, it irked me the way Smith's records were strewn about, lodged in random, private enclaves, estranged. I saw myself battling back a classic collector urge: the desire to gather and serialize. To position everything in relation to everything else. To slot like among like. To write a story.

○

I met Jonathan Hiam at the security desk of the performing arts library on an especially glaring Monday morning. He led me downstairs to the archive. The New York Public Library's record collection is not, it turns out, stored in a damp, underground tomb, but is organized by label on big, white rolling shelves in a fluorescent-lit and well-ventilated basement. While we wandered through the collection, I resisted the urge to throw my jacket on the ground and start pulling 78s from the shelves, chucking their paper sleeves into the air, like a chimpanzee devouring a pile of ripe bananas. I wanted to hear everything, immediately.

Hiam told me he'd been looking into the acquisition of Smith's collection, but that the library's early donation records had been inconsistently kept. Now the process is streamlined and well documented, but it wasn't always: records came in and they were put on the shelf. Maybe a carbon copy of an acceptance note was slotted into a folder somewhere, maybe not. For some reason, Hiam said, there was virtually no information about music donated between 1958 and 1968. Smith's 78s may or may not have been marked with his initials. The library likely sent Smith a letter of receipt, and someone probably filed a copy of it somewhere (which would provide at least a date and the size of the donation; Hiam thought it was unlikely it would be itemized), but finding it would take some time. He promised me he'd try.

The library's several hundred thousand 78s aren't technically in circulation—you can't check one out and tote it home—but patrons can request to hear whatever they want while they're in the building. The retrieval process is delightfully weird, and after I'd browsed the contents of the archive with Hiam, I was keyed up to try it. Per Hiam's instructions, I located the lone microfiche machine on the second floor, which is positioned behind the reference librarian's desk and requires the rather brazen unhooking of a temporary railing to access. There, I thumbed through a Rolodex, compiled in 1985, of purple microfiche negatives listing the library's archived records ("You might be one of three women who have sat here," Hiam snickered after he spotted me settling in). I picked a random track from the *Anthology*—Chubby Parker's "King Kong Kitchie Kitchie Ki-Me-O," a whistle-heavy novelty song from 1928—found the appropriate slide (they're organized alphabetically by performer), and slid it into the base of the Micron 780A (a gray, boxy machine that incites brief, Proustian flashbacks to 1989). After wiggling the reader around for a bit, I found an entry for the record, complete with matrix and serial numbers. I wondered, immediately, if this was Smith's copy—the ur-copy, as it were, maybe even with a tiny "H.E.S." carved into the label!—and eagerly filled out a paper slip, pressing hard enough to ensure the carbon copy was legible. I rode the elevator back up to the third floor and tentatively handed it to the clerk at the A/V playback desk. He told me to take a seat. "This might take a while," he warned.

"Like ten minutes?" I ventured.

"Maybe more than ten minutes."

Once the slip is submitted, a call is placed to a librarian in the basement, who rises from his or her desk and starts scouring the shelves. Because the microfiche hasn't been updated since 1985, and because these records are so infrequently accessed (some have likely remained untouched since their acquisition), this process can be vexing. Records aren't always where they're supposed to be. When the requested 78 is finally located, it's carried to a dark, studio-like room where an audio engineer places it on a turntable, makes any necessary adjustments (changing the speed, weighting the tone arm, equalizing the playback), and pipes it upstairs to the waiting patron, who sits in an ergonomic office chair and listens on a cushy pair of studio headphones.

I waited a while, fiddling with the buttons of my coat. I watched a boneless old man in an oversize blazer repeatedly fall asleep and startle awake: tipping to the right, popping back up, drooping left, up. Every few minutes, the A/V clerk trudged over and told me they were working on it. Hiam appeared, smiled, and apologized. After forty-five minutes, I started to feel a little guilty. I had a perfectly playable CD of "King Kong Kitchie Kitchie Ki-Me-O" at home. I also had an MP3 of the song on the iPhone shoved in the back pocket of my jeans. I owned two physical copies of the *Anthology*. Besides, this particular 78 might not actually be Smith's, and even if it were, I wouldn't be able to touch it, and besides, what exactly did I think I was going to learn by listening to it this way? I told the A/V clerk that it was okay, I'd come back another time. "We have to find it anyway," he said.

"I know," I answered.

I took the elevator back down to Lincoln Center. A guard searched my bag on the way out. All he uncovered was a half-eaten granola bar.

○

I realized fairly quickly that flying south to claw around for Ralph Rinzler's index cards and Mike Seeger's bootleg tapes was a useless errand. I told a lot of people not to worry about it, and nearly all of them appeared relieved. I no longer knew why I was so preoccupied with gathering or in any other way quantifying Harry Smith's 78s—what I thought they could tell me about music or art or humankind, how I thought they might augment or guide my own experience of collecting.

My prying did yield one interesting footnote. The New York Public Library presently holds an uncataloged copy of the Cincinnati Jug Band's "Newport Blues," an instrumental cut recorded for Paramount in 1929 and included on the second disc of the *Anthology*. I only learned of its existence after spotting it in a display case at an NYPL event, and gasping. Hiam helped me arrange to have an archival transfer of the record sent to Chris King, who had previously suggested that he could listen to a good transfer, compare it to his original first-pressing LPs of the *Anthology*, and tell me if the NYPL's copy was, in fact, the source copy—if it had "Smith's DNA on it," as he put it. A few days after he received the CD from the library, King sent me a note. "I'm very certain that the copy of 'Newport Blues' (PMT-12743/21100-2) that was used on Smith's collection (from the original first pressing of the LP set, Vol. 2 Social Music, Dances No. 2, Band 40) is the same copy that is held in the NYPL," he wrote. "The main evidence is that on the CD transfer, there is a rather predictable non-musical artifact found at thirty-five seconds, forty-one seconds, forty-two seconds, and forty-three seconds that corresponds identically with a more muted non-musical artifact found at the same time spreads on Smith's track. This non-musical artifact is above the frequency range of the normal ambient surface noise that an N-Paramount of this time period would have. I think it must be a pressing bubble or other defect in the shellac pressing, possibly caused by the use of ground up chairs or bovine bones, maybe both."

A few weeks later, on a trip through Virginia, I stopped by King's studio to hear the comparison for myself. He made a braised pork shoulder in veal sauce, and after supper we carried cups of red wine into his music room. He played me the CD transfer; I noted its particular crackles. He played me the LP; I noted its particular crackles. I looked up and nodded. As far as I could tell, King's assessment was sound. I knew, at least, where one of Smith's records was.

I still can't quite explain why the *Anthology* has endured in the way it has, why it matters so much to people, why it matters so much to me. New musicians still routinely find their way to it; in the last decade, I've interviewed scads of emerging bands, folksy and not, who vehemently cite it as an influence, to the point where I'm suspicious of their intentions and nervous about the *Anthology*'s sudden muscle, its ability to indicate a certain kind of cool. Between 1999 and 2001, Hal Willner, working with the gloomy Australian rock musician Nick Cave, staged a series of tribute concerts to Smith and the *Anthology* in London, New York, and Los Angeles. A slew of contemporary artists— Steve Earle, Wilco, Beck, Sonic Youth, Lou Reed, Van Dyke Parks, Elvis Costello, Philip Glass, and plenty more—signed on to pay homage to Smith's work. The results were collected as *The Harry Smith Project: The Anthology of American Folk Music Revisited*, a two-CD, two-DVD boxed set that's a perfectly passable tribute, if low on surprises.

When I asked her about the *Anthology*'s continued vigor, Singh told me flatly that she thought it was magic. "He was a magician, he was interested in magic," she said. "As you said before, [it's in] the juxtaposition of songs—one song next to another, they rub up next to each other and they create this frisson that's almost a third thing. You know you're in the company of really true, good art when there's just something else that's there. There's this spark that you remember afterwards that's unexplainable in a way. And the *Anthology* is that for me and so many people. It's so many undiscovered worlds," she continued. "And it's the weirdest thing, every time you listen to it—and I've listened to it hundreds and hundreds of times—you think, Wait, was that song there before? Were they next to one another? How could that be?"

Singh believes Smith's vision—his philosophy, his narrative, his fingerprints—was paramount to the set's survival. "Anybody can make a mix tape, for God's sake," she snorted. "Everybody does. Every old boyfriend makes a mix tape and thinks it's a perfect expression of their love."

For years, rumors circulated that, following Smith's cremation, a handful of his acolytes blended his ashes with wine and chugged him down. Even if this is untrue—and his longtime companion and so-called spiritual wife, Rosebud Feliu Pettet, told me it was nonsense—I can still understand the desire to internalize a guy who believed so deeply in internalization. The *Anthology* works best when you consume it whole. Marcus called it a lingua franca—a password that grants access to a mystical folk brotherhood, a shibboleth—but I like to think of it as more personal and self-actualizing, like the EAT ME cake in *Alice in Wonderland*.

Smith received a Chairman's Merit Award at the Grammys in 1991, just nine months before he died. He was honored for his work on the *Anthology* and "his ongoing insight into the relationship between artistry and society, his deep commitment to presenting folk music as a vehicle for social change." It took two adult men to help Smith onstage to accept his certificate. At one point his foot swung for a stair and missed, like a dog's leg thrashing at some phantom, unreachable itch.

"I have arthritis, so I had to have this young man help me up here," he said when he arrived at the podium. He smiled, happy and calm in a tiny tuxedo, no tie. His long white hair was pulled into a ponytail. "I'm glad to say that my dreams came true," he declared.

"I saw America changed through music."

startled and as my friend Glen tells it, he saw the blood drain from my face. For sure I had never seen a John Hurt record in my life."

I was introduced to Salsburg by our mutual pal Mike McGonigal, a music writer who collects obscure gospel 45s and runs the excellent literary magazine *Yeti*. McGonigal called him a "sweet and smart dude," which is as apt a description as any, but it also discounts the almost disconcerting purposefulness with which Salsburg conducts his life: if all of my stuff were indiscriminately pitched into a Dumpster before my body went cold, I'd want Nathan Salsburg to find it. He is a person who knows what to do with things.

Salsburg was in Brooklyn screening unseen footage from *American Patchwork*, a documentary series born of Alan Lomax's travels through the southeast, when we agreed to meet for lunch. It was deliriously hot—New York had been subsumed, momentarily, by the sort of deep, otherworldly swelter that almost makes you shiver—but I somehow still figured it was a great idea for us to split a fried-chicken sandwich and several beers in an un-air-conditioned restaurant a few blocks from my apartment. Salsburg was forgiving, still game to talk records despite my frequently vocalized suspicion that the entire universe was about to return to ooze. I wanted to hear more about what he'd found in Kentucky. The heat lent our conversation a feverish tinge.

The John Hurt 78 Salsburg's friends unknowingly heaved out of Wahle's house that day—"Stack O'Lee Blues" / "Candy Man Blues"— was recorded for Okeh Records in New York City on December 28, 1928. It's one of only six 78s Hurt made (and saw issued—a total of twenty sides were recorded) before retiring to his hometown of Avalon, Mississippi, and resuming work as a sharecropper. In 1963, following the success of Harry Smith's *Anthology* (which included two of those twenty songs), he was "rediscovered" by the collector Dick Spottswood and the musicologist Tom Hoskins, and eventually recorded more material for Piedmont, Vanguard, and other small labels. "Stack O'Lee Blues" is about a nasty guy—"That bad man, that cruel Stack O'Lee"—who nonchalantly slaughters another guy for his Stetson hat.

Hurt's performance of the song is empathetic and delicate, but it's the flip side I've always found galvanic. "Candy Man Blues" is a hilariously dirty song about a guy with "a stick of candy just nine inch long." Girls, as you'd imagine, can't get enough of it: "If you try his candy, good friend of mine / You sure will want it for a long, long time / His stick candy don't melt away / It just gets better, so the ladies say," Hurt sings. His sweet, almost chaste voice infuses the raunchy lyrics with an impishness that's hard to replicate or to shake. While "Stack O'Lee Blues" / "Candy Man Blues" isn't astoundingly valuable by rare 78 standards (in 2008, a copy in not-great condition sold on eBay for $375), it's still precious. I could see why Salsburg was spooked by its appearance atop a heap of trash.

After he'd taken quick stock of the boxes in the garage, Salsburg, then thirty-one, motored back to the Dumpster with his buddies in tow. It was the middle of the night, full moon. "I was shaking the whole time. It was by far one of the most exciting moments of my life," he said. "We jump in the Dumpster and find box after box. My friend Joe goes down, he's being held by his belt, he comes up with a Blind Boy Fuller record. We got a great big box of LPs, which included all three volumes of the original *Anthology.*" They took whatever they could find, hauling it to Salsburg's car. The next morning, Salsburg dutifully contacted the Dumpster company and got permission to see what was left inside the house. "I slept for like three hours and called the guy and he said, 'Anything you can get out of the house is going to be a favor to us.'"

Wahle's domestic situation, Salsburg learned, was grim. There was a toilet "petrified in shit" and a mound of dirty newspapers spread atop "a waxy camp mattress, government-issue, springs across a frame," which Wahle may or may not have been using as a bed. (As far as Salsburg could tell, Wahle probably slept in the same room as his records.) Salsburg stuffed his Tacoma with 78s, LPs, and other potentially useful ephemera: Wahle's correspondence, his songbooks, decades of receipts, catalogs, and bank statements, and a cobbled-together, fast-action Smith and Wesson revolver Salsburg eventually had to have destroyed because it was so unstable. (When he found it, it was in a shoe box, wrapped in two paper towels, and loaded with rubber bullets.) "I took all the records I could get except the bottom two boxes in the back lower right corner, which were encased in mold. I picked them up and they started crumbling. I imagine there were some records in the middle of those boxes that I could have gotten, but my truck was so full and I was so crazy that I was just like, Fuck it." He paused for a few seconds before adding, inevitably, and with resignation: "I'm nervous about what was there that I didn't get."

It seems worth noting that Wahle had died only one week before—he'd lived, happily or not, with all that decomposition.

Wahle's 78 collection contained around 3,500 records, most by hillbilly artists, many in pristine condition. "I don't think he even listened to them," Salsburg said. "A lot of the LPs were sealed, but he attached notes to them with his remarks about which stylus to use. In some cases there were four copies of a single Jimmie Rodgers record, lots of triplicates of Uncle Dave Macon records. He just *got* them," he continued. "There were a few boxes and mailers that weren't even opened."

Salsburg, who was born in Wilkes-Barre, Pennsylvania, but reared in Kentucky, had purchased and cherished many LPs in his lifetime, but hadn't yet been ensnared by the lure of 78s, in part because he knew how expensive the good ones had become and how engulfing the hobby could be. Still, he admitted that the tactile experience of playing a 78 for the first time was singular, even for him. "There was an intimacy about it that was different from other intimate musical moments that I've had with stuff of this era," he said. "Because first of all, it wasn't a palimpsestuous experience. It wasn't listening to a 78 put on an LP or on a CD, or a 78 put on an LP put on a CD. It was the 78 itself. As I was listening, I didn't know what was going to happen, and then it ended and I had to flip the record over," he explained. "That's the experience of 78s that people talk about."

When we first spoke, Salsburg was still trying to clean and catalog his haul. "There are records where I've never heard of these people, I have no idea what this music is," he said. "It's a total revelation and it's exciting. But you also realize how much of this stuff is just mediocre. I feel like part of the problem is that it's so easy to fetishize them because of their age and because of their rarity. The rarest record I think I've found so far is a late-period Earl Johnson record, with the Clodhoppers or whoever it was, doing a song that a lot of folks were doing at the time called 'When the Roses Bloom for the Bootlegger,' which is a parody of 'When the Roses Bloom Again'—a pop song. It's not a very good song. But I've been told that it's maybe the second or third known copy, and it's probably the cleanest. It catches light every which way, and it might be [worth] two grand to three grand. But it's not great. There are great Earl Johnson records, but I found myself treasuring this one more than I do the others. And I don't like that feeling."

Fortunately, there were better things tucked into Wahle's cardboard boxes: records that were both unusual and great. "I did find a copy of that Arthur Miles record. The throat-singing cowboy. That was in there," Salsburg said.

I scrunched up my face at him. I'd never heard of Arthur Miles, or of a throat-singing cowboy.

"Oh my God, you've gotta hear it." Salsburg started grinning; the way he spoke about the music he loved was irresistible, catching. "It was this dude who recorded in Dallas in 1929. He did two sides, "The Lonely Cowboy," parts one and two. It's just the story of him being lonesome on the plain, and in the middle of the song he throat-sings. In the ledger it says 'Vocal Effects,' but it's throat singing. Or something like it. He's creating overtones. It might be humming and whistling at once. But he just came up with this thing, in place of the standard-issue yodel of the day. It's so ingenious."

When I finally heard Miles go (Salsburg sent me a clip a few days later), I was equal parts flummoxed and delighted: sporadic yodeling was common for country and western singers in the 1920s, and they occasionally imitated the throbbing twang of a Jew's harp, but what Miles does sounds more like *sygyt*, a form of throat singing native to the

Tuvan region of Siberia—a kind of overtone vocalization that resembles the wavering call of a loon, as filtered through a dozen down pillows, and, well, throatier. It was, to pinch one of Lomax's categorizations, remarkable. In a 2008 interview with Eli Smith, the producer and host of *The Down Home Radio Show*, the collector Pat Conte said he found Miles's technique unambiguous. "He's a throat singer, that's for sure," Conte said.

"What knocked me out about it is that I had been listening to a lot of these throat singers from central Asia—Siberia, Mongolia, places like that—and here was another example of this music, but right here at home. And Miles, it's the damnedest thing, he's just absolutely one of the very best," Conte declared. "You can explain it any way you want. There are certain Native American singing styles that have some elements of that—harmonic singing where the partials are kind of choked off. Arthur Miles, I think he's worked it to the very highest level of the art. He's a total master of the style." Conte did note one other recorded instance of a rural American singer employing the technique. In the late 1950s, the collector Eugene Earle had gone to visit Dick Burnett, of the once-popular banjo-and-fiddle duo Burnett and Rutherford. Burnett was blind in one eye from a robbery gone awry and nearly eighty years old, but still working, somewhat miraculously, as a small-appliance repairman in his native Kentucky. Using a reel-to-reel recorder, Earle taped Burnett performing in his home, and according to Conte, toward the end of their session, Burnett said: "I used to cut a lot of monkey-shines with this one! I'm gonna sing you a song, but the song is in my throat!" And then, Conte explained, "He sings 'My Old Kentucky Home,' and does a perfect rendition of this old harmonic singing." Conte paused. "And then the tape runs out."

Nathan Salsburg was just beginning to indulge the idea of turning Wahle's collection into a boxed set of several CDs or LPs. He'd devised a unifying theme (three discs, titled *Work Hard, Play Hard, Pray Hard*) and hooked an interested label, the San Francisco–based Tompkins Square. He already had a few favorite records, songs that couldn't easily be heard anywhere else, like Red Gay and Jack Wellman's two-part "Flat Wheel Train Blues," a train-imitation piece recorded for Brunswick in Atlanta in 1930. It's the only thing Gay and Wellman ever made together, and that's about all anyone knows about it; there are fewer than a dozen extant copies. Salsburg had uploaded both sides, which had previously been undigitized, to YouTube. I listened to the song—basically a rote narration of a train trip, complete with coal shoveling and spirited pep talking—approximately 175 times before I made myself walk away from my computer. Gay's fiddle, craggy and loud, successfully approximates a steam whistle; Wellman giddily bangs away on a guitar. They take turns on the vocals, which are more spoken than sung, and affectless in a flat, Appalachian way that can sound almost lifeless to modern ears.

Salsburg had warned me about a particularly devastating bit toward the end of part two, about a minute and forty seconds in. As the ramshackle train approaches a crossing, a mule scampers up and tries to outrun it. The train passes, the mule cries, and someone, likely Wellman, pauses to mutter: "You'd holler too like that if you was to get left." It is one of the oddest, kindest bits in the whole of American music, a moment of extraordinary empathy, and it shatters my heart every single time I hear it. Over lunch, Salsburg called the song "hilarious and beautiful and melancholy"—the mule, he said, reminded him of *Au Hasard Balthazar*, the 1966 French film directed by Robert Bresson about the parallel sagas of a farm girl and her mule—and it was all those things, all at once.

That night, while I sat in on Salsburg's lecture and screening (it was presented as part of the Brooklyn Folk Festival and held in a crowded gallery near the waterfront in Red Hook), I couldn't stop thinking about Wahle's records, stacked willy-nilly in a Dumpster, coated in ketchup and trash. He was a middling collector ("I wouldn't make too big a deal out of Wahle," Sherwin Dunner warned me when I inquired about his general standing) with a dubious affinity for cornball country songs sung by smooth-voiced goons like Gene Autry or Roy Rogers (Wahle had five copies of Autry's 1949 rendition of "Rudolph the Red-Nosed Reindeer"). But he also seemed like a useful object lesson for any aspiring gatherer: records won't love you back. They won't pack up your house or pay for your funeral. Even collectors as esteemed and celebrated as Harry Smith—or as seminal as James McKune—can't account for their stuff after they're gone. "This guy, he had no contingency plan for them," Salsburg said. "He had nothing. He just lived among them. Like T. S. Eliot said, 'These fragments I have shored against my ruins,' or whatever the line was." (That was it.)

The four sentence obituary that ran in the *Louisville Courier-Journal* that spring was appropriately dismal: "WAHLE, DONALD PICKETT, 75, passed away March 23, 2010. He is survived by his brother, Robert J. Wahle; two nephews, Robin and Charles Banks; and one niece, Shannon Miller. Cremation was chosen. There will be no service."

Shortly after I pulled up alongside Salsburg's yellow, shotgun-style house in the Clifton neighborhood of Louisville, about a mile east of the Ohio River, he began snickering at my rental car, which I was only able to identify as a "Dodge Whatever," a designation he found hilarious. The important thing, apparently, was that it had a spoiler, and possibly a racing stripe, and was white. I'll admit there was something humiliating about even standing near it. It lent all peripheral proceedings an undignified air.

Salsburg had agreed to let me rummage through Don Wahle's papers, which were then stored in deteriorating cardboard boxes in his laundry room. I could tell Salsburg still had a complicated relationship with the material, which at one point he half jokingly called "a two-ton albatross." I saw how it might be disconcerting to become the default material warden of a man you'd never met and whom no one could tell you anything about (although Salsburg would have happily received them, no family members ever emerged; when I tried to contact them myself, my letters were not returned). Salsburg was also in the unique position of knowing, via his work with the Lomax Archive and his own self-edification, how precious some of this material was. Although there was eventually some (limited) money and (limited) glory involved, I'm also not sure he could have ever walked away in good conscience.

By now, Salsburg was deep into the prep work for *Work Hard, Play Hard, Pray Hard*, the set culled from Don Wahle's collection. The rubric itself had originally been conceived to organize discs recorded under the auspices of (and held by) the American Folklife Center at the Library of Congress, which, since 1976, had collected "images, sounds, written accounts, and a myriad more items of cultural documentation" to "facilitate folklife projects and study." The AFC eventually swallowed up the Archive of Folk Culture, which had been established by the Library of Congress in 1928, and it now billed itself as one of the largest collections of ethnographic material from the United States and around the world. Even before he found Wahle's records, Salsburg had an organizing principle and access to raw material. But it turned out Wahle's collection made better fodder.

"The idea was to do work songs—songs about occupation or songs about hard times or songs about being broke or whatever—and then novelty songs and dance tunes, and then sacred material," Salsburg said. "I was interested in that rubric initially because the stuff at the American Folklife Center was recorded 'in the field'—it's music that accompanied folks' lives, songs that were sung at religious observances, ritual events, songs that were sung in church; then songs that accompanied work, songs that were directly related to people's livelihoods or lack thereof; and then songs people entertained themselves by," he explained. "That's a bit of a specious distinction—plenty of people made commercial recordings of very local and occasional material—but I thought it would be interesting to do something that was a little more concrete: expressions of real people's lives in their contexts."

Most 78 collectors deal exclusively with commercial recordings: 78s that were made and pressed by a label, then sold to whomever could afford them. With field recordings, there's often no artifact—collectors can't, for example, attempt to collect all of Alan Lomax's master tapes. But some collectors also maintain an aesthetic distinction between the two forms—they'll argue that field-recorded artists were often coerced or manipulated into performing, or will point out that the equipment used by a folklorist in the field was inherently shoddier than whatever a label would have had at its disposal. There's also the question of curating—of imposing an outside narrative on random forms, which, in some ways, is the folklorist or song collector's chief prerogative.

When I asked Chris King about the metatextual difference between a field recording and a commercial record, he broke it down this way: "The distinction is that commercial recording studios would give a full master or even two full masters to an artist that could perform solidly whatever material they brought to the studio, whereas the folklorist in the field was seeking to flesh out their particular interest, narrative, vision, or imposition, and that guided their taste when they selected both the subject and the expression that they wished to convey," he offered. "The collector as recorder, in the field, was the arbiter of taste and selection, whereas the studio engineer or A&R guy would only reject artists that couldn't hold it together for three and a half minutes. The filter was one person's taste or curiosity versus another person's cold call (can they even tune the fucking guitar)."

For Salsburg, though, it was more about stakes. When he came upon Wahle's records, he realized he could digitize and distribute that material using the same categories he had in mind for the AFC holdings. And unlike those field recordings, some of the commercial records Wahle spent his life amassing were in danger of being lost. "The experience of finding the records, of seeing where they had come from—the whole thing is an object lesson in how rare, how fragile, how forgotten, how underappreciated . . ." He stopped. "Not to further fetishize 78s, but think about how many records were just thrown away, where someone was like, 'The fuck is this old thing? It's heavy and I can't play it, I'll throw it away.' I feel like this project wouldn't be nearly as fun and rewarding and important to do if these records didn't come from whom and where they came from."

The limits of Wahle's collection were also part of what made it so usable; there was a smallness to it that felt germane to Salsburg's entire concept. It was real: "My idea was that it would exist as a kind of counterbalance to the Harry Smith set, because it wasn't wrapped up in all that mystical shit," he said. "The idea was that I would be applying categories to something that made sense in everyday life: work and play and religious experience. Granted, Harry Smith makes Songs and Ballads and Social Music make sense as discrete categories. But they're all bound together by this occult ontology, which I think is a needlessly complicating factor. It calls a bunch of people to it who wouldn't otherwise be interested because of its presentation as this purported mystical document." Instead, Salsburg's model was fiercely proletariat, both in content and in presentation, and as much as I loved the *Anthology*, his point felt valid—Salsburg's categories were accessible, almost intrinsic. It was a life cycle every American would understand.

Salsburg had promised to take me to see Wahle's house, but in the meantime, I wanted to nose around Wahle's things for a little while. I figured I could employ all of my dubious investigative reporting skills to conjure a fully formed portrait of his life—his loves and devastations and whatnot.

Reader, I failed. If Don Wahle's correspondence were a meal, it would be boiled potatoes. He saved everything (receipts, bank statements, brochures, catalogs, shopping lists), but it was all so fiercely banal it was hard to keep going after a while. Digging through it felt like watching a never-ending marathon of a low-budget reality show called *Paperwork*. Here is what I know: he saved old scraps of paper with different-colored scribbles on them, as if he were endlessly testing out his pen collection. He wrote in a thick, slanted script; his words looked as if they were being blown to the right by some unseen gust of wind. His best and most amusing quality was his periodic cantankerousness. Don Wahle was fond of a harshly worded letter. He had a lot of complaints, and he aired them freely. One of his bank statements included a letter of apology from the bank's manager, an E. R. Spelger: "Dear Mr. Wahle: Thank you for calling to our attention the fact that you did not receive a receipt for your deposit of November 19th, which you dropped in our night depository."

Using only his rescued papers, it was tricky to ascertain exactly what Wahle did for cash. According to a November 14, 1958, statement—typed on thick yellow paper and issued by the Citizens Fidelity Bank and Trust Company of Louisville—he had a respectable $135.15 in his bank account. But by 1970, it seemed he was out of work entirely: he received a letter from the Department of Economic Security's Division of Unemployment Insurance stating that there was work available for him at something called "Protective Services, 141 East Woodlawn, Louisville, Kentucky," and that he should report to that employer immediately.

His collecting, however, continued apace. In 1958, Wahle was invited to be included in *Burke's Register of Record Collectors*, a kind of *Who's Who* organized by a man named Vincent Burke, who lived at 172 Thompson Street in Greenwich Village. The enclosed letter requested additional nominations. "The forwarding of lists of active collectors is most important in our efforts to make record collecting the greatest hobby of all," Burke wrote.

Wahle kept endless want lists and corresponded frequently with other collectors, although those conversations were usually restricted—almost aggressively—to the task at hand, and personal asides were limited, if not nonexistent. My favorite set of correspondence began in April of 1959. It was with a record dealer named Victor Dozewiecki of Saginaw, Michigan, who must have responded to Wahle's request for Gene Autry records for sale or trade. Dozewiecki was on the hunt for Autry, too, although he was more interested in the objects than what they might contain and didn't feel any need to pretend otherwise, writing, on May 23, 1959, "I don't care in what condition the Autry records are which you may have to trade, just so I don't already have them."

Mostly, Dozewiecki got mad at Wahle for not responding promptly to his letters and requests for information. On September 12, 1959, in green pen, he wrote: "Dear Don: Some time ago, I requested of you to send me listings of Gene Autry records you wish for me to pick up for you. You stated that you would send lists. I have been waiting for a long time now and still no lists from you. I can't wait any longer for you to send me your lists. Everyone I'm connected with will be sore at me if I don't locate some of their wanted records soon. I can't put off record-hunting any longer while waiting for your 'Wants Lists.' I'm sorry but the record collectors will have to cooperate if they want any further assistance from me. As far as I'm concerned there will not be any further business transactions between you and I. Any letters from you will not be accepted. I must have cooperation if people want any of my help in reference to their record wants."

But by early November—after, I presume, Wahle had finally sent off his want list—they seemed to have reconciled. Dozewiecki agreed to help, but added, "However, when I send you letters I would appreciate a reply without too much delay. When you find it impossible to answer my letter without delay, please send me a postcard so that I'll know you received my letter." You can practically see his face getting red, flushed with indignation and rage. Over the next dozen or so letters, Dozewiecki found new and compelling ways to complain about Wahle's lack of promptness. Then, in December, he suddenly told Wahle he was giving up the hunt altogether and selling his entire collection. It included "nearly every different song Gene Autry has recorded from 1929 to 1944."

"I have a lack of space in my apartment, so the records must be sold," he wrote. "It's too difficult for me to try to relocate due to the present day conditions of the labor situation, also too many personal belongings." When Wahle didn't respond quickly enough, he got agitated again. "I wish to move to a different part of the country, and this matter of records you want to purchase from me is keeping me from doing so." He started bullying: "I honestly don't believe the price I stated for the Autry records of interest to you is too high. I know of people who have paid $1,000 per one record, same people have purchased quite a few records for the same stated price. Many people have paid hundreds of dollars for one record. I have never let prices stop me when I wanted certain records." They eventually made a deal, or what appeared to be a deal, but Wahle—of course—waited too long to answer. In March 1960, Dozewiecki wrote: "Is there some particular reason you will not send me a reply??????? I just can't keep writing letters to you and not receive any answers. I have too many problems on my mind, too many things to take care of." This one ends with "Please do so now, please, please." In a different letter from the same month, he blamed Wahle for derailing his entire life: "I can't wait much longer, I wanted to move months ago but decided to delay the trip for a short time so that you could secure the Autry records of interest to you."

By the next month, Dozewiecki was through with Wahle entirely, or so he claimed. "I'm not waiting for a reply from you after the stated date [April 16] so help me God. I've lost too much time thru this business of records."

That evening, Salsburg and I sat down to dinner at a Vietnamese restaurant, and over steaming bowls of *pho*, I told him how hard it had been to pinpoint Wahle, to isolate the man amid his stuff. His smile was sympathetic: he'd tried, too. I asked if he felt like he knew Wahle at all, if he could discern some portrait, some narrative. "He was religious, apparently, or at least later in life. There was some Bible stuff, there were Billy Graham materials, there were some 45s of banal, white Texas preachers. Nothing good." He shrugged. "He had a bunch of random Christmas shit. I think he was big into Christmas."

Don Wahle was already making me doubt my mulishly clung-to belief that a collection always represented something about its keeper—

that it functioned as an omniscient mirror. For Salsburg, Wahle's records told a confounding if not infuriating story. "The best part of the collection seems to have been accumulated in spite of Don Wahle," he said. "Part of me is sometimes like, 'Don, you are a fucking idiot.' Because there are times when I know that he had the opportunity to get awesome records and didn't, because he was too busy tracking down a Gene Autry record. So there were moments when I swore at him to myself, just purely for reasons of my own taste. But I also think there's something to be said about the records that were really peculiar in their context. A lot of these records are really weird. The late-twenties and early-thirties really rural string-band stuff—that's when that sound was totally falling out of style. Here's this genre in its only real commercial iteration—at least for the decades till the folk revival, when it was rerecorded or reissued on small-batch LPs—and they're capturing these highly localized traditions, performance styles, repertoires. Before the onslaught of the industrial Nashville sound that smoothed out so many of the edges. Those records are often rare because there wasn't much taste for them then outside of their communities; not in the marketplace. And those are the ones that are the most exciting in this collection." They're the same ones that Salsburg believed Wahle acquired by accident, as part of wholesale lots or through some other inadvertent means.

We talked more about the various hazards of collecting: what it can do to you, how a person might end up like Wahle. How, if mismanaged, the urge can manifest as a kind of egomania, a macho possessiveness. "Well, it all has to do with the territory, right? You're the one who controls this body of work," he said. "That seems very male to me."

Strangely, I hadn't thought about collecting explicitly as a means of control, although it was true: collectors might be generous about lending or digitizing their stock as a rule, but they did get to decide how and why and when that would happen, if at all. Everyone else had to go through a middleman, a label, an archive. Collectors had not only the glee of direct access but also got to experience the giddy, near-nefarious delight of discovery, of cramming their personal flag into a piece of exclusive shellac. "It's a different kind of personality that doesn't want that mediation," Salsburg said. "They want to be the one who discovers it. Look at the people—the dudes—who went looking for the Northwest Passage, or Columbus, or whoever else."

After dinner, we took Salsburg's redbone coonhound, Ruby, on a long walk around his neighborhood. One thing Salsburg was fairly certain about was that he thought of Wahle's records as things to be passed on and shared, in one way or another—via the release of *Work Hard, Play Hard, Pray Hard* or by selling or loaning them to interested parties. I chidingly pointed out how that didn't sound like something a real collector would say: to be so cavalier and fluid regarding ownership. He laughed. "I'm not a real 78 collector. That's the thing. Collectors are really particular about the curatorial aspect of their collection. This isn't curation. Don wasn't a curator. He just found all the records he could find and brought them in. For me, I feel like it's an inheritance." He shrugged. "I don't really feel a great sense of possessiveness over them."

There was, though, the smallest bit of satisfaction in giving Wahle's life's work a flash of validation, especially when it had come so close to unceremonious annihilation. Salsburg admitted it felt nice. "To be like, 'All right, you crazy old codger. Here we are. You have a legacy. You have your legacy.'"

○

Late the following morning, I met back up with Salsburg at his home, and after a breakfast of kale and scrambled eggs, he drove me to Wahle's two known Louisville residencies, as discerned by the addresses on his correspondence. We rolled past gentlemen's clubs with blacked-out windows (HIRING ALL POSITIONS!) and several strip malls, past fast-food huts and the Magic Sparkle Car Wash. The first house (on Keller Avenue, just a few yards from Interstate 65) had been razed, likely to make room for a proposed airport expansion; while we crept past the empty grass lot, I half expected to see 78s poking out of the soggy ground, like little black crocuses sprouting through the snow. The windows of the second house—the one where Wahle was living when he died—were still boarded up with plywood when we parked alongside it and got out. It was a two-story redbrick house with white clapboard shutters. A few scrawny, misplaced-looking columns awkwardly beset a poured-concrete porch. Salsburg was quiet.

I dug the tips of my boots into the mud of Wahle's front yard—I felt self-conscious, nervous, like I should have been able to understand more about Wahle from his choice of porch light (it was standard issue). My failure to arrive at any insightful new conclusions, I worried, indicated a broader crisis in reporting. I wanted to kick a loose stone in the foundation and suddenly discover a lost journal, a trove of love letters, a statement of purpose, a clue that I could triumphantly rush back to the lab. What did it mean, Wahle's records getting tossed like that? What did they mean to him? What comfort did they proffer? Instead we walked the perimeter. A dog barked. It was cold. I told Salsburg I thought I'd seen enough.

Twelve

But There's Another Part of Me That Finds It Kind of Disgusting

●

Jonathan Ward and Excavated Shellac, Victrola Favorites,
How to Curate, Ian Nagoski, Richard Weize and Bear Family Records,
Elijah Wald, The King of the Delta Blues Singers,
"They're Looking at the World and Seeing It as Untenable"

●

W ork Hard, Play Hard, Pray Hard was released in the fall of 2012 to effusive reviews. NPR called it "exemplary"; the *New York Times* cited it as one of the best boxed sets of 2012. Salsburg had asked me to contribute a short essay—along with Sarah Bryan and John Jeremiah Sullivan—to the accompanying notes, and I'd happily written about some of the bracing work songs he'd culled and presented from Wahle's collection. In late 2013, Salsburg's notes were nominated for a Grammy.

After the *Anthology,* compilations sourced from the holdings of 78 collectors weren't rare birds, exactly—Richard Nevins and the late Nick Perls had been putting them out on Yazoo for years, as had the collector Chris Strachwitz, who runs Arhoolie Records, and Marshall Wyatt, who runs Old Hat Records, among others—but in late 2012, music that people liked to call "authentic" (which was often used as a stand-in for "old" or "rural") was enjoying a mysterious but fervent renaissance. A younger generation of collectors and producers—Salsburg, Ian Nagoski, Jonathan Ward, Robert Millis, and Frank Fairfield, to start— were assembling compelling, thematically organized compilations of previously unheard material from the 78 era for newer reissue labels like Tompkins Square and Dust-to-Digital. The folks involved didn't necessarily hew to conventional wisdom regarding how a set should be constructed and what it should include. There was both an embrace and a rejection of Harry Smith's template, of what collectors were expected to do, of what curation entailed.

In the late 1990s, the Seattle-based collectors Robert Millis and Jeffrey Taylor hung a condenser microphone in front of a Victrola VV-210 "Lowboy" phonograph and started recording 78s from their collections directly to cassette. The pair produced ten thirty-minute tapes (all long-out-of-print now) for their label, Fire Breathing Turtle; those tapes eventually became the basis for a two-CD set released by Dust-to-Digital in 2008 and titled *Victrola Favorites*. The *Village Voice* called it "a bewildering array of exotica, religious chanting, and bar-room bawls from an equally bewildering array of countries," but what's most remarkable about the collection isn't necessarily the material (the collector Pat Conte's multivolume *The Secret Museum of Mankind*, which first appeared on CD in 1995, covers comparable musical ground) but the accompanying book, a 144-page collection of related images (labels, advertising, sleeves, Victrolas, needle tins, and more). The songs themselves are presented without discographical information, save the title, artist, and country and date of origin, and *Victrola Favorites* is more of an exercise in evocation—in the thoughts and feelings music induces—than a traditionally educational text. It seems to purposefully avoid the imposition of any narrative at all, beyond whatever the listener might write for herself. Even the images—like a photograph of a dark-haired woman in a long white dress, her arms hanging flatly at her sides, singing into a microphone at what appears to be a midcentury Tiki bar—are more suggestive than explicitly didactic.

"We knew right away that we wanted to make a compilation that was about the experience of listening and discovering these old records. We were not so concerned with historical context," Millis told me later. "For us they were still living, breathing, potential-filled objects that could be approached like a new song heard on the radio or at a show." He considered the images and music to be "two separate but equal" stories, and believed there were a variety of valuable ways for collectors and researchers to frame and present the contents of their collections. "I think historical narratives, be they about music or records or politics or whatever, always deserve to be reexamined and recontextualized," Millis explained. "And personal narratives can be very interesting, revealing a lot about the person doing the narrating as well as what he or she is narrating about."

The original cassette series "both inspired and befuddled people," Millis said. I find them transporting. I understood there were a lot of different ways for collectors to introduce old songs to new ears.

○

"What I worry about is the fact that the more visible it is, and the more it's regarded as something in the public domain, people want a piece of it," Nathan Salsburg said. I was back in Brooklyn; we were talking on the telephone, and I'd asked about the reissue boom. "They want to curate it. Because it seems to be totally democratic if not anarchic: it belongs to us, there's this not necessarily misguided sense of it as our collective inheritance. So everyone is a curator now. I don't have a problem with that in and of itself, but personally I feel a responsibility to do right by it and not merely use it as a vehicle for my own aesthetic or, you know, my own goofy ideas about the blues."

When I pestered him to define it, Salsburg said he thought of a curator as "the mediator between the observer and the observed," which struck me as an extraordinarily humane and graceful way of thinking about a complicated process. "The role is to reveal and not obscure. Fundamentally, it's to impart something true to someone. Not in a didactic way—not to bang you over the head with 'Here is folk, here is what it is!' " He paused. "This stuff is underheard, it's made by people who are either undervisible or invisible, and it's about ways of life that are either gone or have been neglected by culture and society. They deserve—and not out of romanticism—our respect."

The urge to romanticize lost cultures, particularly in an era in which our grasp on the tactile and the "authentic" seems particularly tenuous, is strong if not overpowering. I told Salsburg that it felt like a hard thing to do—to keep your eyes from glazing over with nostalgia or wild, chimerical visions. Old records can be so peculiar and thrilling—it's a challenge to keep all those tropes from infecting their analysis and presentation. Salsburg was careful to differentiate romanticism from enthusiasm. "Enthusiasm, even if it's a romantic enthusiasm, feels like a respectful approach to the stuff," he said. "But I distrust myself as a romantic," he added. "When it comes time to represent it, all of this effusiveness about songs being emanations or some music of the spheres is just dumb. It's silly—it's taking it too far. But I'd never put a song on something that I didn't like because I thought it was an edifying text. It should always be good first."

He worried, sometimes, about his own prejudices, all the biases that come with being a human being alive in the world. "I misunderstand records and lyrics and contexts and genres all the time," he said, "because my first approach to them is subjective, as opposed to understanding them in the kind of greater historical or musicological or cultural context that an anthropologist or musicologist would. But that's where the joy is."

I nodded. I was no longer sure if there was any honest way to tell any story.

●

The collector Jonathan Ward runs a website called Excavated Shellac, which is "dedicated to 78 rpm recordings of folkloric and vernacular music from around the world." In late 2011, Dust-to-Digital asked Ward to compile and edit *Opika Pende: Africa at 78 rpm*, a four-disc collection of one hundred never-before-reissued African recordings from 1909 through the 1960s. When I found out Ward had plans to visit New York from his home in Los Angeles, I asked him to dinner in Brooklyn. I was getting more and more interested in the idea of subjective curation: how it worked, what it could or should accomplish, what it might have already wrought.

Ward was bright and articulate, with rectangular eyeglasses and traces of gray hair at his temples. Excavated Shellac is updated a couple times a month, when Ward posts a transfer of an ethnic record generally unavailable elsewhere. "Ethnic records": that's what collectors call most foreign recordings. Ward, for his part, wasn't into the appellation. "'Ethnic records' is a complex term that needs to be trashed, in my opinion. 'Ethnic records'—come on. That's jive," is what he said about it. The posted MP3 was usually accompanied by a short essay in which Ward would give a bit of historical or musical context and then talk briefly about why he liked it. The sharing part—that visitors could download the MP3 and be on their way with it—was essential to the entire enterprise. As Ward wrote on his "About" page: "Record collectors are eccentric people. I don't even like the term 'record collector.' They've been parodied far too many times. Accurately, I might add. But I could not live with myself as a 'collector' without at least one person I could share sounds with. So this blog is for my friends, and for you, stranger."

Ward was immediately adamant about his limited role in the dissemination of old sounds. "The attention should be about the research and the music and not on the collector and his personality," he said. "I have no desire for that at all. The story is in the grooves. It's not in the basements. I don't think my whole name is on that website at all. I'm 'JW.' I don't list my name because there's part of me that feels the more you deify the collector, the further you are from the music," he continued. "And collectors love attention. I can understand that. It's great when you find someone who says, 'Wow, you're into that, too?' That's awesome. But there's another part of me that finds it kind of disgusting."

Over spinach salads and tomato soup, I inquired about the origins of Ward's collection. He'd grown up on Martha's Vineyard. "I was a hyperactive kid, and my parents were like, 'We've got to give this kid something to do.' And my mother said, 'Why don't you collect something?' I was three or four, no older than five. So I said, 'Like what?' And she said bottle caps. And I said, 'Good idea.' I just remember, as a kid in my little winter jacket, picking bottle caps out of the gutter and putting them in my little winter jacket. And I did that for another year and a half—just accumulating any bottle cap that was around." Eventually, Ward got into records via his mom's old Beatles LPs, then Captain Beefheart, and then finally, in the early nineties, he started buying 78s at flea markets.

"I walked into [the now-defunct New York record shop] Records Revisited and asked for the rarest blues. 'Yeah, do you have anything by . . . ?' I was like twenty-four or something. And the guy was like, 'Not today!' And then I quickly realized that what I was asking was ludicrous," he laughed. "But the guy was nice enough, and this is how you figure it out. You make errors and you figure it out on your own, and I'm glad I did that rather than consult the ninety-eight other collectors to figure out what to like and what not to like. That's one of the reasons why I collect in the sphere that I collect in—because I don't have anybody telling me what's good and what's not," he said. Ethnic records hadn't yet been surveyed and ranked in the way rare blues 78s had. There was no established hierarchy or sense of weight.

During our conversation, Ward was frank about how he believed certain visions may have dictated specific narratives about American music—particularly, how the blues had been codified as the rarest, the most hard-sought genre, in part because of who it attracted and what they heard in it. "Oh, there's music all over the world that's equally as rare," Ward said. "Let's not say more rare, because those [blues] records are incredible, they're rare, and they represent a very interesting piece of Americana in a very finite period of time. But that same thing exists in many other places. It's just: does it captivate white dudes?"

It was the same subjectivity that Salsburg had been wary of, and the question felt paramount to something. If we understand 78 collecting as a partisan act with extraordinary consequences—the music from the 78 rpm era that gets collected is also, by default, the music that is preserved and endures—then it's possible we're all inadvertently conflating personal stories with objective ones. The music we have, the music we know best, might be the product of a few individual, even aberrant visions.

In his book *Escaping the Delta*, the musician and author Elijah Wald tackles all the "romantic foolishness" written about the blues by collectors and fans: "As white urbanites discovered the 'race records' of the 1920s and 1930s, they reshaped the music to fit their own tastes and desires, creating a rich mythology that often bears little resemblance to the reality of the musicians they admired," Wald writes. It's a grand delusion that was perpetuated, perhaps, by the Blues Mafia, but probably had much earlier origins; as Wald points out, there was a good chance "it was part of the blues legend from the beginning, a colorful way of marketing a new style." Regardless, the collector's preoccupation with outsiderism had curious consequences. "By emphasizing obscurity as a virtue unto itself, they essentially turned the hierarchy of blues stardom upside down: the more records an artist had sold in 1928, the less he or she was valued in 1958," Wald explained.

The prior summer, I'd become particularly engrossed by a new collection released by Tompkins Square called *To What Strange Place: The Music of the Ottoman-American Diaspora, 1916–1929*, which collected the work of musicians from Anatolia, the eastern Mediterranean, and the Levant region of the Middle East who lived in the United States and recorded 78s in New York City between World War I and the Depression. It was assembled and produced by a then-thirty-five-year-old collector and writer named Ian Nagoski, who had stumbled upon the whole box of source records in Baltimore and paid five dollars for it. Nagoski and I had e-mailed a few times; he had strong and cogent ideas about why people collected rare records, and what the consequences of those impulses were.

Nagoski was familiar with Wald's theories, and he agreed with the basic premise of his book. "Skip James does not represent prewar blues. Barbecue Bob does. Barbecue Bob and Tampa Red, they sold like crazy," Nagoski said when I finally got him on the telephone. "Skip James is a weirdo. He's a freak. He doesn't really fit in, and the fact that he's such a big part of the blues canon is a direct result of the blues canon having been written by white men."

Another danger of the canon having been engineered—accidentally or on purpose—by collectors is that scads of things were excluded, either because they didn't conform to a collector's particular taste or because there just wasn't enough time or space for anyone to properly process them. "When I began collecting seriously and contacting other 78 collectors and going to their houses, they'd see this kid come in, and I'd say, 'Yeah, you got any records for sale?' And they'd say, 'Yeah, all those over there. Those are the ones I don't want from this big buy that I did in New Jersey or New York. You can go through those and see if there's anything you want,'" he explained. "So I'd go through 'em and [the pile] would be full of gospel. Full of incredible jubilee quartets and preachers and stuff. [Older collectors] weren't the slightest bit interested because it didn't fit into their vision of this quasi-demonic, earthy, raw folk-music thing. It was too middle-class, or too aspiring middle-class."

Those sorts of omissions were inevitable: collecting is a hobby, not a responsibility. "Everybody does the sixteen-second test, where you drop the needle, you listen to the first verse, and you go, Okay, I know where this is going. I'm not going to be needing this in my life," Nagoski said. "Everybody has this established sense of what is good. And life is short and you can't listen to everything."

I decided to drive down to Frostburg, Maryland—a small mountain town about two and half hours west of Baltimore, wedged in the little strip of Maryland between West Virginia and Pennsylvania—where Ian Nagoski had recently moved. I booked a room at a place called

Failinger's Hotel Gunter, which opened on New Year's Day in 1897 and had a storied, if perplexing, history outlined in one very long paragraph on its website. ("The basement of the hotel had unique features of its own including a jail and a game cock fighting arena.") I found both its price (seventy-five dollars a night) and its tagline ("Nothing Like It Anywhere Else") irresistible. When I arrived, the place appeared to be populated mostly by stuffed animals and dolls. There was a mannequin museum in the basement, alongside a scale replica of a coal mine and a massive taxidermy display, which included a red fox eating a whole squirrel. On the way up to my room, I couldn't stop myself from taking a picture of two teddy bears posed, midsip, at a miniature, doily-covered tea table. It was that kind of vibe.

That afternoon, Nagoski welcomed me at his door, and after a lunch of cheese and olives at his kitchen table, we wandered down the street to buy some beer from the corner store. After we'd picked out a six-pack, Nagoski told me the cashier would almost certainly ask him about me later. "It's a small town," he said.

Nagoski had soft brown hair that fell to just below his ears, a fuzzy beard, and kind blue eyes. His record room, on the second floor of his home, was charmingly rumpled: there were empty and full cardboard boxes, piles of pennies, rolls of packing tape, a couple toothbrushes, stacks of books, and scattered 78s and LPs. Unlike the music rooms of other collectors I'd visited, Nagoski's wasn't an exacting space. It seemed more like the office of a distracted college professor.

One of the things Nagoski and I had spoken about on the phone was the question of why people collected anything, and why a person might collect 78s specifically. It was something he'd thought about a lot already. "Some people are just really good at listening to records. It's a real talent." He shrugged. "When you get to a certain level of knowledge, and can start passing that along to people, that's really exciting and really beautiful." For Nagoski, the understanding and presentation of the material was just as important as its acquisition. "I see that in 78 collectors over and over again—they're dying to express, to someone who wants to know, how beautiful the whole thing is. The *Ghost World* generation of [Terry] Zwigoff and [Robert] Crumb and innumerable others, these guys are definitely discontents in a Freud's *Civilization and Its Discontents* kind of way. They're looking at the world and seeing it as untenable. The world is sick. And yet here is this thing that affirms that there's something about it that's beautiful. But it's forgotten, or lost, or separate from day-to-day reality. But if you could just put it back together, then you could reconstruct this gone world, this kind of life that was once worth living, and make that into your own life, and then it would be okay or tolerable for you."

Occasionally, there was enormous power to be had in that sharing. In *Escaping the Delta*, in a chapter titled "The Blues Cult," Wald talks about how "for most modern listeners, the history, aesthetic, and sound of blues as a whole was formed by the [Rolling] Stones and a handful of their white, mostly English contemporaries." But the Stones and their ilk were taking their cues from reissue compilations conceived of, produced, and sourced by 78 collectors—the ones who preceded Salsburg, Ward, Millis, and Nagoski.

In the early 1960s, after the Blues Mafia was well established and enough 78s had been canvassed and hoarded away, reissue collections began appearing on long-playing, 33⅓ rpm vinyl. Pete Whelan was the first to reissue Charley Patton, on his Origin Jazz Library label in 1960; the records were sourced mostly from Whelan's collection, with additional contributions from Bernie Klatzko. One year prior, the writer Samuel Charters had compiled an album for Folkways called *The Country Blues*, which was designed to accompany his book of the same name. Like the *Anthology*, it became a kind of guiding document for the folk revival, but most 78 collectors considered it too commercial, including, as it did, top sellers like Leroy Carr and Lonnie Johnson. Shortly after its release, Whelan delivered a retort LP titled *Really! The Country Blues* that featured more obscure bluesmen like Henry Thomas, Son House, and Skip James. (Like Patton, James had never been reissued before Whelan thought to do it.)

Then, in 1961, Columbia Records put out *King of the Delta Blues Singers*, a mono collection of sixteen Robert Johnson sides. It was the first time those songs had ever appeared outside of their original shellac. Columbia executives were ultimately convinced of the music's import by the set's producer, the collector, critic, and talent scout John Hammond, who had recently signed Bob Dylan and would eventually go on to bring Leonard Cohen and Bruce Springsteen to the label. As Wald writes, Hammond "had a gift for persuading other people to share his enthusiasms." Hammond had been interested in Johnson for decades. He'd even tried to get Johnson to perform at a concert he was organizing at Carnegie Hall in late 1938, not realizing that Johnson had died in August of that year. (In a particularly prescient move, Hammond instead rolled out a phonograph and played two of Johnson's 78s to the assembled crowd—already Johnson had been reduced to ephemera; already his music was an exalted object, sacred, fascinating, and distinct.)

Because no one knew what Robert Johnson looked like (and wouldn't—or not really—until a tiny, postage-stamp-size photo was uncovered in the early 1970s), the cover of *King of the Delta Blues Singers* featured an illustration of a faceless black man wearing farm clothes, hunched over in a chair playing a guitar. Most of the cuts were pulled from Hammond's personal collection or from the shelves of the collector (and fellow Columbia employee) Frank Driggs, with the exception of "When You Got a Good Friend," "If I Had Possession Over Judgment Day," and "Traveling Riverside Blues"—which had previously been unissued and were taken from surviving metal masters.

The Johnson set, especially, was a big deal. Eric Clapton lost his mind when he heard it: "It came as something of a shock to me that there could be anything that powerful . . . At first it was almost too painful, but then after about six months I started listening, and then I didn't listen to anything else," Clapton wrote in 1990. Keith Richards went similarly nuts: "I was astounded at what I heard. It took guitar playing, songwriting, delivery to a totally different height," he declared in his 2010 autobiography, *Life*. In 1990, Columbia would issue another

or not and if they can actually open up to them," he continued. "It's a compensation for all kinds of male skills that are supposed to be present in adolescence that may not be present, so you compensate with other things—the superiority of specialization in some arcane field. Science-fiction nerds and baseball-card guys, motorheads. Wanting to talk about your sound system first and your marriage months later. But literally having a shared aesthetic experience of a particular style of speaker could be the foundation of a lifelong, very, very deep male friendship."

I am not male, but by the time I stumbled back to the Hotel Gunter—we'd gone in for another listening session after finishing up at Dante's, this one capped by a spin of Okeh's infamous Laughing Record, a 78 recorded in 1922, of a man and a woman cackling crazily while funereal-sounding music plays—I was feeling warmly toward most things. I took my place amid the dolls and relics, artifacts enduring in a new world.

●

I was introduced to Richard Weize, the owner of the German reissue label Bear Family Records, by Chris King, who had overseen the mastering for several Bear Family releases, including 2011's *The Bristol Sessions, 1927–1928: The Big Bang of Country Music*, which collected all the tracks from Victor Records' famed recording stint in Bristol, Tennessee. (Those sessions yielded the world Jimmie Rodgers and the Carter Family; it netted King another Grammy nomination for Best Historical Album.) King put us in touch over e-mail. Bret and I were going to be traveling from Berlin to Amsterdam and planned to stop in Bremen, a city on the Weser River in northwestern Germany, not far from the Bear Family headquarters. "Yes, we are approximately 25-30 miles from Bremen," Weize wrote. "It is probably best to come here to see what is going on." I accepted his invitation for us to stay the night at his farmhouse.

Bear Family was founded by Weize in 1975, who has since (rightly)

declared it "a collector's record label." Although the company has released plenty of one-disc compilations, usually focused on a single
artist, Bear Family is still best known for its elaborate boxed sets, which
are pricey and startlingly comprehensive: in 2005, the label released a
seven-CD set featuring 195 different versions of the German pop song
"Lili Marleen," which was written in 1915 and most famously recorded
by the cabaret singer Lale Andersen in 1939. Weize's products aren't for
dabblers. But he serves his particular customers with particular aplomb.

Bear Family reissues a lot of rockabilly, bluegrass, folk, world, pop,
oldies, and blues, but Weize's primary focus has always been on country
and western music. Although he owns thousands of his own 78s, he
collaborates frequently with American collectors, who help source and
notate his releases. I was curious about the way prewar American music
had translated globally, and especially how a specialty German label had
become so synonymous with the propagation of rural American music.

Bret and I pulled up to the Bear Family farmhouse in our rented
BMW at just past dusk. It wasn't all that far from Bremen, but the
landscape was pastoral, and Weize's sprawling home was surrounded
by tall, imposing trees and huge plots of farmland. The sun was dipping
below the horizon, but I could still discern the giant carved wooden
bear sculpture (with cub) that beset the front door.

Weize answered my knock in denim overalls and a plaid shirt. His
long, scraggly gray hair was pulled into a low ponytail, and he was
sporting a robust beard and small round eyeglasses. Weize and his
wife, Birgit, graciously invited us in, and after a supper of sausages and
potato casserole, Weize offered to walk me through his 78 collection,
which he keeps in a barn adjacent to the main house. It took a while to
navigate it all. He commands a staggering amount of media: LPs, CDs,
reel-to-reel tapes, and 78s, all organized on wooden shelves reinforced
with metal beams. Weize didn't know precisely how many records he
owned, and he didn't seem to care that much. We walked for a long
time. The barn felt endless. Huge chunks of Weize's collection had
been acquired in wholesale lots or auctions, and there was no way one

person could have heard even half of it in a single lifetime. It was odd and overwhelming to see all those records corralled in a barn in a quiet corner of Germany, most now thousands of miles from where they'd been written and recorded.

Weize, who was born in 1945, had always been interested in American music. "Everybody in Germany was interested in American music," he said. "I bought my first record in 1956. It was 'Rock Around the Clock' by Bill Haley, and I got infected, real bad. Records were precious then, not like today, when you can get music anywhere." Weize has an exacting German accent, but there's a gruffness—an imperfection—to his voice that makes it oddly musical, almost soft, even when he's calling someone "a stupid idiot." (As he often does.)

Eventually, we settled in his office, a cavernous space filled with books and antiques, many of them bear related. A large Stetson hat box was balanced atop a filing cabinet. I sat down in a yellow, RCA Victor-branded vinyl chair. "I work with collectors, but more on a professional basis—I'm not looking for things for myself," Weize said. I was trying my best not to stare at a bear rug—the animal's head still intact, its plastic teeth bared, snout frozen midattack—spread across the floor just to the right of his desk. "If I go to somebody and say, 'My name is Richard Weize from Bear Family,' they're very open. But the records are precious to them," he added. "Let me say something: a collector is a nut, regardless of what he collects. And if he takes things too seriously, if he can't laugh at it, if he doesn't find it amusing, if he can't see that he is a nut, then that's about the time to put him behind bars."

Weize partnered with collectors to source his releases—he had to—but they were also his primary foils. "I have collectors who come up to me and say, 'On your last release, why did you mess it up?' And since I try to be perfect, my heart sort of sinks into my trousers," he admitted. "And I'll say, 'What did I do?' 'On that one track, you faded it two seconds early!' And I'll say, 'Thank you very much.' I don't need that stupidity. Kids are dying in Africa, and we are already wasting our time on stupid things, and in addition I have to waste my time on something like that?" Weize tried to maintain some sense of perspective on the whole enterprise. "I live for it, twenty-five hours a day," he said. "But still, there is a life next to it. Birgit, she doesn't like collecting, she doesn't know anything about it, she does what she wants, I do what I want, and we're getting along fine. But you have to be aware that it's not the center of the world."

That night, Bret and I slept peacefully under a framed poster of Mickey Mouse. The next morning after breakfast, Weize brought me to the Bear Family office, also on his property, where a few of the label's employees were prepping sets for shipping. It was an impressive display: big square boxes of CDs lined up on shelves, wrapped in plastic, ready to be pulled and sent off to whomever had beckoned them.

Just then, I felt extraordinarily overwhelmed by the heft of the collector's preservationist mission. Seeing all that music—so much of it recorded, as it was, in tiny American towns, by artists deeply unaware of the people they might one day reach—being packaged up for global dissemination was humbling. I thought of Salsburg and Ward and Nagoski; I thought of every 78 collector I'd met. They may have written this story imperfectly—they may have imbued it with skewed narratives and faulty parameters—but they couldn't have possibly foretold the scale of its retelling.

|| *Thirteen* ||

Luring Me Out Here for Nothing but a Damn Bunch of LP Records!

●

Joe Bussard's Basement, Fog, Alexis Zoumbas, "Original Stack O'Lee Blues," Black Patti, Scrambled Eggs, "Vernon Stalefart"

●

The upmost peak of Afton Mountain seemed like a reasonable place to meet someone—poetic, even. A few weeks prior, Chris King had agreed to ferry me from Charlottesville, Virginia, to Frederick, Maryland, to meet Joe Bussard, one of the foremost living collectors of prewar 78s and already the subject of dozens of feature stories and even a short documentary film, 2003's *Desperate Man Blues*. I thought King might make for a useful conduit. Bussard, now seventy-seven, had a wide-reaching reputation for equal parts capriciousness and charm: he was politically conservative, particular about his meals, prone to fits of cackling, deep into fart jokes, unimpressed by the last six decades of American culture, and real fucking serious about records. A lot of folks were angling to get into his basement. He and King had known each other for fifteen years and enjoyed what King called "a pretty fast rapport." There was also this remarkable fact: when King was six or seven years old, Bussard showed up at King's parents' house and bought Les King's entire stash of 78s. Ten thousand records, stacked in whiskey boxes in the basement, handed off to Bussard for ten cents apiece. "I remember it vividly," King said. "Dad had mint runs of Jelly Roll Morton, mint runs of the Skillet Lickers on Columbia. Dad had shit that God hadn't seen."

And now Bussard did.

Our rendezvous spot was King's idea. It seemed, at the time, like the most convenient move. I had to ditch my car somewhere so we could travel together, and Afton made geographical sense, given its proximity to Interstate 64, which would take us halfway to Frederick. Still, it arrived with a caveat: "I initially felt that we could leave a vehicle at the top of Afton Mountain where an abandoned hotel is falling in on itself, but then I remembered that crowds of people converge there to sightsee and smoke crack," King wrote a couple days before I left New York. I didn't think anyone would be terribly interested in pilfering the contents of my thirteen-year-old Honda—its seats littered, as they were, with Kit-Kat wrappers and promotional CDs and old newspapers—and eventually, he acquiesced and sent directions. "Taking 250 West, as you crest the mountain, there is a monstrous parking lot on the left . . . This is the place where hotels go to die. I'll be there at 9:00 a.m."

I had driven down to Virginia the day before and spent the night with Bret's parents in nearby Barboursville. I woke early on the morning of our meet-up. It was mid-February, equal parts frigid and damp. I got dressed by putting on every item of clothing I could find in my suitcase. On the hour-long drive toward Afton, I curled my mitten-clad hands around the steering wheel and cranked both the heater and a CD-R of *Five Days Married & Other Laments*, a compilation of Epirotic laments and dance songs culled from a stack of battered Greek and Albanian folk 78s King had junked on a family vacation to Istanbul a few years prior. It was King's latest release for Long Gone Sound, and, like all of his collections, it was deeply personal. It comprised exclusively rural folk songs—"the song and dance of the *volk* and the village," he explained in the notes, which existed "largely as a rustic, primal counterpart to *laîki* or urban popular music, such as *rembetika*." Before I left for Virginia, King had reluctantly e-mailed me the MP3s along with a PDF of the liner notes. "I've already been accused of being a cultural fascist but could I also be an aesthetic one by suggesting that you read the notes to *Five Days Married & Other Laments* while listening to it . . . at least one time through?" he'd asked. "You know how I am about context."

I eventually burned the files to a CD for my drive. I suppose if it hadn't felt dangerous (and crazy), I would have taped the notes to my dashboard.

Although I first met King as a collector and producer, I was beginning to know him as a writer, too. Most week nights, after he'd put his daughter to bed and retreated to his music room, he drank red wine and worked diligently on short fiction or on the notes to his sets, which, in addition to the standard annotations, always contained some essayistic screed probing the nature of sound itself. As someone already over-invested in the question of why certain records made me feel certain things, I read them hungrily. King was acutely compelled by a variety of sonically dissimilar genres, and I frequently bugged him to clarify the overlap, to isolate the precise emotional center, the draw—the thing that made him pursue certain 78s with heart-stopping fervency but remain unmoved by others. Rarity meant something to him, whether he admitted it or not, but I was curious about what else he was listening for. His notes, I knew, were where he worked that shit out: posed the unanswerable questions, tried to understand his role in the exchange.

Reading the introduction that accompanies *Five Days Married . . .* , I could tell he'd been probing those desires, questioning why he needed what he needed. "That the tunes captured on these old 78s are conter-minous with other equally intense musical expressions . . . the doomed pleas of Amédé Ardoin, the confident desolation of Geeshie Wiley, the unharnessed exuberance of Michael Thomasa, is significant," he wrote. "Exactly what is the significance? What is the pit in our bellies that hollows out this epistemic hunger and, consequentially, what would sate this apparently irrational drive for a reasonable narrative? Can something in words explain that which must come before vocalization?"

Thinking about it on the drive toward Afton, the question almost made me queasy. Was King right to wonder if the "that" which came before vocalization—the specific rapture or agony that inspired a song— was inherently prelinguistic, inexpressible? Maybe the alchemical or spiritual flash that powered the art-making impulse was too raw and unimaginable to be parsed; maybe the question itself was naïve. But it felt particularly germane to this release. Even for fans of scratchy old blues records, the songs on *Five Days Married* . . . are aurally challenging (the modal structure is "implied," the duets "asymmetric"), marked by wild, keeling melodies that sound a lot like wet, airless sobs.

The precise sound of the Albanian folk tradition is hard to describe: it is mournful and plaintive, focused on unholy-sounding violins and endlessly circling melodies. King rolled his eyes every time it got called "droning," but there was a mesmerizing rhythm to it, a hypnotic, repetitive whir. Perhaps because the meters and instrumentation were so fundamentally unfamiliar, I couldn't ever get past the sorrow and yearning they contained. It was all I could hear. I was, as King suggested, seized by an irrational drive for a reasonable narrative. It made for dizzying listening, and that morning, I was having a weird go of it in the Honda.

The weather didn't help. Afton Mountain is a harrowing drive even on a clear day, and when fog consumes its summit, it's a little like steering through a storm cloud with a blindfold on. Several years ago, the Virginia Department of Transportation installed a stretch of terrifically expensive runway lights—834 LED bulbs in total—along the highway edge, illuminating the width of the road but otherwise doing very little to aid with general visibility. Considering the elevation (it's a 1,900-foot tumble down into the Shenandoah Valley), it's not the kind of place you'd want to casually drift off course—and yet, as VDOT's regional manager Dean Gustafson once explained in a press conference, "The lights can't help you see cars in front of you." I like to imagine there was a bit of foreboding in Gustafson's voice. That his eyes darkened. When the visibility dips below fifty feet, you're taking the presence of empty road in front of you on faith.

Having briefly lived in Charlottesville, I was vaguely cognizant of the fog situation, and I figured I would leave early, drive slowly, and wait patiently for King at the appointed location. What I didn't quite realize was that it would be impossible to locate the appointed location. I couldn't see anything at all: not the road, not the front end of my car, not other cars, not an abandoned hotel parking lot populated by drug-addicted miscreants. I crept up the mountain, leaning so close to the windshield that the tip of my nose left little prints on the glass. I periodically peered out the driver's-side window, hoping for a break in the fog. Then, suddenly, I was rolling downhill. All I knew from King's e-mail was that the lot would be on my left, and that if I reached the summit and started to descend, I'd gone too far. This went on for a while: me inching up the mountain, figuring out I was angling downward again, making an inadvisable U-turn, repeating the process. Eventually, on one of my re-ascents, I spotted a turnoff point and flicked on a blinker—an excessively civil gesture—before pulling into what I thought might be a parking lot, but in reality could have been someone's front yard or merely an expanse of air. A few seconds later, I saw remnants of a crumbling stone foundation in my headlights. I put my car in park and slowly unwound the rest of my fingers from the steering wheel. A grinning truck driver pulled up alongside my car, flashed his lights, and motioned for me to roll down my window. I made a barf face at him. Because King didn't have a cell phone, I wasn't sure how to tell him that I was here or to find out if he was even still coming. It wouldn't have been unreasonable for him (or for anyone) to turn around. I sat there, idly drinking coffee, turning *Five Days Married* . . . off and then back on again. I didn't know if King would see me in my car, or my car in the lot, or the lot itself, but I figured I'd wait until the fog cleared a bit before giving up entirely.

I finally spotted a sliver of his blue Volkswagen, peeking through the whiteness. It eased up alongside the Honda. I could see King's face—which looked particularly pale—through the passenger-side window. I felt a weird mixture of horror (it occurred to me in that moment, and not undramatically, that I'd inadvertently endangered his life to get to some records) and relief that he'd not only made it to our meeting point, but appeared physically unscathed. I unlocked my doors and lunged blindly toward his car, finding a handle and collapsing into the passenger seat. I wanted to embrace him. Instead we exchanged looks of incredulity. King removed his eyeglasses and wiped them clean. He handed me a paper sack full of ham biscuits. "Breakfast," he said.

While I pulled off my mittens and unwound my scarf, King explained that Bussard had called him earlier that morning and said he wasn't feeling well and that maybe we should come up some other time. King had somehow anticipated Bussard's antipathy and preemptively prepared a retort ("This lady came all the way from New York City with her notebook and pens!" I imagined him saying), which was enough to get Bussard to temporarily half agree, telling King we should call him when we were getting close and he'd decide if he could see us. I was grateful for King's insistence, if slightly nervous about being unwelcome. We rolled out of the lot and toward the highway.

In the months since Hillsville, King and I had developed an unexpected but hearty bond, marked by a shared appreciation for the transformative possibilities of music: we were becoming friends. Our relationship was enacted mostly over the telephone. I would call him and whine about various existential ailments, he would play me curative 78s, and then we'd talk about records until one or both of us got tired. Our drive to Frederick progressed much in the same way. I chewed a biscuit and filled him in on my life in New York. King was working on a compilation of folk songs by the Epirotic violinist Alexis Zoumbas, and he played me a few tracks while we sliced through the fog, which was finally beginning to dissipate, fading into a cold, clear mist. Zoumbas's violin fluttered, cried. Maybe it was the stress of the morning's journey or the anticipation of breaking into Bussard's basement, but after a few minutes, we both had tears in our eyes.

"What do you hear there?" King asked. He wiped his cheek with a handkerchief.

"Longing," I said. I looked at him and then out the window. It was the same question, followed by the same response: what spurred people to need songs, what spurred people to make songs, how overwhelming it was to hear those motivations (the familiar ones, especially) reflected back at us now, in this car, a century after their initial airing, clear through the crackle, all those unchanging human needs. First, it reminded me of something the writer George Saunders once described as a "powerful thing to know: that one's own desires are mappable onto strangers." Then, it reminded me of a piece of paper Nathan Salsburg had shown me, found amid Don Wahle's things: a letter from the collector John Edwards with the words CHIEF WANTS written in all capital letters. Here we were, still wanting. "Longing, yearning, regret, unspecified hunger," I ticked off to the side-view mirror.

"Yeah," he sighed.

Eventually, King would tell me the little he knew about Zoumbas. Through a collector friend, King had found a short promotional biography written in Greek and, after translating it, had enough information to contact a few bureaucratic offices and hunt down some relatives. He was able to piece a narrative together. Or, as he put it: "I have a fairly decent dossier now." Zoumbas was born in 1880 in Epirus, a contentious chunk of land between the Pindus Mountains and the Ionian Sea. In 1913, toward the end of the second Baltic War, during an uprising in his village, he and another man tied stones to "a porcine Turkish landlord named Iakoub" and threw him down a well, killing him. "It's one thing to kill a man, it's another thing to tie him up with fucking stones while he's still alive and throw him down a well," King said. Zoumbas left Epirus and immigrated to the United States in 1914. By 1923, he was accompanying the popular Greek singers Marika Papagkika and Amalia Baka. In the latter part of the 1920s, he recorded several dozen violin solos; those were the records King was interested in. One essential bit of his story was missing, though. Zoumbas had disappeared mysteriously in 1930. "Perhaps he was swallowed up by the same abyss that he threw Iakoub into," King said.

Weeks after our trip to Maryland, when I ran the scarce details of Zoumbas's life back by King for factual confirmation, he explained how the arc had been complicated. "Curiously, what we are certain that we know has become more qualified by unanticipated and perhaps unwelcome ambiguities," he wrote. "There appear to be two narratives associated with Zoumbas . . . a Greek and an American one. Your summary of the Greek narrative is correct. The American narrative, based on a 1930 Census, some passenger lists, a naturalization record and a draft card (???!!!) suggests a slightly different story. The Census gives his birth year as 1885 but his draft card gives 1883. The Census also gives his naturalization as 1910, not 1914. Both of these [discrepancies] can simply be explained as Zoumbas giving incorrect information to both appear younger (which I admire) but also to mess up the system if he indeed committed a crime," he continued. "Perhaps the most curious US document is a passenger manifest from July of 1928. According to this list, Zoumbas sailed back to Greece in February of 1928. This would have been very expensive for an immigrant musician but also extremely risky if his killing of Iakoub was still regarded as murder."

King was about to travel to Corfu and Ioannina in northern Greece, near the Albanian border, with his family in tow. He was anxious to resolve all biographical incongruities in advance of the new set's release. He'd been making appointments, doing the legwork. "All of these additional narrative details will be reconciled (or not!) . . . I've arranged meetings with some relations as well as the local historian," he said.

Before King left for Europe, I received a package in the mail containing a vinyl test pressing of *Five Days Married & Other Laments* and another CD-R in a clear plastic case. There was a blue index card Scotch-taped to the front of it. King had used his Remington to type me a short note: "Amanda, which one of these pulls at the human thread

more?" The CD contained two of Zoumbas's most mournful performances, "Lament from Epirus" and "Albanian Nightingale." Both tracks
were unlistenable to me after a while, containing, as they did, a kind of
unfathomable sadness. Although Zoumbas recorded many 78s in his
lifetime, working often as a backing musician, these two sounded like
someone being turned inside out, with every single one of his organs
suddenly exposed to cold air. "They're completely unlike anything else
he ever did," King said when I called him that night. I don't know if
Zoumbas had been splayed by guilt, or just further subsumed by whatever led him to commit murder in the first place. It all sounded so
human, sourced from some dark recess of the soul. I thought of Shake-
speare: "The fault, dear Brutus, is not in our stars / But in ourselves."

And I understood, for a moment, what collectors meant when they
moaned about what was lacking in contemporary music: that pure communion, that unself-consciousness, that sense that art could still save
us, absolve us of our sins. We know better than to expect that now.

○

King preferred to consume a special kind of chicory coffee roasted and
ground by hand in Louisiana, but on this trip, a Dunkin' Donuts iteration, acquired at a gas-station annex, was going to have to suffice. While
we waited at the counter, I offered to pay for his cup. It seemed like a
small gesture, given the morning's circumstances. "Okay," King agreed.
"Because I only have five thousand dollars in hundred-dollar bills."
King had his sights on a couple of Bussard's rare Cajun records. He was
"actively lusting"—his words—after two upgrades: Dennis McGee and
Sady Courville's "Mon Chere Bebe Creole," Vocalion 5319, and Blind
Uncle Gaspard and Delma Lachney's "La Danseuse," Vocalion 5303.
King had them both in E-minus condition. Bussard had them in E-plus.

After a couple hours on the road, we were finally approaching Bussard's suburban neighborhood. It was my job to call and see if he would
concede to answering the door. Despite years of reporting, I still find
making ordinary phone calls harrowing if not full-on terrifying, and

knowing that the recipient might be unwilling was only aggravating my latent dread. I dialed, frowning at King. Bussard answered with an earsplitting hello. I stammered some kind of introduction. His voice crinkled and shifted, like a sheet of newsprint being balled up and then smoothed out. I'd been warned he was a loud speaker, and I held the phone a few inches away from my ear. I laughed a lot, at nothing, and kept thanking him for having us; this seemed like a better approach than actually asking him if we could still come over. He eventually conceded. I think what he said was: "Come get me and buy me lunch."

King had filled me in on the lunch routine. Bussard frequented a diner called the Barbara Fritchie. (It was named after a local Civil War heroine who, at age ninety-five, purportedly ran into the street and waved a Union flag at Stonewall Jackson's men in an effort to distract or reroute them; it is likely an apocryphal tale, although that seems to bother no one.) He often insisted his visitors drive him there for a meal before he let them into his basement. At this point, he'd been eating at the Barbara Fritchie for over thirty years, sometimes three times a day. King had escorted him many times. "I would suggest the 'Wedge' as it is likely the healthiest item there and it is loam green," King said of the menu. "I don't really recommend it," he added. "I just suggest it."

We pulled off the highway and into Frederick, a midsize, mostly working-class city frequented by Civil War buffs. (In addition to the Fritchie mythology, Abraham Lincoln delivered a speech there, on his way to see General George McClellan following the Battle of Antietam; there is also a Museum of Civil War Medicine and a cornucopia of brass plaques commemorating war-related events.) Bussard's brick house, which he shares with his daughter and grandchildren, is on a quiet residential block. He came loping outside as soon as the Volkswagen eased into the driveway. He was tall and gray-haired, and so thin that he bent a bit in the middle, like a stalk of wheat waving in the breeze. That morning, his hair was sticking every which way. A gold medallion hung from a thick rope chain around his neck, visible in flashes at the collar of his plaid flannel shirt. I climbed out and shook his hand, and then immediately crawled into the backseat. That was the pose I instinctively assumed: a kind of weird, nervous deference.

I'd heard a lot about Bussard's collection, which consisted of around twenty-five thousand country, blues, Cajun, jazz, and gospel 78s, nearly all from the 1920s and '30s, impeccably and mysteriously filed on floor-to-ceiling shelves in an order Bussard knew but wasn't sharing. ("Oh, it's in my head," is all he'd say about it.) Between 1956 and 1970, Bussard operated a record label called Fonotone out of his basement, possibly the last 78 label to ever exist. He recorded new material and old-time songs using a fifty-dollar ribbon microphone slung over a pipe and a cutting machine he bought for thirty dollars from a local college. In the decades since its dissolution, Fonotone has earned its own cult following, and in 2005, Dust-to-Digital issued a boxed set containing five CDs of the label's material, housed in a cardboard cigar box and packaged with a nickel-plated bottle opener imprinted with the Fonotone logo.

Besides Bussard's clout as an eccentric—a surefire cred booster—Fonotone is significant because it was the first label to release the guitar work of John Fahey. In 1959, a then-eighteen-year-old Fahey made his way to Bussard's basement to tape a few things from Bussard's collection, and, like many of Bussard's visitors, he ended up recording a track for Fonotone. Bussard dubbed Fahey "Blind Thomas" and listed his work as "Negro blues" in the Fonotone catalog despite Fahey being a young, white college student from nearby Takoma Park. Fahey would repeatedly trot this joke out over the ensuing decade—it was, of course, the origin of his whole Blind Joe Death routine. On "Blind Thomas Blues," itself now a coveted 78, Fahey plays guitar and sings in a put-on "blues voice" that at first seems offensive in a head-cocked, are-you-serious way, but is actually pretty hilarious: "I make erry'body feel bad when I come around, haha!" he barks, a mantra I suspect many collectors are tempted to adopt as their own. Somehow, Fahey and Bussard had distilled the authenticity scramble that would become a defining neurosis for young Americans a half century later, and lampooned it just as quickly.

Today Bussard was recovering from a cold, which made his voice even gnarlier—preburnished, as it was, from decades of smoking two-dollar cigars in a minimally ventilated basement. Although he could be very sweet, he was prone to griping, especially when he was hungry. During the five-minute voyage to the Barbara Fritchie, he hollered about King's driving, President Obama, liberals, liberal media ("Of course, you listen to liberal channels, you're not gonna get the news—gotta go to Fox, the only one, the only one you're gonna hear the truth on. Don't believe me? Watch it one night, you'll never go back to the others!"), and the various physical ailments plaguing his body, including the bug he'd apparently picked up from one of his grandchildren.

The outpouring of dissatisfaction didn't slow down after we arrived at the restaurant, which was recognizable by its turquoise roof and the fifty-foot candy cane in the parking lot, on display year-round. Bussard liked the Barbara Fritchie in part because there was no canned music pumped in, so he didn't have to manage his boundless ire for modern songs. The three of us sat in a vinyl booth near the back and ordered promptly. Bussard requested a cup of coffee drawn from "a fresh pot." He and King caught up a bit on collector gossip—who was getting what, and from where. Then our eggs arrived.

"Oh, no, no, no, no," Bussard shouted. "Somebody screwed up them eggs! No way. *No* way. I don't want these damn eggs, I ain't eating, no, no, no."

Our waitress, a gentle-eyed woman in her mid-twenties, jogged over. "What's the matter, hon?" she asked.

"Tell Carlos to fix my eggs for me."

"He's the one on the grill right now. How do you like them?"

"Every morning I come in here, he fixes 'em, don't have any problem. I ain't gonna eat these things. I want 'em wet."

"You don't want them cooked all the way?"

"You oughta know that," he snapped. She picked up the plate, apologized, and assured him his breakfast would be prepared just how he liked it. Her ponytail bounced in place on her way back into the kitchen. I squirmed a little, shot the ponytail a sympathetic look. King, for his part, gracefully attempted to change the subject, first talking about his daughter and then about the collector Ron Brown. Bussard didn't want to hear any of that. He had grievances to air.

"I couldn't eat eggs like that. Horrible looking. Good God. They're the horriblest-looking scrambled eggs I've seen in my life! God. Those flakes?"

We exchanged nods of solidarity: Horrible eggs! Unconscionable eggs! Finally, hoping to deflect further attention from his soured breakfast, I asked Bussard about his adolescence: how he got into records, and what he had done, or would do, to get more of them.

Bussard's family had money, so steady employment was never a pressing concern. He began collecting as a kid (birds' nests were his first obsession) and became interested in music via Gene Autry, whom he still calls his favorite singer. Once he was gripped by the call of 78s—and it was a Jimmie Rodgers record that finally sealed it—Bussard spent much of the 1950s and '60s, from the moment he got his driver's license on, combing southwest Virginia and the surrounding coal country for 78s. It's a region that can feel culturally and geographically impenetrable, as insular as it is beautiful, but Bussard barged through anyway, knocking on doors and holding up a 78 to whomever answered, asking if there was anything that looked like that in the attic, and could he have a little peek, and what about five dollars for the whole stack? It was boots-on-the-ground grunt work, pointedly removed from the estate-sale lurking most contemporary collectors indulge in. "I've been in places, met people you wouldn't even believe," he said.

Bussard sometimes employed his boyish charisma as an acquisitions technique. I realize, given the events just described, that he maybe doesn't sound like much of a charmer, but there was something attractively impish about him—a mischievous, glinting quality that made people do whatever work was necessary to get him to smile and start hooting. "I went to one place down below Stanley, Virginia," he recounted. "Woman who answered said, 'There's been two men here buying a couple months ago, and I didn't like them. I told them I didn't have any. But *you* come on in, love.'" He grinned. "I have the blues in my voice."

Although stock has diminished considerably in the last fifty years, that particular corner of Virginia remains a hotbed for 78 activity, in part because it retains its citizens, and in part because those citizens are typically descendants of farm owners or miners who collected steady paychecks and sometimes had a little extra money for records. This is true, especially, of blues records: find out where African-Americans with a bit of disposable income lived and worked in the late 1920s and early 1930s, and you've got a shot at finding something good. It was what drew King and me to Hillsville, and it's what seeded Bussard's collection. "The best two states are Virginia, West Virginia. Got more records there'n any place," Bussard explained. He could tell just by looking at the exteriors which houses were going to have the best records inside. "Old houses," he said. "I liked the ones with the honeysuckle growin' over the porch. You go up to the door, get a draft of air, you can smell 'em. They oughta make a perfume outta that! Oh my God."

"There's no better smell," King agreed.

"My God, I was always interested in records," Bussard continued. "I went out every chance I got and used all the money I had. It was nothing to go out on a weekend and come back with a thousand records. Unload the car. Come down for a few days."

"It was like that when I was in college," King said, nodding. "You ever been to Princeton, West Virginia? There'd be a flea market every five miles—twenty or thirty tables would be set up, and inevitably somebody would have old records. And if they didn't have old records there, they'd have old records at home, so I'd go to their house."

The waitress redelivered Bussard's eggs—now properly scrambled—and he laughed like a wildman. "Thank you, darlin'!" he boomed. While we ate, King and Bussard exchanged a few more junking yarns, trading grunts of respect and (from Bussard, at least) the occasional dismissive barb. At my prodding, King had started talking about a bunch of dealer stock he once found outside of Louisville, Kentucky. "They were all in thirty-count boxes—everything was in a thirty-count Columbia box. Across the top, it said 'Columbia Records, Stay Away from Heat and Steam,' and right below it, stamped in red ink, was 'December 7, 1934.' They'd stamped the boxes and sealed them up. This guy'd had them in his house for the longest time, unopened. Then he put them in a car in his backyard. Just boxes and boxes and boxes and boxes of Columbia dealer stock, nothing later than December 7, 1934, in a car in the backyard."

Bussard noisily slurped his coffee. "Yeah, there are a few Columbias ain't worth a shit," he grumbled.

These days, Bussard mostly trades with other collectors. "I don't go house to house anymore, I quit that," he said. He did periodically attend estate auctions around Maryland, but only if the auction announcement said there would be old records, and even then, he was typically disappointed, if not fully enraged, by what he encountered. "Went to an auction, drove through the whole town, walk in: LPs," he recalled.

Bussard immediately got into it with the auctioneer. "Oh, I was pissed. I said, 'They're not old records!' I said, 'You don't know what the hell you're talking about.' He got snotty. I got snottier. I said, 'Luring me out here for nothing but a damn bunch of LP records! They're not old!' They heard us all over the whole building. I went outside and he followed me outside and said, 'Don't come in here.' I said, 'With a dumbass like you, I don't wanna come in there,'" Bussard spat. "I know I shouldn't have done it, but I don't care. When you get my age you don't give a damn anymore. The hell with it, you know?"

Bussard was married for nearly half a century to a woman named Esther Bussard, who passed away a few years ago. In 1999, she confessed her feelings about her husband's habit to the writer Eddie Dean, who was reporting a story about Bussard for the *Washington City Paper*. "I've never touched one of his records, or anything in his room, because I respect it—that's his room," she told Dean. "Even though I sometimes feel resentful and bitter, I still respect him for what he has done. He has a fantastic collection, and I realize this because I appreciate music, and I appreciate his saving it for history." It was hard to discern more about Bussard's personal life as it existed beyond his basement. Every story he had seemed to revolve, in one way or another, around his collection. He even met Esther while on the hunt for records. Bussard was on the CB radio airwaves asking around about 78s when he encountered her father, who eventually arranged for an introduction. He knew his daughter enjoyed music.

Like most collectors, Bussard can pinpoint exactly when he believes certain genres began their inevitable descent into mediocrity and, eventually, atrociousness. "Country music was over in 'fifty-five. Last gasp. Bluegrass music died, well, a couple years after. It's crabgrass now. The guys singing now, they just don't have it. Best bluegrass was mid-forties, late forties, early-middle fifties. Jazz was over in 'thirty-three," he rattled off. "They lost that beautiful tone—every band had it, the most beautiful saxophones, clarinets, trombones, they just had a certain sound. I don't know what the hell it was, but after 'thirty-three it was gone." Bussard believed rock 'n' roll was a terrible joke, was incensed by midcentury crooners, and even retained some special vitriol for singers like the 1920s pop-country star Vernon Dalhart, whom he called Vernon Stalefart. "People today are so starved for talent, for music," he seethed. "Hey, listen to this computer crap!"

Eventually, we finished our eggs and coffee and headed back to Bussard's house, his mood now noticeably brighter. He led us inside through the garage, around the kitchen, down a set of stairs, and toward a locked wooden door. The ground level of his home was in a state of mild disarray—two obese cats lounged amid piles and piles of stuff—but the basement was an impeccably appointed oasis, an homage to recorded sound. The walls were lined with memorabilia: record labels and sleeves, photographs, mementos, newspaper articles, advertisements, a signed letter from the astronaut John Glenn ("Dear Mr. Bussard, Thank you for your interest in and thoughtfulness in writing about the flight of the Friendship 7 spacecraft and for enclosing a token of appreciation"). The floor was carpeted, perhaps to preempt an accidental record-cracking should a 78 ever slip from his fingers. A couple school pictures of his granddaughters were Scotch-taped to the wood paneling above his desk. A vintage bar cart was parked in the corner, covered with cassette tapes, papers, and an open box of Honey Maid graham crackers. Nearby, a trash can was overflowing with cassette wrappers. If you call him up, Bussard will make you a tape of almost anything in his collection for a small charge, but he doesn't mess with compact discs. To wit: "CDs are crap!"

Every one of his shelves was festooned with a little cardboard warning, typed in all caps on his Smith-Corona: PLEASE DO NOT TOUCH RECORDS. It had never even occurred to me to try. In his *Washington City Paper* story, Dean wrote that many consider Bussard's collection "the most vital, historically important, privately owned collection of early 20th century American music," and nearly all the collectors I'd spoken to agreed on its import. Bussard had things other people didn't even know they could want. That it was privately owned seemed both vital (Bussard knew exactly what he had and why) and incidental, in part because Bussard was famously generous with allowing producers or fans to make transfers or tapes of his records. In that way, it felt more useful than an archive, where records tended to languish, unplayed. Bussard's collection lived.

Before King and I had finished shrugging off our coats and tossing them onto his couch, Bussard was firing up his turntable and asking me what kind of music I liked.

"She likes sad songs," King said.

Bussard pulled a disc off the shelf and pointed to a chair near a speaker.

Watching Joe Bussard listen to records is a spiritually rousing experience. He often appears incapable of physically restraining himself, as if the melody were a call to arms, an incitement it would be immoral if not impossible to ignore: he has to move. He sticks his tongue out, squeezes his eyes shut, and bounces in his seat, waving his arms around like a weather vane shaking in a windstorm, spinning one way, then another. At times it was as if he could not physically stand how beautiful music was. It set him on fire, animated every cell in his body. He only broke to check on me: did I like it? He didn't wait to find out.

"All that for a quarter!" he shouted.

"What a beautiful tone! Oh my God!"

"It's like they're right *there*! You can hear *everything*!"

We went on like this for a while: Bussard scurrying over to his shelves, putting a record on the turntable, going nuts. He periodically held his hands up midsong, his palms out, like "Stop."

"Listen to this," he'd say. His voice was serious. "It's taking everything." When I tried to make a quick note in my notebook, he swatted at my hand with a record sleeve, imploring me to pay better attention. To be held in rapture.

A couple hours passed in a haze of playback. Then, during a brief break in his set, Bussard erupted into his most famous junking story, a tale he clearly relished recounting, even now. It was the one about how he uncovered a stack of fifteen near-mint Black Patti 78s in a trailer park in Tazewell, Virginia, in the summer of 1966. This was what I'd come—what everyone comes—to hear.

After J. Mayo Williams left Paramount Records in 1927, he started a Chicago-based race imprint called Black Patti, named after the African-American soprano Matilda Sissieretta Joyner Jones, who'd earned the nickname because of her (supposed) similarity to the Italian opera singer Adelina Patti. The Black Patti label was festooned with a big, preening peacock, printed in muted gold ink on dark purple paper. (According to 78 *Quarterly*, the late collector Jake Schneider once described it as "the world's sexiest label.") The Black Patti catalog—a total of fifty-five discs—included jazz songs, blues, religious sermons, spirituals, and hokey, vaudeville-style skits; it was designed to compete with (and, hopefully, outsell) Paramount's race series. The performances were recorded at several different studios, then pressed into shellac and shipped from the Gennett Records plant in Richmond, Indiana. Black Patti lasted about seven months. Not much is known about why the label collapsed, although it likely proved financially unsustainable for Williams and his two partners (Dr. Edward Jenner Barrett, the son-in-law of Paramount cofounder Fred Dennett, and Fred Gennett, a manager of Gennett Records), who unceremoniously shrugged the whole enterprise off in September of 1927. According to Rick Kennedy, the author of *Jelly Roll, Bix, and Hoagy: Gennett Studios and the Birth of Recorded Jazz*, it was Gennett who ultimately yanked the plug.

Now Black Pattis are wildly desired things, having been pressed in deliciously small quantities of one hundred or fewer each and sold in just a handful of stores in Chicago and throughout the South. After I told King I'd spent a few weeks trying to track down sales or distribution records to no avail, he tried but failed to suppress a guffaw: "They didn't keep ledgers for this material," he said. With a few exceptions, there are less than five extant copies of each Black Patti release, and some have never been found. In 2000, Pete Whelan dedicated an entire issue of *78 Quarterly* to the Black Patti: its cover features a dark, nearly indiscernible figure with gold eyes emerging from the shadows and holding two Black Patti labels where her breasts would be. The tagline reads: "The most seductive feature ever!"

Although I'm not sure I find them quite so arousing, Black Pattis are certainly mysterious (that same issue of *78 Quarterly* describes them as "historic, bizarre, and idealistic"). Most of the artists Williams recruited are now ciphers, with names like Steamboat Joe & His Laffen' Clarinet or Tapp Ferman and His Banjo. A pipe organist named—confusingly—Ralph Waldo Emerson recorded five sides for Williams in 1927. Stylistically, the label was something of a mixed bag, but for collectors, its pull is unnerving.

In the summer of '66, Bussard was on the road, running his usual

Appalachian route in a Scout pickup. He thinks he must've had a buddy with him, but that bit of the legend is incidental, at least as far as Bussard is concerned. He got lost looking for a flea market. That sort of thing happened to him a lot. "So old dummy, old dumbass, I s'pose I made a right turn instead of a left turn," he explained. There was a pause. "Best left turn I ever made."

Bussard was getting into the story now, his blue eyes flashing like two synchronized traffic lights. "So I got down the road about a mile and thought, There's no flea market down here. There's an old man walking up the road, and so I ask him, and he says, 'Yeah, it's up there up the road.' I said, 'You goin' up? Hop in!' And I had a tape playing, some strange stuff. He says, 'You getting that on the radio?' I said, 'No, it's a tape.' He said, 'That figures,' because, you know, he knew damn well there wasn't anything on the radio any good. And we went up there and walked around and I didn't find anything, of course. Then I told him what I was looking for." Bussard was doing all the voices now: his, the old man's. " 'I got a gang of them back at the house.' "

Bussard drove the man the twenty-five miles or so to his house, a little shotgun shack behind a trailer park. "Sloppiest-looking place you'd ever seen—looked like a flood had hit it. And we went into this shack, and he goes down a hall, turns left, pulls a box out from under the bed," he continued. Bussard felt that familiar churn of anticipation in his gut, but he knew deals like this could curdle quickly. The records might be garbage, or the man might decide at the last minute—when confronted with a stranger's barely contained eagerness—that he didn't want to sell after all.

"[The box] had so much dust on it—like snow, like a blizzard." Bussard leaned in and mimed blowing the dust off the surface. His cheeks puffed up and deflated, like a cartoon's. Bussard's whole life would be changed—nearly defined—by the next five minutes, but he didn't know that yet. "First record I hit was an Uncle Dave Macon. Average. Carter Family. Charlie Poole. And then the first Black Patti. I went down a little further. Three more! Phew! Finally I got to the bottom of the box, and there were fifteen of 'em. I said, 'Where'd you get these records from?' He said, 'Oh, some guy gave them to my sister in 1927, we didn't like 'em so we put 'em in the box under the bed.' I said, 'What do you want for them?' and he said, 'Ten dollars.' And I said, 'Ten dollars.'"

Bussard paid the man and booked it to his truck. Almost immediately after he got back to Frederick, word got out about his find and offers started accumulating. First, Bussard said, was the collector Bernie Klatzko, who drove down from New York City and offered him $10,000 for Black Patti 8030, "Original Stack O'Lee Blues," performed by Long Cleve Reed and Little Harvey Hull, the Down Home Boys. Although some Black Patti masters were also issued by other labels, like Champion or Gennett, and often with the performer using a different name, "Original Stack O'Lee Blues" was released by Black Patti exclusively. And in 1966, Bussard's was the only known copy in the world. "So then after that happened, Don Kent called, he came down, offered me more. I had other offers. Went up to twenty thousand dollars, then twenty five, then thirty, then thirty-five, then up to fifty thousand dollars." Bussard darted over to the shelves. "Don't look at where I keep it!" he said, pulling the record down and trotting back to his desk. He held it out to me in a way that suggested, "Take a nice long look, drink it in, but don't you dare touch." A mammoth grin spread across his face.

After Bussard felt I'd been sufficiently wowed by the sight of it, he pulled the 78 from its paper sleeve, laid it on his turntable, and wiped the surface with a record-cleaning brush that resembled a blackboard eraser. Although Bussard repeatedly told me his was, in fact, still the only surviving copy of "Original Stack O'Lee Blues" on earth, King later whispered that he'd heard another had been uncovered and was in the possession of an unnamed collector in California.

All anyone knows about Black Patti 8030 is that this particular performance was recorded in a Chicago studio in May 1927. The song itself (also known as "Stagger Lee," "Stagolee," "Stack-A-Lee," and other phonetically similar variants) is a tremendously popular, oft-adapted American murder ballad, first published in 1911—after the folklorist

John Lomax acquired a partial transcription from a Texas woman, and the historian Howard Odum submitted it to the *Journal of American Folklore*—and first recorded in 1923 by Fred Waring's Pennsylvanians. It was likely written sometime in the very late nineteenth century. "Stack O'Lee" tells the story of the Christmas murder of a twenty-five-year-old levee hand named Billy Lyons, who was shot by a St. Louis pimp named Lee Shelton, who also went by the nickname "Stack" or "Stag." According to Cecil Brown's *Stagolee Shot Billy*, Lee was part of a gang of "exotic pimps" called the Macks who "presented themselves as objects to be observed." They wore specially cut suits made from imported fabric—a nod to Parisian style—and wide-brimmed Stetson hats. The hat was important. As Brown wrote of it, "In that era it was a mark of highest status for blacks, coming to represent black St. Louis itself . . . To hurt a man symbolically, one could do no worse than cut his Stetson." Brown also points out that Freud believed that in dreams, at least, a hat was a symbol of "the genital organ, most frequently the male," and that knocking someone's hat off his head functioned as a kind of proxy castration.

That night, Shelton and Lyons were drinking in the Bill Curtis Saloon, a local bar and meetinghouse owned and operated by its namesake. It was also the default headquarters of the Four Hundred Club, a social and political organization composed of influential black men; Shelton was its captain. An 1896 story in the *St. Louis Globe-Democrat* described Curtis and his operation like this: "Though the Morgue and the City Hospital are regularly supplied with subjects from his headquarters, his popularity never declines, for it is generally conceded that he is acting as a public benefactor in allowing undesirable members of colored society to be dispatched in his place of business."

Shelton and Lyons were seated at the bar, imbibing, exchanging thoughts. They were colleagues of sorts, if not necessarily pals. The conversation shifted, as it sometimes does, to a contentious topic—politics, maybe—and to augment or possibly accelerate the skirmish, Lyons decided to swipe Shelton's prized Stetson from his head. Just reached up and swatted it off. It was a power move: childish but hu-miliating, nearly inconceivable in its hubris. Shelton demanded its re-turn. There is no transcription of this exchange, but I imagine it was heavy. Lyons wouldn't give it up. So Shelton whipped out his revolver, unloaded a few bullets into Lyons's stomach, and—rather coolly, and with no outward indication of distress—reached down to collect and reposition his hat. Then he strolled out.

Lyons ultimately died from the wound, and Shelton was tried, con-victed, and jailed in 1897. (Curiously, he was pardoned and released in 1909, but was reincarcerated just two years later for robbery and assault, and died in prison, reportedly of tuberculosis.) There is a Tarantino-esque brutality to the story, which has to do with pride, vengefulness, and retribution, and all the accompanying lines in the sand, and if you were to maybe drink a whiskey and think about it for a bit, you know, what else was Shelton gonna do? Play keep-away with a petulant twenty-five-year-old? In his home bar, with his peers looking on? The narrative was swiftly adapted as a folk song, and, as with almost any story, the details change depending on who's telling it. Woody Guthrie, Bob Dylan, and the Grateful Dead have all recorded notable takes; the Dead's is set in 1940 and told from the point of view of Billy Lyons's girl, Delia, who hunted down Stagger Lee on the night of Lyons's murder and "shot him in the balls." Beck's 1996 single "Devil's Haircut" was also an adapted version of the myth: "I had this idea to write a song based on the Stagger Lee myth. The chorus is like a blues lyric. You can imagine it being sung to a country-blues guitar riff," he told *Rolling Stone*'s Mark Kemp in 1997.

There is nothing particularly interesting, from a contextual stand-point, about "Original Stack O'Lee Blues"—it's just another take on a song everyone was already singing, performed by two people who don't appear to have had much of a commercial career beyond it, al-though they did record a few other songs for Gennett, likely in the same session. Bussard's interest in it was partially because of its scar-city, but had more (according to him, at least) to do with its aesthetic superiority. He thinks everything about it is perfect. King doesn't quite agree, although he acknowledges the enduring lure of a Black Patti. "I don't think that the label's cachet has diminished too much in the last twenty or thirty years," he told me later. "Probably the only thing that has diminished are those collectors willing to shell out obscene money just for a rare-label disc that may or may not have much musical interest or power."

Bussard spent a few minutes making sure he had the needle he wanted, and then lowered it onto the record. His face went slack. He winced. His shoulders started scrunching up and down. It is, indeed, a lovely performance—particularly when Reed and Hull lean in to harmonize on the chorus, their voices entangled in just the right way. There is something sweet and melancholy in the guitar, a sense that violence is sometimes inevitable, that Billy Lyons and Lee Shelton were destined to destroy each other, like lovers or enemies, like we sometimes do. As soon as it was over, I thanked Bussard for playing it for me, and I meant it. He was still riled up, shaking his head back and forth.

It was getting late, and I could tell King was ready to get back on the road. He didn't like driving at night. He started rolling a cigarette. Bussard, who had finally quit smoking a few years back, turned to me. "We gotta get him off that shit."

"You wanna hold him down and I'll steal the tobacco?" I offered.

"For a certain record I'd do it," King said. "I'd quit." Bussard guffawed. He knew what King wanted—those Cajun upgrades. There was something else, too. While Bussard had been pulling records, King had spotted a file copy of the accordionist Angelas LeJeune's "Perrodin Two Step" / "Valse de la Louisiane," and now he didn't want to leave without it. For most collectors, spotting a record you need is not unlike getting your hands on someone who means a tremendous amount to you, pressing your face into their neck, and letting whatever incalculable combination of pheromones and memory do its thing on you: that first inhalation, that impossible relief. It's an overwhelming, unshakable feeling of need. Still, King kept his cool, as he does. He is a patient, thoughtful negotiator, unafraid of waiting it out, always capable of managing his pining. (Externally, at least.)

Bussard now owned so many rare records that he had become nearly impossible to trade with. Anything you might think to offer him he probably already had, so the game was mostly in upgrades these days. He had told us earlier that he was looking to bump his copy of Frank Hutchison's "K.C. Blues" to at least an E-plus. "Yeah, some son of a bitch had to strip that," he said, holding out the record and pointing to damage imparted by a Victrola and its weighty tone arm. "Damn windup."

Frank Hutchison was a white guitar player and West Virginia coal miner who recorded forty-one sides for Okeh Records between 1926 and 1929 (Bussard's sweet spot, chronologically speaking); his spritely, harmonica-bolstered version of "Stackalee," which sees Billy Lyons begging for mercy, was included on the *Anthology*. Hutchison died in 1945 from complications likely due to alcoholism. King owned "K.C. Blues"—an instrumental guitar rag with a memorable spoken interlude, during which Hutchison declares he's "just getting right on good red liquor"—but his copy wasn't in any better shape.

"I don't think there's a clean copy of this, Joe," King said.

"Somewhere!" Bussard howled.

King was going to have to try cash for the LeJeune.

"I don't want to get rid of it unless you got a lot of bucks you wanna throw away," Bussard said.

"I only brought a lot of bucks to throw away."

"I'm thinking."

King opened up his wallet and pulled out a little piece of worn-out white paper. He slowly unfolded it. "Last time I visited you, and you let me actually go through your Cajun records—this was the list of them. You didn't let me know you had the LeJeune. You didn't tell me you had the LeJeune or it would have been on that list. And as you can see, right here, I have this one and I have this one, but I don't have the one you have," he said, holding up the paper. "So you're breaking my heart."

"Well," Bussard said. He went back to his shelves and started pulling down more 78s to play for us. This went on for a while: Bussard requesting absurd amounts of money, King emitting a string of increasingly exasperated sighs. King finally decided to let it go for today. He'd call Bussard in a few days and try to work something reasonable out. (His plan would succeed: a few months later, King would get the record for the price he wanted. "Visited Joe today and picked up the file copy of the LeJeune, which I will send an image of via WeTransfer," he e-mailed. "I Am Happy Now.") Tonight, though, we had to get back to Virginia.

Leaving Joe Bussard's basement is about as hard as getting in. It's possible there is nothing Bussard likes more than playing music for people. Since 1956, when he started a pirate station out of his home, he's been an avid radio producer; he presently cohosts a show called *Country Classics*, which airs every Friday night on Atlanta's WREK. As we were putting our coats on, he grabbed an acoustic guitar, laid it across his lap, and started playing a blues riff using a screwdriver as a slide. Then he began telling me about the various phonographs set up around his basement. Then he ran over to a filing cabinet, opened a drawer, pulled out a maroon-and-gold-patterned tie, and told me it was the tie Hank Williams was wearing the day he died. "The undertaker took the knot out of it," he said. "Hank never unknotted a tie. He'd just throw it away. He only wore 'em once." I got the sense that one could stay in Bussard's basement for days and miraculous things would never stop happening. But it was late and starting to snow. King and I said our good-byes and thank-yous and retreated to the Volkswagen.

The drive back was menacing: the snow gave way to rain, which gave way to sticky clumps of ice, which fused to the pavement. We stopped for Indian food in Harrisonburg and debriefed. King thought Bussard was overinflating the price of the LeJeune for my benefit (and he was right), but he agreed that I'd gotten a fairly authentic basement experience: a bit of sass, a bit of playfulness, access to a whole lot of priceless records. We spent the rest of the drive to Afton talking about love and death in song, in part because it seemed like we might not actually make it back up and down the mountain, given the deteriorating weather conditions. When we finally got back to my car, it took fifteen minutes of scraping to clear the ice from its windshield, which did not portend particularly well for the state of the road, no longer visible through the ever-prodigal fog.

King and I exchanged ominous farewells and white-knuckled it out of the parking lot. It was a slow and terrifying drive back to Barboursville. Bret's parents greeted me with a cup of bourbon, which I consumed in one desperate gulp. When I finally checked my phone, there was a new e-mail from King. He'd made it home. No new records, but at least he was alive. It was something.

Fourteen

An Obsessive Need for Things to Stay the Same and an Immersion in Arcane Knowledge

○

Sarah Bryan, "Skokiaan," Girls, OCD, David Linden,
Autism, the Pleasure Circuit, Neurobiology,
"Pleasure Is Replaced by Desire; Liking Becomes Wanting"

○

Sarah Bryan and I admired the coral-red armpits of the three-inch African stick bug cowering in her small, outstretched palm. I am not a bug person, exactly, but this particular creature possessed uncommon corporeal charms—chief among them that it looked more like a stick than an insect, and I like sticks just fine. It spoke to Bryan's intuitiveness—and, perhaps, her mercy—that she didn't attempt to cajole me into cradling it; these were her stick bugs and I was an interloper with a notebook and a hotel pen, ill equipped to contain or embrace such things. The bug remained motionless in her hand. I wondered, for a moment, if it was gearing up to lunge at my face. Bryan looked at me with pity and laughed. The stick bug was lowered back into its habitat and we retreated to the kitchen, filled our plates with cold salads and fresh fruit, and settled on her living room couch to talk.

Bryan, who edits a bimonthly music magazine called the *Old-Time Herald*—a lively and vital read for collectors and fans of old-time music—is a vegetarian and an animal enthusiast, and, in addition to the aforementioned terrarium, her Durham, North Carolina, home contained two sweet calico cats, a big yellow dog, and an aging parrot. It also contained shelves and shelves of 78s culled by Bryan and her husband, Peter Honig, who had invited me over on a balmy spring night. I was so riled up about hearing some of their records—I'd already spotted a Charley Patton 78 hanging on the wall over their Victrola—that I could barely keep my hands still through supper.

I'd spent most of the day in the archives of the Southern Folklife Collection at the University of North Carolina at Chapel Hill, where a patient young archivist named Aaron Smithers had played me a stack of Blind Blake 78s—all Paramount pressings—in the archive's cool, dark recording studio while I made goony faces, scribbled notes ("Holy shit!") in my notebook, and tried my best not to think about what Chris King and I had lost at Hillsville. In 1983, the university had acquired the John Edwards Collection, an assemblage of around ten thousand vernacular 78s culled by the Australian-born collector John Edwards, who died in California in 1958. Edwards's good pal and contemporary, the collector Eugene Earle, managed the donation of his records first to UCLA and then, twenty-one years later, to the University of North Carolina, after it was determined that the materials would be "more effective" if housed in the region where this music was born. (Earle eventually handed over his own collection of nearly eighty thousand 78s, 45s, LPs, and transcription discs to the SFC, too.)

Blues scholars had long assumed Blind Blake was a native of Jacksonville, Florida, per the address erroneously given by Paramount, but in late 2011, after his death certificate was dug up and published by a team of collectors and researchers (Alex van der Tuuk, Bob Eagle, Rob Ford, Eric LeBlanc, and Angela Mack), it was revealed that he was actually born six hundred miles north in Newport News, Virginia, and had died in Milwaukee, Wisconsin, in 1934, of pulmonary tuberculosis. Either way, Chapel Hill did seem like a more appropriate depository for Blake's music, which was pivotal in the development of the Piedmont blues in the late 1920s, a regional guitar style named after the Piedmont plateau (the chunk of land between the Atlantic Ocean and the Appalachian Mountains, stretching, roughly, from Richmond to Atlanta) and marked by a complex fingerpicking style that mimics the loping syncopation of ragtime. There's a lightness to Piedmont blues that I've always eschewed in favor of the Delta's rougher, more disreputable tone, but there's something irresistible about Blake's soothing, dignified croon, the way his fingers skip over his guitar strings, the giddiness of the entire enterprise. Even when Blake sings about trouble ("When you see me sleeping, baby, don't you think I'm drunk / I got one eye on my pistol, and the other on your trunk," he promises in "Early Morning Blues"), he sounds playful, almost mischievous.

Despite most collectors' contentious relationship with academia and with archives in particular, many still posthumously bequeath their records to institutions rather than burdening their already strained estates with thousands of pounds of shellac. The Southern Folklife Collection's curator, Steve Weiss, estimated that nearly 95 percent of the SFC's holdings were sourced from private collections and not from other archival or commercial institutions. Interestingly, Weiss was grateful for collectors' contributions, and not just to the archive he oversees but to the broader notion of folklore as a viable academic pursuit—a field that didn't really blossom until the 1950s and '60s. "At the time, there really wasn't serious academic study of vernacular music," he explained. "And I think one of the things collectors did is they brought a lot of (a) interest, and (b) legitimacy to the serious study of this work. They really have preserved the music, and they've promoted the music, too. They are archivists in their own way," he said. "Maybe even more so than some professional archivists." While there was sometimes tension between collectors and academics, there was symbiosis, too.

Back at Bryan's house, I babbled to her and Honig about the university's blues holdings and everything I'd seen and heard that day. Bryan, who has long, wavy brown hair and pink cheeks, listened sympathetically. I asked her if she remembered the first time she ever heard a 78. "I remember vividly," she replied. "Peter and I were friends at the time. I was living in northern Virginia and he was living in Charlottesville. I went down to visit him with a mutual friend. I was already into the music—playing it and listening to reissues—but Peter knew that I had never heard a 78 before. He picked one up that he knew I would like, which was 'The NuGrape Song,' a twenties advertising jingle from the Royal Crown Cola Company. When I came in, he immediately put it on. I was so distracted by the fun of hearing it I didn't think that much about the tone of the record at first. And then he put on another record he knew I loved, which was 'Diamond Joe' by the Cofer Brothers, a rough Georgia string band from the twenties. And for that one, I had settled down enough to listen, and I was just totally knocked out by the intimacy of the sound. I had listened to LPs a lot, so it wasn't like I only knew digital music. But just hearing it through wood and metal and the little sheaf of mica . . ." She smiled. "It was really like they were there. I still have a visual image of sitting in Peter's living room and envisioning the Cofer Brothers in the next room. It was that much of an impression." Honig—a man of medium build, with brown hair he combs to the side—beamed and sat up a little straighter in his chair.

While we ate, Bryan and Honig played me selected sides by Uncle Dave Macon, Peg Leg Howell and His Gang, and the Roane County Ramblers. They alternated choosing records, grinning knowingly at each other's selections. (Early on in their relationship, Honig bought Bryan an antique Victrola and stuffed its drawers with records he thought she'd love, which is just about the most romantic gesture I can think of for a pair of courting record nerds.) While a Washington Phillips record played, I bit into a sugar cookie and let Bryan's square-faced cat rub its head on my ear from the top of the couch cushion. I was high on records—on all of it—and prepared to stick my toothbrush in the holder above the sink and stay for as long as they'd let me.

Bryan, maybe sensing I was ready, pulled down one of her favorite pieces: a Zulu drinking tune called "Skokiaan," performed by the Bulawayo Sweet Rhythms Band. She had scored the record at a flea market outside Richmond eight or nine years earlier, buying it from a dealer she and Peter had known for a while—"a very old man named Pop," she explained. "Pop was flipping through his records, because he knew the kinds of records Peter liked, the right kinds of labels. He was putting things aside and saying, 'He'll like this, he won't like this.' And then he came [to 'Skokiaan'] and said, 'I don't know what this is.' Just for the hell of it, I looked at it and I could see from the name that it was African. And he said, 'I'll take a dollar for it.' So I paid a dollar and we brought it home. It's my favorite 78 that I've found."

Skokiaan itself is an illicit African street drink, an occasionally lethal moonshine mixed by so-called Skokiaan Queens who, according to a *Time* magazine brief from 1954, "know how to spike it with enough methyl alcohol to provide the jolt that thrills but does not kill." (In a short review of the song later that year, *Time* loosely translated "Skokiaan" as "happy-happy.") The record was first issued in 1954 by Gallotone, an imprint of the Gallo Record Company, Africa's oldest independent record label. It was written by August Musarugwa, a bandleader from Southern Rhodesia (then a British colony, now Zimbabwe), who recorded it with his band, the African Dance Band of the Cold Storage Commission of Southern Rhodesia, either in the late 1940s or early 1950s. By the time it was released by Gallotone, someone had changed the group's name to the comparably pithy Bulawayo Sweet Rhythms Band. The track reportedly sold an impressive 170,000 copies in South Africa, and eventually Bill Randle, a DJ at Cleveland's WERE, got his hands on a cracked copy that was delivered by a friend, a "pilot on the South African run," according to the September 1954 issue of *Downbeat*. Randle was tickled enough to request a clean disc from the label, which he then played on air four times. Per *Downbeat*,

"The cannonade began. Customers, distributors, retailers all clamored for copies." Shortly thereafter, the British label London—an international partner of Gallotone—released the record in the United States (Bryan's copy is a London pressing, label number 1491). "Skokiaan" was a moderate hit, peaking at number seventeen on the Billboard chart that year. The song inspired a slew of covers, including two somewhat joyless iterations by Louis Armstrong, one instrumental and one with improvised vocals, recorded for Decca in August 1954.

A couple years earlier, the Weavers' rendition of "Wimoweh" had squirmed its way into the Billboard top ten (the original version, "Mbube," was recorded by Solomon Linda and the Evening Birds for Gallo in 1939; Pete Seeger supposedly misheard the Zulu chorus of *uyimbube* as "wimoweh," thus creating its new title), and the Brooklyn-born pop sextet the Tokens landed a number one record with a further adapted version, now called "The Lion Sleeps Tonight," in 1961. But for plenty of American kids, "Skokiaan" was their very first introduction to world music created by non-Americans, and it was revelatory.

Here's a simple truth: if you want to make someone's day, play them "Skokiaan." If they've never heard it before, they will never forget you. Musarugwa's wobbly saxophone carries the melody, and its particular tone is unlike anything else I've ever heard. His performance isn't frantic or even drunk—it's sweet and effortlessly joyful, a slipped guffaw, a good, long laugh. It's one of the most human sounds ever committed to record.

Bryan told me it took her a while before she could listen to it without crying.

Although I continued to stubbornly insist that they were out there, silently compiling killer collections, Sarah Bryan was the only female 78 collector I'd managed to locate and meet. I knew there was at least one other—in 2010, a woman named Sherry Mayrent donated her collection of nearly seven thousand Yiddish and Hebrew 78s to the University of

Wisconsin–Madison's Mills Music Library—but record collecting in general is a predominantly male enterprise, and 78 collecting almost exclusively so. Nearly every time I asked a collector if they knew of any women in the game, they squinted and said something vague. Someone, somewhere, maybe. I don't know.

Collecting anything requires a singularity of focus, but 78 collecting demands an almost-inhuman level of concentration. There is a violence to the search, a dysfunctional aggression that vacillates between repellent and endearingly quirky. It's intimidating to outsiders, and it feeds on sacrifice. Although many collectors managed to maintain healthy, even thriving relationships, for others, the needs of friends, partners, family members, wives, girlfriends, and associates were consistently ranked below the acquisition of new records. I wondered, sometimes, if women were unable (or just less likely) to make those kinds of choices. This was certainly true in America in the 1940s and '50s, when the first wave of collectors—men like James McKune and Harry Smith—were establishing the rules of the trade and the seeds of world-class collections.

Given my profession, I was already accustomed to being the only girl in the room, but the gender divide in collecting had, like everything else, started to feel personal. There are so many broad, unsatisfying generalizations about gender that get trotted out to explain the different ways men and women experience music fandom: there is the idea that women, temporarily incapacitated by unmanageable waves of passion, are incapable of comprehending how guitars work (it's hard to understand anything through constant tears). And that men, unsettled by deep connections, need to reduce the experience of music to a series of facts and figures—they need to dissect it so they can comprehend it in a practical, physical way, which in turn makes it less frightening. Obviously, these kinds of theories are reductive if not absurd.

Trying to figure out how and why collectors collect—and how that relates, if at all, to their maleness—is a largely thankless pursuit. In most cases, if you ask a 78 collector to explain his motivations, he'll either laugh it off with a self-deprecating remark or deliver a prepared and earnestly rendered speech about how much and how deeply he loves the music. I would say I bought the latter about 50 percent of the time. It didn't help that, among major collectors, there was a nearly universal refusal to acknowledge that any music recorded in the last sixty-plus years was artistically valuable. This was so insane and maddening a contention (and such a preposterous way to be a fan) that I was, on occasion, rendered functionally speechless. I resisted the urge to force Clash or Prince CDs into collectors' closed fists because I knew it would be a dead cause, and because I suspected that their repudiation of contemporary sounds was almost entirely extramusical. The blanket rejection of twelve-bar rock 'n' roll I sorta understood—one could argue, after all, that most rock music was just a watered-down/gussied-up version of the country blues—but I found the rest of it mystifying, particularly collectors' near-unanimous dismissal of hip-hop. I couldn't understand why men so obsessed with weird, sexualized, obtuse music from ninety years ago wouldn't be at least mildly interested in a contemporary analog. Was it just easier to fetishize something that no longer existed and that they couldn't be expected to participate in? I wondered, sometimes, if a hundred years from now, a bunch of older white men wouldn't be gathered in some hotel conference room, beaming each other MP3s of limited-release Lil B mixtapes—or of any kind of modern music that had since passed into a safe stasis, a realm that allowed for distance, voyeurism.

Obviously, my curiosity about gender only led to other, bigger questions about obsession and love and art and race and money and power and the human brain. Both hoarding and collecting are often linked with obsessive-compulsive disorder and, on occasion, its sister condition, obsessive-compulsive personality disorder. The National Institutes of Health defines the difference between the two thusly: "People with OCD have unwanted thoughts, while people with OCPD believe that their thoughts are correct." OCPD occurs more frequently in men than women (OCD is mostly gender neutral), and at least a few of its eight diagnostic criteria (excess devotion to work, inability to throw things away even when the objects have no value, lack of flexibility, lack of generosity, not wanting to allow other people to do things, not willing to show affection, preoccupation with details, rules, and lists) falls neatly into step with the 78 collector archetype—more so than hoarding itself, which was only recently added to the American Psychiatric Association's *Diagnostic and Statistical Manual of Mental Disorders V* (*DSM-V*) as its own diagnosable medical condition and is marked by "the accumulation of possessions that congest and clutter active living areas and substantially compromise their intended use."

Ultimately, an unshakable sense of what belongs and what doesn't is what distinguishes collectors from hoarders; hoarders are often incapable of getting rid of any object that they've knowingly acquired and stored, whereas 78 collectors, at least, are constantly making complex value judgments. In their book *Stuff: Compulsive Hoarding and the Meaning of Things*, Randy O. Frost and Gail Steketee suggest that "distress or impairment" is what "constitutes the boundary between normal collecting and hoarding," which makes both states impossible to define objectively. Elsewhere, the authors are optimistic about what collecting means for the collector, suggesting that the objects in question are actually just awkward conduits for human connection. "Instead of replacing people with possessions, Irene was using possessions to make connections between people and to the world at large," they wrote of one subject after she gave them a tour of her stuff. ("The advertisement for the tires led to a story about her car, which led to a story about her daughter wanting to drive, and so on.") Although I can see how the collector's drive for historical information could be viewed as a way of making human "connections," I'm not sure I'll ever believe this behavior manifests as anything resembling sociable.

Unlike most OCD patients, OCPD sufferers aren't necessarily bothered by their preoccupations. In this way it's similar to Asperger's syndrome, a high-functioning autism-spectrum disorder that affects more men than women: a ratio as high as ten to one has been cited, and even if that statistic reflects widespread diagnostic problems, it's still striking enough to suggest Asperger's skews definitively male. For *Retromania* author Simon Reynolds and many others, obsessive record collecting appears to mimic symptoms of Asperger's. As Reynolds explains, the disorder "combines difficulty relating to other people with an obsessive need for things to stay the same and an immersion in arcane knowledge."

While I'm hesitant to diagnose anyone with anything—being that my medical training consists mostly of watching reruns of *House* while running on a treadmill at the New York Sports Club—the symptoms did sound awfully familiar, especially the bit about the stockpiling of obscure information. According to the *DSM-IV*, Asperger's is indicated by (among other things) impaired social interaction and repetitive patterns of behavior, including "encompassing preoccupation with one or more stereotyped and restricted patterns of interest that is abnormal either in intensity or focus." But, as with the diagnostic criteria for nearly every psychiatric disorder, and particularly the many that exist on a spectrum, Asperger's is a vague and subjective diagnosis. In fact, the syndrome was removed entirely from the *DSM-V* and bundled with autism instead. Now what was once called Asperger's is just considered a milder form of Autism Spectrum Disorder. A mark on a line.

●

The links to autism and OCPD were compelling, but as far as medically diagnosable conditions go, collecting still seemed, to me, to most closely resemble plain old addiction. Collectors were always desperate for the next hit, and their reliance on the continued acquisition of 78s was often troubling to them, if not fully debilitating.

Intriguingly, if that addiction supposition is true, there's scientific evidence that collectors actually might enjoy music *less* than noncollectors, which would also explain, to some extent, the head-heart paradox and their focus on information as a substitute for (or unnecessary supplement to) the emotional satisfaction of music. The neurobiologist Dr. David J. Linden, a professor of neuroscience at the Johns Hopkins University School of Medicine, outlined the phenomenon in his 2011 book *The Compass of Pleasure*: "Do you, like many, think that drug addicts become drug addicts because they derive greater reward from getting high than others? The biology says no: they actually seem to *want* it more but *like* it less," he writes. "Pleasure is replaced by desire; liking becomes wanting."

As anyone who's ever lusted after something knows, that kind of deep, bone-tingling want can be a potent motivator. Linden recounts an experiment in Montreal in 1953 wherein two neuroscientists accidentally figured out how to stimulate the brain's complex, interconnected reward center by misplacing electrodes originally intended to control sleeping cycles in lab rats. When given the choice of food, water, or pressing a lever that would deliver a brief shock to the implanted electrodes, thus activating the brain's so-called pleasure circuit, the rats consistently chose the latter. (The experiment was later re-created, successfully and unethically, in humans.) "Self-stimulating male rats would ignore a female in heat and would repeatedly cross foot-shock-delivering floor grids to reach the lever," Linden writes. "Female rats would abandon their newborn nursing pups to continually press the lever. Some rats would self-stimulate as often as two thousand times per hour for 24 hours, to the exclusion of all other activities. They had to be unhooked from the apparatus to prevent death by self-starvation. Pressing that lever became their entire world."

We all find different ways to press that lever, and, importantly, to limit its pressing: such is the civilized experience of pleasure. In my drunker, more hedonistic moments, I think that life is long and hard and why shouldn't we press the stupid lever if it makes us happy? Why shouldn't we forgive each other our lever pressing? But the issue is never the payoff itself (although for many addicts, there are clear physical penalties), it's the external consequences: the rat ditching her baby, the addict forsaking his family, the long, hurtful trail of busted relationships and soured promises. We measure the problem of addiction by its fallout. As Linden writes, addiction is nothing more than the persistent pursuit of something in the face of "increasingly negative life consequences." The ramifications, however catastrophic for everyone involved, aren't always potent enough to combat that want.

Some people learn to manage the cost better than others.

After reading and rereading his book, I finally contacted Linden and asked if he'd be willing to talk me through some of the neurological impulses behind the pursuit of pleasure and to discuss how the collector's quest might or might not be biologically ordained. Maybe collectors were just addicted to records—or, moreover, to the acquisition and categorization of records. But I suspected it wasn't quite that simple.

Linden, it turns out, is one of those infuriatingly smart people—bubbling over with ideas that seem premeditated even as they're being extemporaneously rendered—who makes you immediately feel like you need to recomplete your entire education beginning with third-grade science. After I explained my basic questions about gender as it related to collecting and my two-bit observations about the similarities between the archetypal Asperger's patient—as I understood him—and the archetypal 78 collector, Linden immediately brought up the work of Simon Baron-Cohen (a cousin of the comedian and *Borat* star Sacha Baron Cohen), who published, in 2006, a little book called *Pre-Natal Testosterone in Mind*, a groundbreaking and oddly gripping study ("This is a book about a scientific journey," it opens) of how prenatal testosterone affects postnatal development and behavior.

"The astonishing thing was that prenatal testosterone was extremely predictive of how these kids, both males and females, would fall out among a spectrum of behaviors," Linden said. "And what Baron-Cohen believes—and I think it has some validity—is that autism is just extreme maleness. In other words, the kind of differences in cognitive style and personality that you see on average—now, of course, this is broad strokes, obscuring all the tremendous variation amongst individuals—but if you're looking at the average cognitive differences between men and women, men are more object oriented, less person oriented, they hold gaze less, they're less socially intelligent, they're less verbally fluent, they have a reduced ability to generate language quickly," he continued. "There are a number of things you can test. And of course within both male and female populations, there are a lot of variations: there are females that are more malelike and males that are more femalelike, and at the extreme end of maleness, basically, are your Asperger's and autism patients who are not exclusively but overwhelmingly male. And so when I'm hearing about your Asperger's-y collector guy, this is what comes to mind," he finished. "I wonder what their prenatal testosterone was like."

I wondered, too.

I remembered, then, a 2005 op-ed Baron-Cohen had written for the *New York Times* titled "Is Autism an Extreme of the Male Condition?," which had appeared not long after Lawrence Summers, then the president of Harvard University, delivered a controversial speech in which he suggested that women were inherently less suited to careers in science. (He chalked it up to "a different availability of aptitude at the high end.") Baron-Cohen was more diplomatic, but essentially made the same claim, citing a slew of psychological and biological testing: "In my work I have summarized these differences by saying that males on average have a stronger drive to systemize, and females to empathize," he wrote. It seemed possible, then, that the overwhelming maleness of 78 collecting couldn't ever be chalked up to any one social, cultural, or even personal cause. The need to compile and systemize might have been imprinted into the collector's brain long before the OB nurse could squeal, "It's a boy!"

Linden had plenty of other ideas—enough to convince at least one willfully naïve, poetry-reading person that every single humiliating

habit or weird fetish she'd ever secretly indulged was actually a function, in one way or another, of her particular human body. "I don't
mean to say we're all the slaves of our genes and our chemistry," he
said, chuckling. "What it means is that your experience modifies your
brain—it's a two-way street. Your experience in the world changes
your brain, starting in utero and throughout your whole life. That's
what makes your memories, that's what makes you an individual. And
your genetics and your brain's function influence your behavior, your
cognitive processes, your emotions, et cetera," he said. "The substrate
is all biological, even if the origin is sociocultural."

We also talked for a while about the thrill of the chase (of not
knowing when or if or what you'll find, the lure of what's new and
what's next), another common experience of pleasure that Linden believed was dictated, at least in part, by basic biology. "The journey is
the destination. I think that's fundamental," he said. "It's something
that really seems to be deeply true in terms of the biology. In other
words, people have this rational economist's model that randomness is
anxiety-producing. Not knowing is only a negative, and it's only when
we win that we get rewarded. The brain imaging does not seem to be
supporting that notion. It seems to be supporting the notion that to a
certain degree we are hardwired to get a buzz off of uncertainty. And
probably there is genetic variation that some people get more of a buzz
off of uncertainty than others. I don't know if you've talked with compulsive gamblers, but they'll tell you that the winning is the least of it.
It's the action that they crave. And maybe this is in some way analogous
to your collectors, who really enjoy the pursuit."

Beyond the exhilaration of the search, Linden agreed that the collector's insistence on discovery and knowledge—on having enough
information to both locate and then properly contextualize a record—
could also have neurological origins.

"We like a sense of agency," he said. "We like to plan, execute that
plan, and then get information that that plan has succeeded. That's
something that is fundamentally human, and it gets expressed in dif-

ferent ways in different people," he continued. "This is also what makes firearms so attractive. You sight down the barrel, you imagine what's going to happen, you pull the trigger, you hit some targets, you can see that your plan succeeded. Once I asked my father, 'What is it that you like about playing the stock market so much?' And he said, 'I love being right.' When I think about your collector guys who take pride in their knowledge about their collections and go to great lengths to learn about and get a particular disc, I can only imagine this sense of agency is somehow involved in the pleasure they're feeling in the process. My suspicion is that these guys also have very particular ideas about their food and about their living space."

"Yes," I muttered into the telephone. "Yes."

It hadn't previously occurred to me how rightness—in this case, about the aesthetic and cultural worth of this music—could become such a potent narcotic, although I suppose whole wars have been fought over less-quantifiable certainties. Collectors may have been intimidated by contemporary culture (or socially inept, or sartorially challenged, or whatever else), but they were rarely timid about the righteousness of their work. They believed.

That unwavering intensity is the 78 collector's other defining attribute. It certainly accounts for their marginalization and also for their occasional unpleasantness. Linden had convinced me of the neurobiological basis for the collector's behavior, and how those habits might be inherently gendered; I also felt like I had a pretty good handle on the various sociocultural reasons why it could feel good—very good—to indulge these particular wants.

But the more I thought about why, the less I cared. I still don't entirely believe that the collector's work is driven exclusively or even predominantly by appreciation, but on occasion (if I spend enough time listening to Blind Uncle Gaspard in Chris King's music room, say, or if someone plays me "Skokiaan" late at night while simultane-

// Fifteen //

Who Wants to Hear a Story About a Boy Learning Guitar from a Book?

●

Michael Cumella, Jerron Paxton,
Commodification, Whiskey, Brooklyn, the Future

●

East Ville Des Folies is a beer and whiskey festival held at Webster Hall, a nightclub and concert space in the East Village that, in the 1910s and '20s, at least, was noted for its public embrace of hedonism and hip clientele (F. Scott Fitzgerald, Man Ray, and Marcel Duchamp were supposed regulars). These days, though, it's just another mainstream concert venue in a fully gentrified neighborhood in downtown New York City, remarkable only for its cavernous layout and the fact that there is a bathroom attendant.

The festival had a speakeasy vibe, by which I mean the aesthetic was old-timey in the most blanket sense possible. Some attendees were sporting partial costumes: polyester flapper dresses, felt bowler hats. For reasons I could not entirely understand, the live entertainment included burlesque dancers, trapeze artists, and "circus acts." I was there to meet Michael Cumella, who hosts WFMU's Antique Phonograph Music Program and had been hired to stand on a low black stage and DJ 78s from his collection on two windup portable phonographs.

When I arrived and checked in, I was handed a little plastic cup, which I could use to request samples of craft beer or artisan whiskey. Already this seemed like a treacherous way to spend a dark, midwinter afternoon. I weaved through the crowd—the event was sold-out—elbowing toward the stage, stopping midjourney to procure a nip of rye. I introduced myself to Cumella, who was wearing high-waisted pants, a bow tie, and suspenders. He had just finished explaining a phonograph horn to a young woman in velvet platform shoes.

Over the last few years, a seemingly insatiable appetite for bespoke wares had awoken in New York and other American cities, and with it came an attendant fascination for times gone by—a mass enthrallment with the decades before the age of mechanical reproduction, when everything was hand-crafted with, the presumption goes, extraordinary care. Frankly, it was sort of vague, the whole thing. It included vintage taxidermy, Edison bulbs, enamel dishware, pre-Prohibition cocktails, red lipstick, dropped-waist shirtdresses, vests with pocket watches clipped into place, and so on. Cumella had seen it coming: subscribers of the new-old aesthetic would need someone to DJ their weddings and events. Nothing would shatter the mood faster—sour your whiskey sour, even—than an iPod dock and a bunch of tangled-up cables. He called his service "Michael Cumella's Crank-Up Phonograph Experience" and promised it would "thrill your guests' ears and eyes." His calendar was full through the spring.

Since 1995, Cumella's radio show had been a must-stop for 78 collectors visiting New York and a must-listen for fans of early-twentieth-century recordings as played on period-appropriate machines. Most collectors deliberately eschewed the original players because their tone arms—those heavy, monolithic limbs—were too rough on the records, gouging out the grooves, but Cumella was nonchalant about any potential damage. "I'm not that guy, the preservationist guy—I'm the use-it-and-destroy-it guy, I've firmly established myself as that," he said. He liked the synchronicity of it all. In the WFMU studio, Cumella used a Victrola XIV, which was introduced around 1910, an Edison Standard D model phonograph, which sold from 1908 to 1911, and a Victor IV from around the same time ("Why, that is the real thing—you can't tell it from the actual human voice!" early advertisements proclaimed). At East Ville Des Folies, he was attracting a bit of a crowd with his setup. Tipsy onlookers seemed shocked that the machines were "real"—that was the word they used, over and over. "Is this real?"

Cumella was playing jazz-age dance bands. There was a microphone pointed into the horn, and the records were being broadcast over the venue's PA. I watched him work for a while, answering questions, cueing 78s, winding his machines. It was a novelty act, but a novelty whose time appeared to have come. I sipped my small-batch whiskey, leaned against a wall.

●

A few months later, Michael Cumella and I met again in the upstairs café of J&R Music World, a hulking relic of an electronics store in downtown Manhattan, across from City Hall. Open since 1971, J&R used to sell records. Now, walking through the ground floor, I grimaced at a few undertrafficked racks of compact discs, at shelves and shelves of dusty-looking computer accessories. We sat at a table and ordered coffee and sandwiches. Cumella was on his way to Brooklyn, where he was meeting with event coordinators at the new Wythe Hotel in Williamsburg. The hotel, which opened in the spring of 2012, had been instantly popular. All summer long, a horrifyingly long line to access its rooftop bar had twisted outside its front door and around the corner.

It was hard to figure out the fate of 78s in the digital era: whether the technology would be fetishized and protected, what might be lost.

I'd recently encountered a handful of younger collectors in and around New York, including the guitarist Jerron Paxton, who, at twenty-three years old, was the youngest of them all. Paxton and I first met at the Jalopy Theatre and School of Music, a small performance space with an old-time bent on Columbia Street in Red Hook, Brooklyn, a few yards from the glowing yellow entrance to the Brooklyn Battery Tunnel. He was teaching a series of guitar workshops on early blues greats—the afternoon we were introduced, he was concentrating exclusively on the Reverend Gary Davis, a fingerpicking Piedmont blues guitarist from South Carolina—to eager packs of aspiring players (per my survey, mostly bearded white men in flannel shirts). Paxton was wearing slacks, brown leather dress shoes, a white button-down shirt, a gray vest, and a black bowler hat. A short silver chain peeked out of his vest pocket, and he periodically tugged on it and consulted an engraved pocket watch.

Handsome and sweet faced, Paxton was refined in presentation—it was an awful lot of look—but he still grinned and called me a dumb fuck when I mispronounced his first name. He'd brought a portable electric turntable and a small box of 78s to play for me, and after his class was over, we clomped downstairs to the basement workshop, where Jalopy co-owner Geoff Wiley repairs and restores vintage stringed instruments. In the venue's main space, a young woman was teaching the basics of vocal harmony, and bits of early country standards—as performed by a dozen singers in training—drifted down through the floorboards. Amid the handmade instruments and spare parts, Paxton spotted a framed piece of sheet music—for "Colored Aristocracy," an old minstrel tune—and yelped. "Where the fuck did you get that?" he asked Wiley, who only laughed in response.

Paxton performs under the name Blind Boy Paxton, and according to local lore (and his Wikipedia page), he started losing his sight at sixteen. He often squeezed his eyes shut in photographs—an approximation, of sorts, of promotional portraits taken of Blind Lemon Jefferson in the 1920s—although as far as I could tell, he saw well enough to get around without much assistance. This, like many self-produced facts regarding Paxton, had a whiff of tricksterism. He was raised by his Louisiana-born grandparents in the Watts neighborhood of South Central Los Angeles and practices Judaism (there was a yarmulke pinned under his bowler hat). Besides 78 rpm records, he collects sheet music, antique razors, and fountain pens. Paxton was wily—while performing, he would adopt a kind of antebellum accent and often said things like "Seeing as I am a colored gentleman, I must play some blues." He graduated from Marist College in upstate New York and, in a 2008 interview with Eli Smith for *The Down Home Radio Show*, half implied he'd been taught guitar by Blind Blake, whom Paxton also claimed had lived to be 108 years old. (He later admitted it was a joke: "Who wants to hear a story about a boy learning guitar from a book?") I sort of liked Paxton's nonsense—it reminded me, at times, of Fahey's long Blind Joe Death con and of the self-mythologizing executed by folks like Ramblin' Jack Elliott and Bob Dylan. While some of it was surely practiced at the expense of his more earnest fans, it was a welcome respite from the self-seriousness that plagued so much blues scholarship and fandom.

Over and over, in the basement of Jalopy, Paxton played me a record and then refused to tell me the artist or title. He took my digital recorder and placed it on the turntable, though, so that I could capture a clear recording of the song to listen to later on, if I wanted to. I got it—that he thought the only story was the music.

Like Joe Bussard, Paxton had an acute and visceral reaction to his records. He clutched his heart, grinned, and danced in place while they spun. He was particularly seized by 1920s gospel songs and sermons, which were more affordable than prewar blues records. He was annoyed by the way those blues 78s had been monetized. He played me a 78 by Blind Joe Taggart and his wife, Emma; Taggart was a gospel shouter from Chicago who recorded under a couple different names in the late 1920s. "This is a fellow who sang the blues, but [then he] sang a gospel song with his wife, so it's worthless," Paxton said. "Like, what the fuck, fuck you! How does Blind Willie Johnson go for several thousand dollars and I got this for thirty bucks?"

Paxton said he collected 78s so that he could be edified by them—could learn songs, discover how to be a better musician. He wasn't particularly swayed by the notion of collecting as a form of historical preservation. "The hell with my children, I don't care, I want this for me—this is *my* stuff," he said. "To quote the New Testament, as they say in Corinthians: 'When I was a boy I thought as a child and spoke as a child and learned as a child. When I became a man, I put away childish things.' I want to become better! I learn from these things. That's why I collect sheet music—to know that Reverend Gary Davis did not write 'Candy Man,' to know that Blind Blake did not write whatever that song is he gets credit for," he said.

Although he likely wouldn't frame it as such, Paxton was a virtuosic acoustic guitar player. Before a pal e-mailed me a YouTube clip of one of his performances (subject: "He's fucking unbelievable"), I'd never heard a contemporary musician play the country blues with quite as much fervor or skill. That, coupled with his affectations, made for an engrossing, almost overwhelming display, and I was reminded again of the half-drunk East Ville Des Folies patrons lurching toward Cumella and his windup phonograph: "Is that real?"

●

Back at J&R Music World, Cumella and I were discussing the Tex Avery cartoon "SH-H-H-H-H-H . . . ," which features a scene soundtracked by the Okeh Laughing Record. "What a weird record, I remember thinking," Cumella said. "Where did that come from?" Cumella, now fifty, started buying records at yard sales and eventually began working as a DJ, first using LPs and 45s. "I had some interest in the pop music of my youth, but then I was thinking about earlier pop," he said. "Schmaltzy fifties stuff, then the hits of the forties, big-band stuff—Glenn Miller, Artie Shaw, those people. Then I wanted to go further back, to the thirties, but there wasn't much reissued. And where were the twenties compilations?"

He bought a Victrola, and his interest in early music developed alongside an interest in the early players. "I took it home, started playing records with it. I didn't know anything about it. I had to go to the library to do research." As I'd witnessed at Webster Hall, people were often flummoxed by his DJ routine. Cumella told me about a recent gig where a guy came up to him and said, "What are these, xylophones?"

"I always have to explain it to people. 'What are these?' 'Is that real?'" he laughed. "I'm getting tons of wedding bookings. I did an event at the performing arts library at Lincoln Center, using records from their collection." Cumella attributed some of the sudden interest in his service to "the *Gatsby* thing. If anything, it's a lightning bolt to a culture. Now everyone is conscious of it, romanticizing it," he said. "Sometimes you realize, *now* is the time for this project. I don't know where it's going, but I can't believe how far it's come."

I didn't think 78s were about to supplant LPs as the accessory of choice for fashionable youth, but it did seem like the medium was immutable, in its way, and that allowed for some timeless appeal—there would always be something profoundly tactile and enigmatic about a 78 and the sounds it contained. Those qualities had allowed the format to endure because they were everlasting and true: humans want to hold things. We want to learn and be changed.

Nowadays, people like Paxton and Cumella are outliers, maybe, but they aren't pariahs; ironically, a subculture that developed in opposition to the mainstream is presently being co-opted by it, as subcultures almost always are. Noted oddballs like Tom Waits have long heralded the format (in 2010, Waits, in collaboration with the Preservation Hall Jazz Band, released two early Mardi Gras Indian chants on 78, simultaneously selling a limited-edition 78 rpm turntable to accompany the record), but now figures like Jack White (of the White Stripes, the Raconteurs, and his own label, Third Man Records) are aggressively lionizing it.

In late 2013, Third Man, in conjunction with Revenant Records, the reissue label cofounded by John Fahey and now run by his former partner, Dean Blackwood, released the first volume of *The Rise and Fall of Paramount Records*, a collection of six LPs, two perfect-bound books, and eight hundred MP3s preloaded onto a flash drive hidden inside "sculpted metal housing" that resembles an old phonograph reproducer.

The whole set is housed in a beautiful oak suitcase stamped with the Wisconsin Chair Company's logo; it weighs 22 pounds and retails for $400. That fall, Third Man threw a release party for the collection at Freeman's Restaurant, a so-called "rugged clandestine Colonial American tavern" in a dark alley off the Bowery in New York, and I showed up with Chris King, who'd worked on the transfers and taken a bus up from Virginia. The whole scene was disorienting. Michael Cumella had been hired to DJ and was using 78s borrowed from the New York Public Library's collection, gathered and delivered by Jonathan Hiam. Greil Marcus wore a black sweater. Young people milled about, drinking artisanal cocktails, scratching their beards, readjusting their skirts.

I felt suddenly and fiercely protective of a subculture I had no real claim to. I wanted 78s to continue offering me—and all the people I'd met—a private antidote to an accelerated, carnivorous world. I didn't want them to become another part of that world. I wanted them to stay ours.

I was reminded, then, of a scene near the end of Stefan Fatsis's *Word Freak*, a book about a cabal of competitive Scrabble players, wherein Fatsis swiftly realizes he's "gone native." "There are days when I'm sure they've forgotten that I'm a reporter," Fatsis writes of his subjects. "There are days when I know I have."

There was a lot I had forgotten.

In 1969, the Swedish folklorist Bengt Olsson and his partner, Peter Mahlin, spent a summer loitering around Beale Street in Memphis, interviewing and recording blues musicians. I'm certain it was hot, thankless work. In 1970, Olsson compiled some of those interviews into a short, now long-out-of-print book called *Memphis Blues*. In it, Olsson recounts a conversation with the guitarist Furry Lewis, who was born in Greenwood, Mississippi, in 1893 and came up playing blues with the Memphis legend W. C. Handy. Olsson never did much editorializing on the page—he just presented the material he'd collected—but there's a quote toward the end of the Lewis chapter that's become lodged permanently in my cortex, repeating endlessly like a koan: "The people I used to play around with, they all done died out," Lewis tells Olsson. "And sometimes I get scared myself, 'cause it look like to me it gonna be mine next. You know, it's a funny thing, but you can do a thing for a-many years, and all of them die out and you still here," he continued. "You know, that's more than a notion if you come up and just think about it."

I had thought about it. And I knew they were all still here, together, etched into shellac, tucked into sleeves.

I could hear them.

Acknowledgments

Ron Brown, Sarah Bryan, Joe Bussard, Michael Cumella, Sherwin Dunner, John Heneghan, Peter Honig, Robert Millis, Ian Nagoski, Richard Nevins, Jerron Paxton, John Tefteller, Jonathan Ward, Richard Weize, Pete Whelan, and Marshall Wyatt let me into their lives and collections, and this book would not have been possible without them. I owe the largest debt of gratitude to Chris King, a source who became a friend, and who was so generous with his time, knowledge, and records that I could spend the next half century thanking him and still not feel like I've said it enough.

Many have written very smart and thoughtful things about 78 rpm records and American vernacular music, and I'm particularly grateful for the work of Stephen Calt, Samuel Charters, Eddie Dean, Sarah Filzen, Kurt Gegenhuber, Peter Guralnick, Marybeth Hamilton, Alan Lomax, Greg Milner, Robert Palmer, Simon Reynolds, John Jeremiah Sullivan, Alex van der Tuuk, Elijah Wald, and Gayle Dean Wardlow.

Additional thanks to the following folks and institutions: the Anthology Film Archives, Susan Archie, Cary Baker, Andy Beta, David Bevan, Clarke Boehling, Delaney Britt Brewer, the Brooklyn Writers Space, Eden Brower, Donna Burrows-Hite, Daphne Carr, Guy Cimbalo, Aaron Cohen, John Cohen, Colonial Pines Resort, Columbia University, Kate DellaFera, Andy Downing, Charmagne Dutton, Chris Estey, David Evans, Will Georgantas, John Glynn, Brendan Greaves, Stuart Gunter,

Jason Heuer, Jonathan Hiam, Karen Hibbert, Grant Hunnicutt, Charles Hutchinson, Elliot Jackson, the Jalopy Theatre and School of Music, John Kim, Fiana Kwasnik, Lance and April Ledbetter, David Linden, Angela Mack Reilly, Rachael Maddux, Luke McCormick, Mike McGonigal, Tom Moran, the New York Public Library, Patty O'Toole, Jonathan Pace, Jeff Place, Jill Plevan, Jesse Poe, Sam Polcer, Kevin Rooney, Josh Rosenthal, Jeff Roth, Steve Sand, Doree Shafrir, Jennifer Shotz, Rani Singh, Kae and Joe Slocum, Alexia Smith, Aaron Smithers, the Southern Folklife Collection, Dan and Mary Lou Stetka, Elissa Stolman, Neil Sweeney, Mike Taylor, Ashford Tucker, Steve Weiss, Bruce and Gail Whistance, Gregory Winter, and Rebecca Winters.

Thanks to all the editors who have strengthened and challenged my writing over the years, including David DeWitt, Stephanie Goodman, Sia Michael, and Mary Jo Murphy at the *New York Times*, Roger Hodge at the *Oxford American*, Steve Kandell at BuzzFeed, Charles Aaron and Caryn Ganz at *Spin*, and Ryan Dombal, Mark Richardson, and Brandon Stousy at Pitchfork. Thanks, also, to Gregory Erickson, June Foley, and everyone at New York University for their empathy and support, and to my students, who require me to think harder and better about music and writing. Extra appreciation to Ryan Leas, who fielded many panicked missives, and August Thompson, who poured me a whiskey the day I finished writing and then massacred me at air hockey.

Some sections of this book originally appeared in the *Oxford American* and the UK music journal *Loops*. I am deeply grateful to those editors and publishers.

Mark Sussman helped with transcriptions and on more than one occasion, offered sage editorial advice. Richard Lucyshyn gave crucial early edits and, a week before my deadline, successfully convinced me to stop working and collaborate on a collection of prose poems "about wieners." For those reasons, among others, he remains one of my most cherished allies. Michael Washburn was the first person to read this manuscript in full; besides being a tremendous writer and reader, he is also a world-class drinking partner and I owe him endless rounds of Eagle Rare. John O'Connor entertained many early chapters, oversaw many revisions, and split many pepperoni pizzas with me at many crucial junctures. Nathan Salsburg was a constant and essential source of support, both in this work and far beyond it, and I am so endlessly grateful for his friendship and guidance.

Copious thanks to my agent, Chris Parris-Lamb, who shepherded this idea into being, and to everyone at the Gernert Company for their help and encouragement.

One of the best things about this project was getting to collaborate with the inimitable Brant Rumble and all the exceptionally kind and erudite folks at Scribner. Thank you.

My parents, John and Linda Petrusich, and my sister, Alexandria, are the best people in the world, and I can't thank them enough for everything they've done for me.

And thank you, finally, to Bret Stetka, who I love very much.

Selected Discography

On 78 rpm

Kid Bailey, "Mississippi Bottom Blues" / "Rowdy Blues," Brunswick 7114, 1929.

Blind Blake, "Miss Emma Liza" / "Dissatisfied Blues," Paramount 13115, 1932.

Willie Brown, "M&O Blues" / "Future Blues," Paramount 13090, 1930.

Bulawayo Sweet Rhythms Band, "Skokiaan" / "In the Mood," London 1491, 1954.

Cincinnati Jug Band, "Newport Blues" / "George St. Stomp," Paramount 12743, 1929.

Blind Uncle Gaspard, "Sur le Borde de l'Eau" / "Natchitocheo," Vocalion 5333, 1929.

Red Gay and Jack Wellman, "Flat Wheel Train Blues Part 1" / "Flat Wheel Train Blues Part 2," Brunswick 523, 1930.

King Solomon Hill, "My Buddy Blind Papa Lemon" / "Times Has Done Got Hard," Paramount 13125, 1932.

Mississippi John Hurt, "Big Leg Blues," Okeh (unissued, matrix 401474-A), 1928.

Mississippi John Hurt, "Blue Harvest Blues" / "Spike Driver Blues," Okeh 8692, 1928.

Mississippi John Hurt, "Stack O'Lee Blues" / "Candy Man Blues," Okeh 8654, 1928.

Frank Hutchison, "K.C. Blues" / "Hell Bound Train," Okeh 45452, 1929.

Skip James, "Devil Got My Woman" / "Cypress Grove Blues," Paramount 13088, 1931.

Skip James, "Drunken Spree" / "What Am I to Do Blues," Paramount 13111, 1931.

Blind Lemon Jefferson, "That Black Snake Moan" / "Stocking Feet Blues," Paramount 12407, 1926.

Robert Johnson, "Cross Road Blues" / "Ramblin' on My Mind," Vocalion 03519, 1937.

Robert Johnson, "From Four Until Late" / "Hell Hound on My Trail," Vocalion 03623, 1937.

Tommy Johnson, "Alcohol and Jake Blues" / "Riding Horse," Paramount 12950, 1929.

Angelas LeJeune, "Perrodin Two Step" / "Valse de la Louisiane," Brunswick 369, 1929.

Dennis McGee and Sady Courville, "Mon Chere Bebe Creole" / "Madame Young Donnez Moi Votre Plus Jolie Blonde," Vocalion 5319, 1929.

Arthur Miles, "The Lonely Cowboy Part 1" / "The Lonely Cowboy Part 2," Victor 40156, 1929.

Chubby Parker, "Davey Crockett" / "His Parents Haven't Seen Him Since," Conqueror 7895, 1931.

Chubby Parker, "Nickety Nackety Now Now Now" / "Whoa Mule Whoa," Silvertone 5011, 1927.

Charley Patton, "High Water Everywhere Part 1" / "High Water Everywhere Part 2," Paramount 12909, 1929.

Charley Patton, "Mississippi Boweavil Blues" / "Screamin' and Hollerin' the Blues," Paramount 12805, 1929.

Charley Patton, "Pony Blues" / "Banty Rooster Blues," Paramount 12792, 1929.

Charley Patton, "Some These Days I'll Be Gone" / "Frankie and Albert," Paramount 13110, 1929.

Ma Rainey, "Ma Rainey's Mystery Record" / "Honey, Where You Been So Long?," Paramount 12200, 1924.

Long Cleve Reed and Little Harvey Hull, the Down Home Boys, "Original Stack O'Lee Blues" / "Mama You Don't Know How," Black Patti 8030, 1927.

Sylvester Weaver, "Guitar Blues" / "Guitar Rag," Okeh 8109, 1923.

Geeshie Wiley, "Last Kind Words Blues" / "Skinny Leg Blues," Paramount 12951, 1930.

Alexis Zoumbas, "Tzamara Arvanitiko" / "Syrtos Sta Dyo," Columbia 56094-F, 1928.

Compilations on Long-Playing Vinyl

The Country Blues, Folkways, 1959.

Country Blues Encores 1927–1935, Origin Jazz Library, 1965.

The Mississippi Blues, 1927–1940, Origin Jazz Library, 1963.

Really! The Country Blues, 1927–1933, Origin Jazz Library, 1962.

The Rise and Fall of Paramount Records Vol. 1, Revenant, 2013 (LP and MP3).

Robert Johnson: King of the Delta Blues Singers, Columbia, 1961.

The Rural Blues: A Study of the Vocal and Instrumental Resources, RBF, 1960.

Compilations on Compact Disc

Aimer et Perdre: To Love & to Lose Songs, 1917–1934, Tompkins Square, 2012*.

American Primitive, Vol. I: Raw Pre-War Gospel (1926–1936), Revenant, 1997.

American Primitive, Vol. II: Pre-War Revenants (1897–1939), Revenant, 2005.

The Anthology of American Folk Music, Smithsonian Folkways, 1997 (CD reissue).

Five Days Married & Other Laments, Angry Mom, 2013*.

Fonotone: Frederick, Maryland 1956–1969, Dust-to-Digital, 2005.

Goodbye, Babylon, Dust-to-Digital, 2003.

Skip James: Hard Time Killin' Floor, Yazoo, 2005.

Robert Johnson: The Complete Recordings, Columbia, 1990*.

Mama, I'll Be Long Gone: The Complete Recordings of Amédé Ardoin, Tompkins Square, 2011.

Masters of the Delta Blues, Yazoo, 1991.

Mississippi John Hurt: 1928 Sessions, Yazoo, 1990.

Opika Pende: Africa at 78 rpm, Dust-to-Digital, 2011.

The Return of the Stuff That Dreams Are Made Of, Yazoo, 2012.

Screamin' and Hollerin' the Blues: The Worlds of Charley Patton, Revenant, 2001.

The Secret Museum of Mankind, Yazoo, 1995–1998.

The Stuff That Dreams Are Made Of, Yazoo, 2006.

Victrola Favorites: Artifacts from Bygone Days, Dust-to-Digital, 2008.

To What Strange Place: The Music of the Ottoman-American Diaspora, 1916–1929, Tompkins Square, 2011*.

Work Hard, Play Hard, Pray Hard: Hard Time, Good Time, and End Time Music, 1923–1936, Tompkins Square, 2012*.

Alexis Zoumbas: Lament For Epirus, 1926-1928, Angry Mom, 2014*.

(*Denotes a release that is also available on LP.)

Index

ι